Whatever's Happening to Women?

Julia Neuberger is a rabbi who was minister at the South London Liberal Synagogue for twelve years. Since then, she has been a Visiting Fellow at the King's Fund Institute, looking at research ethics committees in the UK and she is now a Harkness Fellow, based at Harvard Medical School for six months, looking at issues of professional accountability amongst healthcare professionals and others. On her return to the UK, she hopes to write about how professionals approach their public.

Previous books include *Caring for Dying People of Different Faiths* and the introductions to a selection of political essays in four volumes, entitled *Days of Decision*, on women's policy, disarmament, privatisation and the Bill of Rights and freedom of information.

She is married with two children, lives in London and West Cork, Ireland, loves opera and choral music, gardening, and entertaining, and lists amongst her main recreations in *Who's Who* 'setting up the old girls' network'.

Whatever's Happening to Women?

Promises,
Practices
and Pay Offs

Julia Neuberger

KYLE CATHIE

The cartoon on page 180 is reproduced by permission of Posy Simmonds. Wendy Cope's poem *Men and their Boring Arguments* (page 177) is reproduced by permission of the author and the extract from John Betjeman's *Death in Leamington* (page 159) by permission of John Murray (Publishers) Ltd.

The lyrics of *A Hymn to Him* from *My Fair Lady* (page 133), words by Alan Jay Lerner, music by Frederick Loewe, are © 1956 Alan Jay Lerner and Frederick Loewe USA, Warner Chappell Music Publications. Used by permission.

For acknowledgements of passages quoted in the text, please see the Bibliography which begins on page 209.

First published in Great Britain in 1991 by
Kyle Cathie Limited
3 Vincent Square, London SW1P 2LX

© 1991 by Julia Neuberger

ISBN 1 85626 046 1

Julia Neuberger is hereby identified as the author of this work in accordance with Section 77 of the Copyright, Designs and Patents Act 1988.

A CIP catalogue record for this book is available from the British Library.

Edited by Caroline Taggart
Typeset by DP Photosetting, Aylesbury, Bucks
Printed by Biddles Ltd, Guildford

Contents

Acknowledgements

This book could not have happened at all without the series of conversations between its publisher, Kyle Cathie, my agent, Carol Smith, and myself. To them, my profound thanks for the idea, which we jointly verbalised, and the support, help and encouragement.

To the women friends who gave me so many of the ideas go my gratitude and amusement that we were all thinking the same things at the same time, but in particular gratitude goes to my mother, Liesel Schwab, to Margaret Jay, Barbara Hosking, Felicity Ann Sieghart, Valerie Amos, Joanna Foster, Silvia Rodgers, Barbara Christie-Miller, Heather Neill, Rita Cruise O'Brien, Victoria Neumark, Fiona Maddocks, Frances Jowell, Angela Levin, Sheila Angel, Angela Holdsworth, Celia Goodhart, Carole Stone, Ann Oakley, Joanna Waley-Cohen, Felicity Waley-Cohen, Usha Prashar, Pat Hewitt, Tessa Blackstone, Marcia Levy, Carolyn Faulder, Nigella Lawson, Miriam Rothschild, Helena Kennedy, Jacinta Hogan, Sally King, Lyndsey Brennan, Giana Ferguson, Rabbi Sybil Sheridan, Mary Stott, Polly Toynbee, Tessa Jowell, Melanie Henwood, Helen Ward, Katie Petty-Saphon, Sue Slipman, Emma Nicholson MP, Winifred Tumim, Julia Cleverdon, Penelope Phillips, Ava McKenzie, Liz Vallance, Ros Miles, Heather Brigstocke, Shireen Ritchie, Fran Miller and Elizabeth Clough. With all of them, some more often than others, I have had some of these conversations. They may not recognise themselves in the book, but they are without doubt there.

To the men friends who looked at me bemused when I started talking about the book, but have been funny and helpful and supportive since, my thanks go too: to my father Walter Schwab, to Anthony Lester, Andrew Baillie, Andrew Phillips, Rabbi Hugo Gryn, Martyn Goff, Trevor Clay, Bishop Richard Harries, Rabbi Tony Bayfield, Rabbi David Freeman, Rabbi Nicholas de Lange, Jeffrey Jowell, Michael Neuberger, Peter Kellner, John Lloyd (who thought of the original title, *Paradox Lost*), Tim Clement-Jones, Jim Rose, John Walsh, Phil Ward, Bob Horton, Bill New, Gerald Rothman and Bob Low. It has been harder for them, but they too are in here somewhere, not necessarily agreeing, though most of them did, most of the time. My thanks also to John Marsden, who came up with the title we finally used.

But the greatest debt of gratitude is for the support and tenderness of my husband, Anthony, and my children, Harriet and Matthew. Their concerns are reflected within the book, too, and they put up with my irritation, absent-mindedness and absence throughout the long period of gestation and writing. Whether they will think it was worthwhile is another question altogether.

Julia Neuberger
June 1991
London and West Cork

1
Introduction

I myself have never been able to find out precisely what feminism is; I only know that people call me a feminist whenever I express sentiments that differentiate me from a doormat or a prostitute.

Rebecca West *The Strange Necessity*

WHEN THE NUCLEAR bomb testers were waiting for the result of the mission to bomb Hiroshima on 6 August 1945, they expected a coded message. If the mission was successful, the message would be: 'It's a boy.' If it was a dud bomb, the message would read: 'It's a girl.' As Jane Mills puts it in her book *Womanwords*, 'The scientists and politicians begat a boy bomb – proving their virility by the mass slaughter and subsequent slow deaths of hundreds of thousands of Japanese civilians.'

Messages about 'girlhood' abound, messages suggesting that women are inferior to men and that girls are inferior to boys. It was this sense, this feeling about the inferiority of women and the superiority of men, together with the idea that there were certain roles which men could play and women could not, which led at last to the explosion of Women's Liberation in the 1960s. The bra-burning was perhaps largely apocryphal, but there was certainly a heady onslaught of vitriol poured on to the civil rights campaigners, bastions of '60s feeling, whose certainties women had shared when it came to the liberation of blacks and the poor. Their reply was to shout out their contempt for women in the way they marginalised them in the running of revolutionary organisations, and one of their leaders, Stokely Carmichael, said, to his everlasting shame: 'The only position of women [in the Civil Rights Movement] is prone.'

Yet again women were being told that they were sex objects, and that serious political issues were to be left to the men. What was the history of these feelings about women? Why were women called 'girls' so often, infantilising them? Why did men want to protect women on the one hand and ravage them on the other? Why should Mary Wollstonecraft, one of the heroines of this book, have needed to write: 'Men, indeed, appear to act in a very unphilosophical manner when they try to secure the good conduct of women by attempting to keep them always in a state of childhood.'[1]

The women's movement, a campaign or series of campaigns stretching back over the last two centuries, be it fighting for the education of women or for the vote, for their right to work or their right to property, and latterly for their right to self-fulfilment in many ways, has done incalculable good for women. It has opened up possibilities, suggested new worlds for us to move in, given us hope when there only seemed to be blocked opportunities. Latterly, from the 1960s on, there has been what has been called, loosely, Women's Liberation, or Women's Lib. It began as a movement of anger at the plight of women, yet it subsumed into itself the work done over the years by countless individuals and campaigning groups, trying to improve the lot of women in society, in their families and in their own self-esteem.

Yet something has gone very awry. Many women, and I am amongst them, feel this, not only about the women's movement and its daughter organisations and groupings of radical feminists and peace organisations, but more fundamentally we feel that something has gone very wrong with our society. We, the products of 1960s education, who believed that the world was open to us and that we could do anything, learned from the new and heady thinking of the beginnings of modern feminism in the late 1960s and early 1970s that many of women's problems were directly caused by men. Women were imprisoned, expected to do it all in the home, never allowed to fulfil themselves. In short, life for women was very unfair.

There was much that was true in what Kate Millett and Germaine Greer were saying so angrily in the 1960s and 1970s, be it about the lack of sexual fulfilment for women, or about lack of education, or prejudice at work, or the expectations that women would fulfil men's sexual dreams – body images being men's images, and not the natural shape of women, fat or thin.

And yet the women's movement, or the group of movements it has become, could be argued to have damaged women's lives as irrevocably as the male oppressors have done. For, as with all social revolutions, the tide of the high fashion of feminism went too far – women who stayed at home felt inadequate; women who worked but did not reach real seniority, hit what has been described as the glass ceiling, felt angry and betrayed; women were exhausted rather than fulfilled; and whole tracts of female experience and female desires, the nurturing we were brought up to do and the sense of duty we feel to our loved ones, have been jettisoned for some apparently nobler cause, self-fulfilment in the workplace, alongside men.

It is not clear that women are satisfied with that view of the world. Many of those who can afford it are running away from their first careers and taking up new jobs, or even electing to stay at home with the children until they finally leave home themselves, only a few years from now. Many are challenging the certainty that it is possible to do everything, to run the perfect home, cook the perfect meal, do the perfect job, be respected by colleagues male and female, have the perfect body, always be dressed in the perfect clothes, and be the perfect companion in bed to the delightful and supportive husband, having given quality time – there was no time for quantity time, after all – to the mutually adored children. Women are saying, one by one but too often for it to be purely anecdotal, that they cannot do it all, that they are tired, somehow disappointed, furious at what they hear their male colleagues at work say when a group of female top executives meet and discuss the difficulties of trying to do it all, and that there has to be a better way to run our lives.

The idea that we should make choices between working and children when it would not occur to men to do so, the idea that somehow children need us but not their fathers, the idea that the nanny needs to be looked after as much if not more than the children because we are so dependent on her – all these are frightening in their absurdity.

Why, for instance, should nannies and child-minders so often be exploited by employers who simply are not back on time? Yet they put up with it, some of them because they believe it is important that their female employers work, to support the families, and some of them because they are too economically dependent on their employers to make a fuss. When women make the choice, if choice it is rather than necessity, between work and children, they do it knowing that they are likely to exploit other women in the process. A strong union for childminders and nannies is a long way off.

Yet women do make choices. They agonise over the difficulties, they throw in the towel if things get impossible, they expect to work, these days, but are not supported adequately in so doing, and it all leads to top media women like Maeve Haran writing blockbusters on the theme that one cannot have it all. The truth is that one *can* have it all, but only with some hard choices being made, considerable dedication to organisation and a great deal of exhaustion when the strain shows. And it is hard to accept that the strain which leads to the decision to give it up, is not the natural strain of trying to have it all, but the imposed strain of the idea that children are a private matter, and a women's matter at that. Why is this not a concern for the whole of society, with relatively inexpensive crèches, nurseries and after-school schemes provided by the state, properly run and inspected, and a normal part of life for which one pays if one can afford to, perhaps on a means-tested basis, but certainly without guilt.

The question is how these issues should be addressed. Individual women can easily make deals with individual and beloved men, men who do not lack a sense of justice. But even the fairest minded of men are conditioned, as women are, by the cultural values of society. In a working environment where most colleagues are male, the man who is willing to share sees that less is expected of his colleagues. The atmosphere is not conducive to persuading individual men to help more, to share the load. The need is not for individual negotiation alone, helpful though that is in many couples. Instead, it is for changes in education, in public attitudes to domesticated men, and for the women's movement to realise that in the arena of childcare, if in no other, they have a battle they can fight with employers, with local authorities and with government. But that requires limited objectives, such as tax allowances for childminding, or non-taxable workplace nurseries, rather than the hyped up, and patently politically unacceptable, suggestions about every child having a right to daycare from the age of six months. We would be doing well in this country if we got to the situation where every child of three and four could be guaranteed a nursery place.

These are issues the political parties can tackle, and to some extent, in the Liberal Democrats and Labour Party, they have done so. But the truth of the politics of these issues is that they need massive male support. They also need cross-party support. And that means mobilising women's groups and political groups, it means enabling women to talk about the issue publicly, and it means allowing men to shoot themselves in the feet politically if they answer unsatisfactorily. We are still a long way from that.

After all, the structure of families takes generations to change. Effecting political awareness cannot be done by marginalised groups here. This is where the Women's Institutes, the Towns-women's Guilds, the National Council of Women, the BBC's *Woman's Hour* and all the women's magazines have an important role to play. Many will play it willingly. The radical women's organisations which perceive themselves as the bastions of true feminism have to learn that the old, well-established women's organisations in the UK have a great deal to offer, and their help should be sought and won, if general attitudes, rather than those of a very small number of people in a rarefied stratum of society, are going to see, and feel, the change.

To achieve these aims requires deradicalising. It means taking the issues into the political parties and across them. It means talking about them in *Woman's Own* as well as *Cosmopolitan*, in *Vogue* and *Harper's* as well as *Options*. It means making the connections with rural women as well as urban ones, with part-time working, relatively well-off, well-heeled wives of businessmen as well as with politicised female students. And it means pointing out to the charities and voluntary bodies who rely so heavily on the input of women as volunteers that some of these women's issues fit on their own agendas as a result of the gradual lack of helpers they are experiencing, and, unless a change comes about, will continue to experience.

There also has to be some serious research on the effects on children of different methods of upbringing, with non-working mothers, with part-time working mothers, with two part-time working parents, with two full-time working parents who work out of the home, or with parents who work full-time but at home. The need to look at these issues sensibly and seriously is the more acute as it becomes increasingly acceptable to argue that it damages children for mothers to work. But the downside of this is that if the findings show what some of the more radical women's groups do not want to know, they need to learn to accept that theory, without the experience and its analysis, is not enough to govern human behaviour in the long term, and that very different political and family solutions may need to be sought for caring for children and for the elderly and handicapped.

There has been little desire to study the effects on children and families of working mothers, for a variety of excellent and less than excellent reasons. The first is that the majority of women work because they have no option financially, but that could of course be dealt with by the provision of greatly increased family allowances. The second is the fact that governments have always recruited women into the labour force when necessary, such as in a time of war, and would find it difficult to say that the effect on children of working mothers is such that women ought not to enter the labour market. The third is the issue of self-determination for women, and the fourth is the apparent ineffectiveness of trying to force 'family values' on to the political agenda, where this has been seen as a deeply conservative move to force women back home where they belong.

Yet this is a time when, despite high unemployment, women, particularly skilled and trained women, are urgently wanted and needed in the workplace. Nurses are in short supply, yet there are thousands of them out there, in their homes or in other jobs better suited to their hours of free time, who ought to come back into the hospital service. The same is true of teachers and of other careers, other jobs. And when statistics project vast increases in the percentage of elderly people in the population, we need to take a long, hard look at who is going to be caring for them. If this is not the time when the women's movement, or free groupings of women's organisations, should make a fuss and raise the issues, talk about the problems and put the questions of caring and women's lives on the political agenda, there will not be another opportunity for decades. The women's movement could be argued to have failed in this matter thus far, yet there is still time.

This book is not about the history of the women's movement,

except insofar as it touches the argument, but about the way in which the effects of the women's movement in its larger sense, from the late '60s on, have not necessarily been of benefit to most women. For its beginnings were largely in the reaction to the apple-pie dream of motherhood that swept the USA in the 1950s. Women had been brought into the labour force during the war, but when the boys came back home, jobs were needed for them. They were the source of family support, and they were the breadwinners. Women went back home to be real mothers. Domestic America reigned, and, to a lesser extent, domestic Europe, and particularly Britain, reigned too. But women reacted against their prisons, and the combination of a hatred of enforced domesticity and the cult of personal fulfilment and the 'let it all hang out' philosophy of the 1960s led to a gradual demonstration of 'women's liberation', with books appearing by Betty Friedan, the mother of feminism, and later by Kate Millett, Germaine Greer and Gloria Steinem. 'Sisterhood is powerful' was the clarion call of the early women's libbers, and consciousness-raising was the name of the game. Some of the activities were profoundly political, such as the unsuccessful attempt to get the Equal Rights Amendment passed by every state in the US. But meanwhile some equality legislation was going through, and anti-discrimination, particularly in relation to women and blacks, became important in 1960s thinking.

But gradually there were splits and arguments. Abortion, and 'the right to choose' lobby, was one of the causes of dissent in a society as deeply evangelised as America. But there were issues surrounding lesbianism as well, and the values of feminism meaning that men had to be excluded from the debate. Universities became beset with women's caucuses that refused to talk to men, and women's groups that took a moderate line were described as 'inauthentic' by their more radical sisters. Feminist psychotherapy took off, as did women's studies in the universities and affirmative action to guarantee places for women students. Some of this was marvellous, and some was beset with political strife and increasing tensions and divisiveness. Gradually, women for whom the 'women's movement' had been an important political reality left it for more conventional party politics or for single-issue campaigning, driven out by the endless philosophising and apparently intractable sectarian warfare between lesbian separatists and heterosexual wives and mothers, not to mention a tendency to insist on a 'party line' so extreme about many practical issues surrounding children or husbands that prospects of effecting real change seemed remote indeed.

But this is not to say that the women's movement has been a failure. Far from it, for it has brought an awareness and a richness to life and a source of support and a sense of achievement to many women, and there are few whose lives are not touched by it in some way. But there are also countless women whose lives have been *barely* touched by it, whose poverty and family situation and hopes and expectations are perhaps worse than they have ever been, whose duties of care for children and elderly relatives exclude them from much of the world far more than was the case twenty-five years ago, and whose future looks even bleaker, as the demographic picture shifts and the number of younger women available to look after older ones diminishes rapidly in large areas of the Western world.

These are major issues for the 1990s, and it is the fact that the women's movement, in all its ramifications, has addressed these issues so little that has created an apparent paradox: a movement which claimed to liberate women from domestic chains, but which has succeeded by and large in extending those chains still further, by failing to analyse where women's lives were really heading, and where women most needed help and support and campaigning for better treatment.

Part of the problem lay in what was a general fault of the 1960s, an inability to see individuals within the context of where their lives were. The cause of civil rights for black Americans was taken up by thousands of young white liberals who failed to understand the nature of black history in the United States, or to see that black family structures, very often as a result of white ill-treatment of blacks, were different from those of whites. So too the early women's libbers failed to see how most women's lives were buried under the pressures of caring for husband and kids and family at large and doing a bit of a job as well. Simply to view those women in isolation was profoundly unhelpful, because it told you nothing about their lives.

Yet indirectly and directly, the women's movement has wrought change for many middle-class and middle-aged women. But in some of the most fundamental areas of life, it has not wrought nearly sufficient change, be it in economic terms or in terms of help with the house and housework and children and the generally heavy domestic load women have tended to have to carry, whatever else they are doing.

Indeed, the creation of the 1970s, the 'new man', who was concerned with babies and housework and domestic chores, who cooked and changed nappies and made bread, has rapidly disappeared into oblivion during the materialistic, individualistic, achieving 1980s. There are undoubtedly more men actually pushing the buggies and changing the nappies, but the number of men to be seen at school sports day is pitiful, and the number who can be relied on to take a day off for a child's sickness is even smaller. That is by no means only the fault of the individual men concerned. Employers think men have gone slightly mad if they take a day off for a child's ill-health, whereas employers of women, who complain about the absences of their women employees even though women have an infinitely better staying record in jobs than men, are somehow resigned to the fact that mothers will have to stay at home when their children are ill, and it is, of course, one of the justifications for paying women less and giving them less good working benefits.

So the 'new man' does not necessarily have it easy from his employers or his workmates. Add to that the fierce ambition, the 'get on and make it' philosophy of the 1980s, and it is hard to see how the nurturing tendency that men have and can put to good use can be expected to flourish. And yet men on their own with children, either because they are widowed or because their wives have walked out on them, leaving them with the kids, make remarkably good, tender nurturers in many cases, and tend to suffer much less social isolation than a women would in similar circumstances.

The question then remains of the extent to which the women's movement has changed male expectations of what they need to do in a household and with their children, to what extent they share responsibility for domestic and family matters, and to what extent families are changed by the thinking feminism has brought into the general arena, even amongst those who think it did not touch them.

But the evidence is depressing, with few signs of change and an increasing desire to push women back into the home and caring roles, whilst men get on with the real work. Women still do most of the housework, even if they work full-time or part-time. Where, then, did the women's movement go wrong in failing to convince men that child-rearing was too important to be left only to the women? And was the fault more in the style and so-called stridency of the thinking and campaigning, or in the arguments themselves? Or was it that the arguments fell on deliberately deaf ears, the ears of people who rejoiced in being able to say that these were only the views of women, and not to be taken seriously?

So what are the expectations of our daughters to be? Will they feel that the women's movement, and the feminist philosophy, did them any good? If they feel their lives are easier, or better, or more rewarding, because of the women's movement, then it will be worthwhile, but if, as I suspect, they will look around them ten years from now and see women completely trapped by having to care at home for the severely confused and disabled elderly because there will be no-one else to do it and no public spending commitment to care in the community, then we who were and are feminists, who fought in the '60s and '70s and tried to change men's thought and men's oppression of women, will have failed. And the failure will not even be a dignified one, because if we had thought a little harder, we would have been able to see the demographic and political changes coming from miles away. The writing was on the wall.

It is those issues which the women's movement, now a disparate series of organisations with a few over-arching bodies such as the National Council of Women, and the National Association of Women's Organisations, ought to be addressing. But in order to address them, it needs to be made clearer precisely what the issues are. Some are the obvious ones of equal pay and equal treatment, others are much less clear-cut but none the less important for that.

The equal pay situation has been well-described, and there can be no justification for paying women less than men unless there is some real evidence of material difference. But other forms of discrimination are less clear. The UK's blocking of the European Community's directive on employment protection for part-time workers is a case in point. So too is the lack of opportunity to get out and about because of the absence of childcare and grannycare facilities. On these issues, the major political parties have said all too little, but so have the women's organisations, at a time when the wind was being taken out of their sails by persistent attacks such as changes in divorce legislation which had some deleterious effects on older women, or more and more rape cases being dismissed, or occasional anti-feminist articles being widely quoted.

The new agenda must be to restate the case for justice, to strengthen women's hands by making sure they have legal protection, access to money, including maintenance allowance where appropriate, and an opportunity to go back to work. But the women's movement, or movements, can only do that if they recognise earlier failures, if they see that most women, though by no means all, *do* want to have children, and to care, and to cope, and to be married, and to do a great deal of cherishing. What they do not want is to be told that these are their duties, and then be put in the situation where the logistics of carrying them out are impossible. They do not want to be the victims of a rising divorce rate, with the common phenomenon of women being left on their own to cope, having neither money nor back-up resources to help them manage.

These issues are the legacy of the Women's Liberation movement of the 1960s and 1970s. Can women's organisations, along with the Equal Opportunities Commission, government, political parties, men's organisations, the media and whoever else is interested now manage to change the agenda, including that of separation and divorce and its impact on children? Or will we see more of the same: women at a disadvantage; women largely unaffected by the new thinking feminism brought to our lives; women as drudges and as carers, unpaid, into the twenty-first century?

2
The Family

All our institutions, our traditional attitudes, our laws, our
morals, our customs, give evidence of the fact that they are
determined and maintained by privileged males for the glory of
male domination.. . . That woman must be submissive is an
unwritten but deeply rooted law.

Alfred Adler, psychoanalyst

ONE OF THE issues that has most vexed the West in the twentieth
century has been the nature of marriage and its permanence. In
Britain, we now have one of the highest divorce rates in the
Western world, and by far the highest in the European Community. Between 1971 and 1986, the divorce rate more than doubled in
the UK; according to current figures, one under-sixteen-year-old in
four will experience a parental divorce. Statistics also show that the
majority of families living in poverty are headed by one parent
alone, usually a woman. Twelve per cent of families have a lone
mother, of whom over half are divorced (5% of families) or
separated (2%), with an additional 4% of families headed by a single
woman, 1% by a widowed woman and 1% by a widowed man.
Elderly, isolated, poor women add to the statistics of female
poverty, but the worst problem lies with single-parent families
headed by a woman.

There is a great deal of talk about these families being the product
of some feckless young woman electing to have a baby, without a
proper father for the child, in order to jump the queue on the

housing list, or of older women simply having a baby while they still can, even though they have no permanent man in their lives. These women are perceived as irresponsible and silly. They are also perceived as being many in number, which is a total misconception. In fact, in England and Wales, about half the babies born outside marriage are registered by two parents living at the same address. In Denmark, a country with a massive 44% of babies born outside marriage, only 4% of women who give birth are not living in a couple, and cohabitation does seem to have replaced marriage for a sizeable number of people there. The proportions in Britain and France are much lower. In France, about 12% of women aged 20–24 and 25–29 were living in unmarried couples in 1987, and in Great Britain it was 9% of women aged 20–24 in 1985. These figures are still far from negligible, and illustrate a major social change, suggesting that the number of babies born outside marriage is not directly related to the number of women who are literally lone parents, because the cohabitation rate is so high.

But far more significant for the rise of lone parenthood are the instances where one parent abandons the other, who is left to bring up the children on her, or his, own. It is not a popular view to suggest that divorce should be made more difficult, though moves are under way to change the divorce law and introduce a family court with a possible requirement of a cooling-off period and a definite desire to put the interests of the children first. But the moves are fairly minor. Perhaps there should be a growing rejection of the individualistic view of the 1960s on and a recognition that the emphasis on self-fulfilment for the parents may not be of benefit to the children – indeed, may even harm them.

Piers Paul Read, writing in the London *Evening Standard* in June 1991, pointed out that with all the concern about rising divorce rates, the only clear recommendation of the Law Commission was a mandatory conciliation session in order to sort out the interests of the children. In his view, children are often violently damaged by divorce, even if the bruises do not show. And he argues convincingly, as do many reports, that what parents regard as an intolerably strained atmosphere to live in, unbearable and unfulfilling, can be quite satisfactory for the children. Indeed, with statistics showing that more than three-quarters of a million children in Britain never see their fathers, there has to be some cause for concern, since it demonstrates that only 57% of absent parents keep in touch with their offspring, a 10% decline over a decade.[1]

It is not a fashionable stand to take, yet it seems that if we wish to address the issue of the growing number of children in poverty, and the growing number of single-parent families, we have to think hard about it. We may even have to come up with some very unpalatable views about how responsible it is to bring a child into the world without having an 'active' father for it, be he a husband or long-term live-in lover. Young women who had babies without giving them a father in the nurturing sense used to be supported very largely by families, once we progressed beyond the time when a respectable girl who got pregnant was thrown out and left to fend for herself (though even that is well within the living memory of many eighty-plus members of society). But the support of family is a good deal less common than it was, because people move away from their families, because it is regarded as 'respectable' to have a baby on one's own, and because there has been a mushrooming of informal groupings of friends who take on looking after other friends' babies.

Yet I am not convinced that this is fair to children. Though it is clear that children can do perfectly well with only one parent rather than both, the statistics about the later psychological problems of those who are separated from one of their parents early on, for whatever reason, are hardly comforting. The incidence of such problems is some four times higher than the norm. And the additional strain that is put on one parent must be phenomenal: those who have done the job of parenting along with other work outside the home have found it hard enough when both parents are involved.

This is no argument for taking the moral high ground. To say to young women that they must not have babies without attendant, supportive fathers, would be blatantly absurd, because they would quite rightly put two fingers in the air and say, 'Get knotted,' or a more vulgar equivalent. Nor would it be right to say to young couples that they must not get divorced 'for the sake of the children', for acute tension between parents can put children in extreme danger, and certainly great misery: older children are not uncommonly relieved when their warring parents decide to part.

In Norway, where there is a feminised political system with more than a third of MPs being female, seven female cabinet ministers out of eighteen, and a third-term female Prime Minister, Gro Brundtland, family and childcare issues are at the top of the political agenda. We are a long way away from this in the UK, despite Mrs Thatcher, in particular, being keen to emphasise 'Victorian' family values. If women's political organisations can learn to look at the family as the normal and natural unit – one which may need reform and pressures and new ideas, but a stable and important factor in society – then we might be nearer to sorting out some of the problems faced by people, male and female, young and old, in our midst.

Clearly, a traditional family that allows women no choices is no good to most women. That, presumably, accounts for why so many women leave their husbands when their children have grown up, seeing no purpose in the traditional divisions of labour, and no prospect of future development for themselves. The number of extremely happy divorced women I have spoken to over the years of putting this book together, women in their fifties and sixties who divorced their husbands after twenty or thirty years of apparent nuptial bliss, is phenomenal. They speak of the relief, the pleasure in being able to do things for themselves and to develop their own interests, the vitality they thought was lost twenty years before that they have rediscovered, the encouragement they receive from their children. This says more about the sterility of the marriage they were in than about anything else, more about the acceptance of traditional ways of doing things rather than aiming for a shared role. And it suggests more of a willingness to stay together for the children while the children are small than would appear to be the case with younger people, as the divorce rate continues to rise.

Yet attitudes to children are themselves rather peculiar, particularly in the United Kingdom. The number of children women have is declining in all European countries, which is presumably linked to a loosening of the marriage bonds, as the European Commission's report on 'Lone Parents in the European Community' puts it so delicately. On average, women throughout the European Community are having one fewer child than they did twenty-five years ago. All European countries are also experiencing a rapid rise in child abuse, though the extent to which the rise is in *reported* child abuse or in fact in its occurrence is a moot point.

Several authorities have suggested that there has always been child abuse and that it is simply becoming 'respectable' to report it, in the same way as there is a new-found respectability in trying to counter sexual offences against the young amongst those in prison for sexual offences generally. Whatever the case may be, there are worrying trends in our attitude to young people, for despite the concern about sexual abuse and about physical violence against children, time and again it is the social workers who are held to blame for failing to prevent a tragedy; time and again there is some sort of judicial inquiry, usually excellently prepared by the barrister concerned; and time and again there is no action.

The reported cases are on the increase. In the 1960s, there was Maria Coldwell, the child the family did not love, who died of violence and malnutrition in Brighton, to the shock and horror of the community, which had failed to notice. In the early '80s, there was Jasmine Beckford, four years old and battered to death by her father, who had himself been an abused child, and no-one noticed. The evidence of her mother, that he had hit her 'as you would an adult', not a child, rang in the ears of many of the public who read it. There was an excellent inquiry, but nothing changed. There was Tyra Henry, twenty months old, bitten to death by her father; and many, many others, choked on balls of wool stuffed into their mouths to make them stop crying, or battered or beaten or undernourished. Little girls in Croydon were whipped with electrical flex and kept short of food whilst their baby brother was overfed and much adored. A little boy of three in East London was battered with a billiard cue by his mother's live-in lover and died of internal injuries, in hospital, having been taken there too late with a ruptured spleen. A child of two was put in the tumble-dryer for thirty seconds 'to teach her a lesson' and taken out screaming with fear, unhurt physically, but perhaps scarred for life emotionally.

This is no news, except that it reflects a worrying public attitude to children. An attitude that they are a private concern, not the concern of society. We must not interfere, if they starve or scream or are bruised or withdrawn. And when the family finally fails them, and they are put into a children's home or given to foster parents by a local authority, then yet again we do not interfere. There is an inspectorate for children's homes, of course, but it does not go into every home on a regular, weekly or monthly basis. We do not pay the staff of children's homes a decent salary, or give them training and support as they deal with people who are already disturbed, but who, with care and encouragement and love, could become important contributors to society in the future. Children's homes rarely have open access, nor do they encourage visits from local church groups or 'befrienders' for each resident child. They are closed and distant institutions, with their own violent ways of restraining their residents, as the recent row about 'pindown' – restricting children to solitary confinement in a room with a bed and a chair and no entertainment – has shown.

A society that allows this sort of treatment of children, keeping children's homes at a Victorian level of sophistication and giving no scope for really gifted, talented and devoted staff because it does not support them or train them or reward them, does not love children. Nor does it love children if inquiry upon inquiry merely continues to blame the social workers who fail to stop the worst tragedies. Should we not be asking about the load on young social workers' shoulders, their own lack of training and support in these difficult matters; whether they are the right people to handle these matters, or whether older social workers with specialist knowledge could be more helpful here? Is this not a matter of genuine public concern? Should women, and men, not have something to say about this? Should women, and men, not be going into homes where abuse takes place as befrienders, rather than police? Should we not accept that the children are, to some extent at least, everybody's children, and not a private matter at all?

And does not the contrast in the extent to which families are encouraged and children cared for within the community in other European countries – such as France, with its universal availability of day nurseries, or Sweden, with its provision of kind ladies who look after sick children at home whilst their parents work – and what exists in Anglo-Saxon Britain and America seem very stark? For here an Englishman's home (and an Englishwoman's) is his castle, and no-one may enter it without good reason.

But the protection of children is a good reason. It is right for neighbours to be nosy about the welfare of the children next door. It may be called snooping, but it is also protection, and Childline and other telephone advice services for children in difficulties are of no value if the children are too young to use them. It is here that society has a role to play, in keeping its eyes open. But it is also here that families, grandmothers and grandfathers and other relatives, have a role, and that parents have a duty not to split, when so much of the abuse is in fact perpetrated not by the natural parents but by step-parents, the lovers of the children's mothers, but not the children's natural fathers.

This is by no means universally true. Yet there is enough cause for concern to make a convincing case that part of effective child-protection lies in the child having its own parents at home, and preferably, of course, living in harmony. But homes and institutions alike should be open in a variety of ways to public scrutiny, so that violence has less opportunity to occur behind curtained windows and locked doors, in the privacy and terror of homes that become prisons, whether the family home or the children's home that was used, originally, to give refuge.

These are precisely the sorts of issues that women's organisations should be addressing. They are the concerns of Betty Friedan's 'second stage', as she implores women and men to work together to look at the kind of society we are creating. As women do most of the childcare, and take most of the responsibility for children, it would seem even more a women's issue than a men's, but fundamentally it is a joint issue, an issue for the whole of society, calling into question basic ideas about individual fulfilment and mutual obligation, about whether it is right for parents to abandon each other in separation and divorce at the cost of children's instability and unhappiness, about whether children are not a public concern, a community responsibility and pleasure and our communal future.

The women's movement has so far failed to address itself to this issue properly. It has failed to put high on the political agenda of all the parties the question of how, and to what extent, government agencies should pursue the fathers who refuse to pay maintenance, and it has failed to argue that two parents are better than one. It has failed to recognise that being rooted in a family, preferably a large, generational, wide, welcoming family, is a healthy atmosphere in which a child grows up with the ability to relate happily and securely to lots of adults, in contrast to the one-parent family where there is only Mum. It has failed to see that the insistence on individual rights for women, the 'right to choose', has led to a lack of recognition of the interests of children; that the family, for all its faults, is the best framework we have for the rearing of children, and that therefore a look at families from a feminist perspective, seeing where they can damage women's interests, must be combined with a look at it as a valuable institution worthy of retention.

And in looking at questions about how family patterns change, how divorce and separations, even in societies such as the Irish Republic that allow no divorce, increase and impinge on children, questions have to be asked about the extent to which the self-fulfilment of the individual can take precedence over the welfare of the group, be it the family, or the local community, or the society itself which finds the fragmentation of families hard to absorb. Those questions may challenge the orthodoxies of the 1960s, the age of 'doing one's own thing', and provide answers which refer to self-restraint and community and family duty. This is language that was hardly heard in the heady days of the 1960s, nor in the time of the growth of the modern women's movement in the early 1970s, with its consciousness-raising and its encouragement of women to be aware of the extent to which their chances of self-fulfilment were restricted by the men they lived with and their family responsibilities.

This time round, the discussion cannot be exclusively about women's duty, women's self-restraint, women's self-denial, but about the duty of everyone to consider the effects of their wishes and desires on other members of their families and communities, in all circumstances.

3

Sex

The marriage bed is a peculiarly delusive refuge from the world because all wives of necessity fuck by contract. Prostitutes are at least decently paid on the nail and boast fewer illusions about a hireling status that has no veneer of social acceptability.

Angela Carter *The Sadeian Woman*

ONE OF THE most extraordinary features of the women's movement is that it still has not come to terms - quite - with sex. There are huge numbers of books about sex - Germaine Greer's *The Female Eunuch*, Kate Millett's *Sexual Politics*, Harriett Gilbert and Christine Roche's *A Women's History of Sex* and many, many more. But there are also a large number of curious assumptions, including the radical feminist one that it is somehow better, nobler, more fitting, to do without men, to take one's sexual pleasures from women, to live in supportive women's environments without the threats and the putting down that men do to women, to remove oneself from male society because it is men who have taken all the power as a result of their sexual being.

The problem with all this is that it is vastly removed from the lives of most women, most of the time. Although evidence is mounting that 10% or more women have a lesbian affair at some point in their lives, and there is nothing wrong with that, it is quite clearly the case, as any study of women's magazines or magazines for young girls shows, that women still have romantic illusions about knights on white chargers who are going to come and take them away from whatever mind-blowingly boring existence they are now in, and that they will live happily every after.

If, for instance, one starts reading a classic Mills and Boon romance, beloved by many women across the classes and age range, one finds examples of handsome, tanned, film-star-like men coming to the rescue, practically as if they were knights on white chargers, of damsels in distress, or at least girls with long blonde hair and excellent eyes and teeth and complexions, who work in antique shops or do directors' lunches in the Home Counties. The man is passionate, embraces her, kisses her tenderly and thrust-ingly, and she melts into his arms. They presumably then go off and make love (I use their expression) and get married, in that order these days, and live happily ever after. There is still precious little of such literature about women's affairs with women, although it is a growing genre, with stories which have a distinctly lesbian and romantic flavour to them being written for young girls, such as Susannah Bowyer's *On the Verge*, about a girl who discovers she is a lesbian.[1] Yet on the whole the romantic dreams of women still tend not to include lesbian relationships.

This does not mean that they do not happen. Patently they do, and very often after a woman has been married for some years and has experienced dissatisfaction of varying seriousness with her spouse. There are, too, many women for whom sex with a woman is infinitely more satisfying than it is with a man, for reasons to be discussed below, and they will have lesbian affairs. But it is not part of most young women's dreams to become a lesbian, and the politicisation of it is seen by many less 'radical' feminists as being a mark against joining the ranks of the 'declared' lesbians, not because of their sexual orientation but because of their politics.

Harriett Gilbert argues that 'in learning to value one another as sisters, as friends, as political and personal support, "heterosexual" women in the 1970s and '80s rediscovered each other's potential as lovers.' I cannot help wondering if that is true. Was it not always the case that many, many women were lesbians? Were not many professional women of the earlier part of this century, who had apparently forsworn love and family for the sake of their career, in fact lesbian? In private conversations with several of them that is precisely the impression I formed, and one very distinguished elderly lady showed me a series of photographs of women which she had kept, all of them of lovers from her past, all of them now dead. And there was no suggestion that such liaisons had even been particularly private. In the right place, at the right time, women were quite open about their relationships with other women. Wartime was perhaps the best of all for these lesbian women of enormous professional reputation, because, as officers in the army, it was so easy for them to meet other similarly inclined women and to encourage the relationships.

It must also have been the case that a great deal of lesbian activity took place in the years after the First World War, when the menfolk who would have been husbands to so very many women were killed in the trenches and on the Somme. In her book, Harriett Gilbert virtually says as much, and argues convincingly that there was widespread lesbian activity which tended to be kept quiet except in a few, very privileged circles such as that of Vita Sackville-West and Virginia Woolf. But if the apocryphal story about Queen Victoria is only halfway true, that there was no legislation against lesbianism because she did not believe that women would do such things to one another, does it even suggest a need to keep things quiet, let alone a total absence of sexual activity? Indeed, love letters from women to women remain and were not thought in the least odd. It was quite usual for two women to live together and nobody apparently considered the sexual implications. Only in our so-called sexually liberated age do people raise an eyebrow at women living together, and even then only if they are young.

The difference today is surely in the assertion of lesbianism, and the confusion which has, I believe, been very damaging to the feminist cause, between the political cause of separation from men and the social cause of where one gets the greatest sexual, and community or family, satisfaction and pleasure.

There was much wrong with the attitudes involved in the sex-obsessed '60s, and the 'how to do it' books of the period make hilarious reading. They are all about how to experiment with vibrators and what to wear in bed (definitely not one's specs, which is a bit of a shame if one is short-sighted), and how to have an orgasm. As Harriett Gilbert puts it elegantly: 'These books . . . were, in attitude as much as tone, closer to the instruction manuals that you get when you buy a new blender.' They were distinctly clinical. It was the period, too, of the myth of the vaginal orgasm. Anne Koedt published her paper of that name in 1969, arguing that the route to sexual rapture lay through the clitoris and not the vagina at all. Germaine Greer disagreed, and a heady debate followed. The argument which ensued broke the anxiety women were having as to whether they had had an orgasm at all and had proved themselves in bed with their chain of men, as some of them roared with laughter at the debate itself and others began to realise that something quite important physically was happening to them anyway, wherever it was rooted.

But of course the most important aspect of it all was that it was not really a debate about orgasm, but about whether men were necessary for women's sexual satisfaction. It was only as a result of the sexual liberation of the 1960s that women felt able to talk in this vein at all. In the women's groups of the time, there was beginning to emerge an astonishingly low level of satisfaction with hetero-sexual sex, standard-style, by penetration. Women were agonising over the fact that they had no orgasm, and, indeed, it looked increasingly likely that Anne Koedt was right in her claim that sexual satisfaction came from the clitoris, so it was hardly surprising that women who had no deliberate stimulation of the clitoris by hand or by mouth were not reaching orgasm other than by masturbation, in secret.

This was one of the benefits of the sexual revolution. It actually became possible to say that the thrust of 'Wham, bang, thank you ma'am' was unsatisfactory, to ask for the added refinements of cunnilingus and manual stimulation. In the Victorian era, a woman was presumed to have no sexual desire, and letting her husband wreak his will upon her was the duty of every good Victorian wife. But by the late 1960s and early '70s it was quite possible to say, 'I want my sexual freedom, and I want to explore my sexuality.' It did not necessarily mean making love with women. It was possible to make love with men, on new terms, with new refinements, explaining that there were other things needed than plain penetration.

Yet penetration is what is perceived as 'normal' in sexual terms. Going right back to Freud and his theory of penis envy, there is the sense that a woman needs to be penetrated by a man in order to have a proper sexual experience, which, unlike the Victorians, she should not suppress. It is amazing that women never appear to have been consulted about this issue. Freud is not wholly to be blamed. He was writing in his time and in his place, and at least he thought women ought to have sexual experiences. But he was convinced, as were all the early sexologists, that sexual fulfilment for both sexes lay in penetration by the penis. Ultimately, for women, fulfilment lay in pregnancy, but before that it was essential that she switched from the clitoral stage to vaginal sexuality. Just the thing to reduce sexual pleasure! But he was not to know that, and, as far as we know, he did not ask.

Even more extraordinary – or perhaps it is only to be expected – is the writing of Havelock Ellis on the subject of awakening desire in a new and totally sexually inexperienced and uneducated wife: 'The civilised woman ... has often tended to come into her husband's hands ... in a condition inept for the conjugal embrace, which, if the bridegroom is lacking in skill or consideration, may cause her suffering or disgust. ...' On this Sheila Kitzinger, in *Woman's Experience of Sex*, rightly comments that 'this teaching reflected the power of the Sleeping Beauty myth. The princess is asleep till kissed by the prince who, on approaching the forest, sword in hand, discovers that, as if by magic, clearings appear in the thicket and blossoms replace thorns. Not only is the woman to be woken by the man, but the triumph is made possible by his sword-like penis.' So here we are back at penetration.

In order to understand just how important penetration was thought to be, it is essential to look at legislation, world wide. Almost every possible kind of sexual relations that does not consist in 'normal' heterosexual sex – by penetration by the man of the woman's vagina – is illegal in some state or other in the USA. This includes anal sex with people of either sex, oral sex, various forms of sado-masochism and homosexuality. The reason that lesbianism has been excluded from legislation in Britain may be nothing to do with Queen Victoria at all, but because there is no penetration, so it 'isn't real sex'. Because sex is seen very much from a man's point of view, and because legislation was made by men, whether religious or civil, ancient or comparatively modern, it is always penetration which is taken as the measure of sexual experience, and it is penetration, and the fruit of that penetration in the shape of pregnancy and children, that must be controlled by law. Add to that a civilisation which is basically anti-sex, such as early Christianity, or one that thinks it should be controlled, as in Judaism and Islam, and those forms of sex which do not lead to pregnancy and childbirth are often regarded as lascivious or lustful, or 'spilling seed in vain'. But woman to woman is usually irrelevant, because no penetration takes place, however much pleasure is given or received.

But the extraordinary thing is that, even now, with this possibility, one might have thought, gloriously opened up by a feminist critique of sex and by a study of the history of sex, many books are astonishingly coy about what gives many women by far the greatest pleasure, which is oral sex, or cunnilingus. Sheila Kitzinger, in her otherwise excellent and very informative *Woman's Experience of Sex*, devotes only a page to what she freely admits is what many women 'like best in lovemaking'. And in that page she devotes most of her attention to the fact that both men and women think that the vagina and the genital area are 'smelly' or 'dirty', rather than discussing specific techniques to give great pleasure, such as those she advocates in massage or in manual clitoral stimulation.

Sheila Kitzinger could hardly be accused of being coy about this area, yet it is extraordinary how little discussion there is of what most women obviously enjoy a great deal more than 'straight' penetration. The only true exception is Germaine Greer, in a delightful and typically irreverent piece she wrote for an alternative sex-paper entitled *Suck*, in 1971. In it, she sends up the then fashionable but now wholly discredited vaginal deodorant, by suggesting to the (female) reader that she sucks her own cunt: 'CUNT IS BEAUTIFUL. Suck it and see. If you're not so supple that you can suck your own fanny, put your finger gently in, withdraw and smell, and suck. There. How odd it is that the most expensive gourmet foods taste like cunt. Or is it?'[2]

Germaine Greer, who continued to believe in the efficacy of the vagina for enhancing sexual pleasure, had no time for the pussy-footing around the issue most of the sex advisors were doing. And, of course, she was right. Cunnilingus is a great pleasure-giver. But presumably men, or women, have to find the smell and taste attractive and a turn-on. QED.

The really interesting question is why the whole business of sex became a purely male domain, where women were supposed either to have no sexual feelings, as in the case of 'ladies' in the Victorian era, or to be the constant temptation. Much has been written about the Christian view of the body and the fault must be ascribed to Augustine for arguing that woman was the cause of all evil, the source of temptation, the lure to man. It goes back to the Christian interpretation of the story of Adam and Eve in the Hebrew Bible, where Eve caused Adam to sin: 'I do not permit a woman to be a teacher, nor must woman dominate over man; she should be quiet. For Adam was created first, and Eve afterwards; and it was not Adam who was deceived; it was the woman who, yielding to deception, fell into sin. Yet she will be saved through motherhood. . . .' (1 Timothy 22:13–15).

The response of the Church was to make the body itself, and sexuality, sinful. Attitudes to the body in early Christianity make for extraordinary reading. Nor was it only women's sexuality which was shameful, but men's as well, and there are numerous accounts of ardent young Christian men who castrated themselves in order to be spared the temptation of sex. In his masterly study of such attitudes,[3] Peter Brown discusses the whole question of sexual renunciation and the accusations of promiscuity which were thrown at members of the early Church because men and women prayed together. The role of women was a strange one in that setting, for in many cases, in order to earn the respect of men, they had to make themselves disgusting, wear fouled clothes and renounce any signs of their sexual nature. Only then could they be true Christians.

It is hard, from the vantage point of the twentieth century, to understand these attitudes, but if we really want to explore the nature of sexual relationships and how the Church has influenced them in the West, it is not sufficient to look merely at the medieval Catholic Church with its strong views about women being men's possessions and sex being only for the purpose of procreation. One has to consider the whole nature of sexual renunciation, and the element of temptation that was ascribed to women.

For the Church eventually came up with the perfect, and impossible, role for women in the shape of the Virgin Mary, every man's ideal (and probably quite a few women's as well, given the danger involved in childbirth and the subjection which women suffered in their sexual relationships). The Virgin Mary performed wonders: she gave birth to a child, in this case the Son of God, and remained a virgin. No other woman could match her. Others were either virgins, or mothers, but never both.

This in itself influenced the lot of women considerably. Virginity and chastity came to be major virtues in the eyes of the Church. Yet motherhood was essential for the procreation of the species, and there needed to be a fair bit of motherhood about because infant mortality was so high. Hence the insistence on sex, not as a source of pleasure for either participant, but because of the duty of peopling the earth, for the greater glory of God.

But at least at that date, in the early Christian era and throughout the medieval and renaissance periods, women were thought to be sexual beings. Too much so, really. They were lascivious, and always out to tempt men. But that was surely preferable as an image to the Victorian one of women having no sexual urges, and being subject to the husband's desire because that was the duty of a good wife. It is fascinating to think where that came from, but at least it is clear that it is not part of the early Christian tradition as passed down within the Catholic Church. The non-sexuality of women had more to do with a romantic image of women as eternal little girls, tender and delicate.

Other religions had a different view, however. Hinduism celebrated sexuality with its *Kama Sutra* and wonderful erotic sculptures at Khajurao and elsewhere, sculptures that are equally erotic for men and women. Classical civilisation had allowed women to play a sexual role, from the Vestal Virgins who married later on to the *matronae* of ancient Rome who practised contraception. Judaism insisted that women had a right to sexual satisfaction from their husbands, and there was a list drawn up as to how often a husband of a particular trade or profession might be expected to make love to his wife. It was once every six months for a tanner, who presumably smelled pretty dreadful, and once a week for a scholar. And the wife could demand her satisfaction. Her sexuality was formally acknowledged, to the extent that it was legitimate, in Jewish law, for a man to perform cunnilingus, described as kissing her in her intimate parts, 'in that place', if that gave her pleasure. This was written at the same time as the Christian Church was beginning to reject sex and the body altogether, and the contrast is remarkable.

But Christianity has been infinitely more influential in Europe than Judaism ever was, and it is Christian attitudes to sex and to the perceived temptation set by women that are so fascinating. Gradually, feminist historians of religion, such as Elaine Pagels, are making sense of all this, and male scholars such as Peter Brown are expressing their gratitude to them because of the degree to which they have changed the perception of the early and medieval Church. It is important that this area is fully studied by the women's movement, which has been, until now, all too keen to lambast early Christianity and the early rabbis of Judaism as sexist without examining the true nature of those beliefs. So influential have they been on modern thought that they must be given a fair reading. This is all the more important at a time when religious belief, and specifically fundamentalist religious belief, is coming more and more into fashion, and women are more and more likely to be pushed behind the veil, out of sexual satisfaction, back into the home and out of public office or even appearance in the churches and synagogues.

For, if the forces of conservatism in religion and society at large become more successful, if women are restricted more and more in what they can do and where they can go, as evidence from many Muslim countries suggests is the case, and as parallel social moves in the West appear to hint as well, then it is all too likely that the prevailing morality will once again be that it is all right for men to sow their wild oats, but women must be faithful, and the woman caught in adultery will be stoned under Islamic law and reviled under Christian. As 'Victorian values' and the supremacy of the family are preached again and again, it is time that women took a serious look at that institution, particularly as it relates to sexual fidelity, rather than simply talking about the choices women make to leave their families and go to live in communes in groups of women. That will always be a minority sport. The majority will stay with their children and their families, and be the carers and nurturers as they always were. But will they be faithful?

This is an area the women's movement has not explored. Yet the evidence cited in Annette Lawson's book *Adultery* suggests that married women are less likely to be faithful after one affair than their husbands are. Does this suggest a total dissatisfaction with the pleasures of heterosexual sex, as the radicals in the women's movement would have us believe? Or does it suggest that the sexual liberation of the 1960s taught women that they did not have to put up with any old kind of sex that they were offered, but that they could look around for what was really satisfying, really exciting, and learn more about themselves as sexual beings in the process? Or does it merely tell us that adultery is easier the second time? At least for women?

Annette Lawson's evidence suggests that the incidence of adultery, particularly amongst younger women, occurs precisely because looking for sexual experiences is commonplace amongst women, but she also cautions that women do tend not to separate sex and emotion in the same way that men do. Anne Kelleher, in her superb *Sex Within Reason*, argues hard for marriage being a kind of bondage, following John Stuart Mill's analysis of marriage as a trap and a route into possession of people, not objects. She then states firmly that it is quite possible to have a perfectly good definition of marriage which does not entail the husband owning the wife. That, of course, is absolutely correct, and the question of adultery is then more about the betrayal of trust than about the right to find sexual fulfilment or simply to break loose. Although Anne Kelleher does not wholly rule out adultery as being acceptable within any moral scheme, she is very sceptical about it, allowing only for rare exceptions where it can be described as acceptable. The truth of the matter is that it is far from rare, and that younger women in marriage will be unfaithful more quickly than men.

If this is the case, and evidence suggests that it is, there are many questions to be asked about how women feel about their family lives, their responsibilities and their duties rather than their happiness. Many women I talked to when thinking about this book in its early stages spoke at length about a profound sense of dissatisfaction with their lives, a sense of isolation in the midst of family responsibilities, an absence of real relationships with their husbands, which was what had lured them into taking lovers in the first place. There are men who make very good friends as well as lovers, who genuinely enjoy the company of women more than the company of men, and they are hugely in demand amongst women. This is surely because so many women find themselves married to, and trapped in daily relationships and obligations with, men who may love them, according to their understanding, but have no time or inclination to talk, and who will sprawl night after night in front of the television, watching the sport or the news, and chatting only very occasionally. This was said so often, with such irritation mixed with affection and resignation, by so many women, that it must lead us to question what those women who have taken the conventional path of marriage and children, who love and are loved, really get out of their relationships. And is this where Betty Friedan's second stage of thinking about feminism, with its emphasis on the sexes working together rather than against each other, ought to take us, into examining what has happened to relationships of love, leaving so many people dissatisfied, men as well as women?

What does the women's movement have to say to all this? Is it right that women should be experimenting sexually? Do they merely succeed in 'cutting men down to size' by their early and easy infidelities? Is infidelity as satisfactory a way of reducing men's power over women as getting rid of men altogether could be? These are questions which need women's analysis. The area of heterosexual behaviour amongst women, outside marriage, has received all too little attention from a series of women in the radical political movement whose main concern is to draw women out of heterosexual relationships altogether.

Indeed, the next area for analysis must surely be the good accredited 'feminists' who decide to get married and have a rather conventional family with husband and children. To many of their erstwhile sisters, they are traitors. When discussing this single issue of women's sexuality and its relationship to family organisation, the most common response I got from a variety of women of different backgrounds but with a clear, committed feminist political perspective, was how hurt they had been when they had told their 'sisters' that they were going to marry, and were rejected out of hand. The new discussion may need to be about coming out of the closet as a heterosexual woman with apparently conventional ideas about love, marriage and children, for at the moment such a position can lead to the suggestion that one is 'not a proper feminist after all'.

Yet most of us will marry, and have children. It is the dissatisfactions, the unhappiness, the reliance, for the rich, on psychotherapy and counselling (appropriate in its place, but not as a substitute for conversations and building relationships), the wealth of injured, accepting looks on women's faces, the sense of anomie, the boredom, that really need examination. And that examination must take account of the fact that most of us still want our sexual relationships to be with men. We also want children, and parents, and families, to love and to cherish, and, of course, to be part of, to protect us against the appalling sense of isolation that is the problem of so many of the women I talked to for this book.

4

Birth Control

The day when, misunderstanding the inferior occupations
which nature has given her, women leave the home and take
part in our battles; on that day a social revolution will begin and
everything that maintains the sacred ties of the family will
disappear. . . .

Gustave Le Bon, French scientist.

THOSE OF US who did most of our maturing in the West in the 1960s
learned a slogan never fully to be unlearned, although forever to be
laughed at. It ran: 'Make love, not war.' We were, like most
adolescents at any time or place, alternately thrilled and repelled by
its message. Sex was frightening, alluring, profound, tempting – and,
as teenagers growing up before legal abortion had been introduced
in Britain, very dangerous. I did have one friend at school who left
because she got pregnant. She was, however, a clergyman's daughter, and I believe that it was her parents' influence which led to her
decision to leave and have the baby, marrying the boy 'responsible'.
For plenty of others got pregnant too, but they did not talk about it
in the same way, and they had their illegal abortions in clinics in St
John's Wood, paid for by wealthy, indulgent, 'liberated' Hampstead
parents. But the school, which had hitherto made an appalling job
of educating us about matters sexual, on the grounds that it was for
our mothers to do (most of them thought it was for the school),
decided it had better do something about the situation, which was
plainly getting out of hand.

Hitherto we had been treated to diagrams of the male and female reproductive organs put up on the blackboard in a biology lesson, for us all to copy. Unattractive little girls that we were, we began to snigger, and the embarrassed unmarried biology teacher walked out of the room, blushing, leaving us to our own devices, which consisted mainly of giggling. Now, two years later, at the ripe old age of sixteen, we had discussions about sex with a rather impressive woman who came in and took us off in groups. Of course, no-one would talk openly, and we remained silent as she spoke competently and unemotionally about the Pill, just coming into its heyday, and the diaphragm, and the condom, then still a subject of huge amusement to us all, with its association with illicit sex, which the others did not have. But she persevered, in difficult circumstances, and I am convinced she contributed indirectly if not directly to the numbers of us 'going on the Pill' within the next year or so.

By encouraging us to do this, she was assuming several things. One was that some or many of us were already having some form of sexual relationship. The incidence of abortion, the one schoolgirl pregnancy that I remember and the numbers who later talked about 'going on the Pill' immediately would suggest that she was right. But I do not know for certain, for though we would sit on the radiators on a Monday morning discussing 'how far we had gone' the previous Saturday night – even if it was only watching *That Was The Week That Was* on the box with a friendly arm around one – the lies and half-truths of the sexual competition were so obvious that those who had what we later described as 'meaningful sexual encounters' would never have confessed the fact to that audience. But they might have gone off to the doctor, who would very likely have prescribed the Pill to the under-sixteens, long before the celebrated case brought by Mrs Victoria Gillick in 1985, in which she argued, unsuccessfully, that it was illegal for family doctors to prescribe contraceptive pills to girls under the age of sixteen without their parents' consent.

But in the 1960s freely available contraception for women was undoubtedly considered the norm. We were not concerned with the joke condoms, which allowed men to sow their wild oats. We were talking about sexual liberation. For the first time girls were able to be as carefree sexually as boys. They could sleep with whoever they wanted to, and they could have stable relationships or live in communes. And if you were not 'making it' with someone, there had to be something wrong with you. On the other hand, we had the first serious discussions of women's entitlement to sexual pleasure. The vaginal orgasm was all the rage despite those later suggestions that it did not really exist. Sexual fulfilment was a right. Women had for too long been the victims of male thinking about women's sexuality. Victorian attitudes about sex being a duty were long past, but the idea that a girl should be a virgin at marriage whilst a boy needed to have some experience was still prevalent. Our rejection of this was swift and total.

That was the common thinking of middle-class schoolgirls, anyway. Of course it was not quite like that. The history of contraception is a far more complicated matter than the prescription of hormone pills to hundreds of thousands of immature girls would suggest. It has its origins in a far earlier period, when sheaths made of linen were worn by men to avoid venereal disease, and used with prostitutes rather than with wives. There are, too, plenty of accounts of early forms of contraceptive, including a sort of cap, the *mokh*, in rabbinic literature, designed to protect a girl from getting pregnant too young, if she was still physically immature when she was married, and in a few other situations.[1] As well as this, it appears that the Roman *matronae* used half-lemons as a form of cap, and that the spermicidal properties of vinegar were well known throughout the ancient world.

What is remarkable, however, is that this knowledge was either lost or deliberately hidden from women in the medieval and later periods. When Edward Shorter writes of the fear of childbirth,[2] he does it from the standpoint of women who had no knowledge of safe periods, or for whom the authority of their menfolk and their required submission to demands for sexual relations whenever the men wanted them meant that any knowledge they did have was profoundly irrelevant:

> Put yourselves in the shoes of the typical housewife who lived in a small town or village then. Neither she nor anyone else had any idea when the 'safe' period for women was, and for her, any sexual act could mean pregnancy. She was obliged to sleep with her husband whenever he wanted. And in the luck of the draw, she would become pregnant seven or eight times, bearing an average of six live children. Most of these children were unwelcome to her, for if one single theme may be said to hold my story together, it is in the danger to every aspect of her health that this ceaseless childbearing meant.

In other words, there were no contraceptives, and there were huge risks to women from childbirth. So that the invention in 1838 of a contraceptive in the form of a true cap (as opposed to the diaphragm which came to take its place and is often referred to as the Dutch cap) was a major breakthrough. Its inventor, Friedrich Adolphe Wuilde, took a model of the cervix in wax, made a cap out of latex, and found it was copied very quickly by people producing them in gold, silver, ivory, rubber and platinum. The cap appears to have been seen as a once-in-a-lifetime acquisition, removed only for the menstrual flow. Unlike the diaphragm, which superseded it, it did not need to be renewed, coated in spermicidal cream, washed out and hung over the bath taps to dry (as gloriously described by Germaine Greer in *Sex and Destiny*), but it was essentially the contraceptive device of middle-class women. It was, according to Germaine Greer, advertised in *The Wife's Handbook*[3] as a 'check pessary' and cost 2s 3d a piece.

Quite why the cap fell into disfavour is not clear, though it was certainly in use in some circles before the Second World War, particularly in Germany. It may have something to do with the rather chequered career of Marie Stopes, who obviously advocated it at one point, or because of the confusion caused by Stopes, her biographer Ruth Hall and others between the cervical cap and the diaphragm. What is quite clear is that the campaigns run by both Marie Stopes in Britain and Margaret Sanger in the USA had a somewhat deleterious effect on precisely the people they wished to help. The reasons are these: both women, according to Germaine Greer, were convinced publicists. That in itself suggests they were less than tactful in their approach to the intimate details of people's lives. But far outweighing that consideration, to my mind, was a stated or implied eugenic argument in their preaching, which was that the reason contraception was essential was to control the breeding of the very poor. Stopes herself referred to C3 families, and both she and Sanger translated their eugenic enthusiasm into 'a rhetoric of glorified motherhood and racial hygiene'.

Poor women, with all the fear Shorter has described of the consequences of many children, had nevertheless seen a marked improvement in their own health by about the turn of the century, partly, no doubt, due to increased medical intervention in childbirth, but also because the prevalence of infection had been so massively reduced by universal use of antisepsis and asepsis. The public health moves of the mid to late nineteenth century, to improve sewerage and water supplies, had also helped to transform their lives. The result was that childbirth was not as feared as it had been, and that the desire to limit the families of the poor (and, of course, as it later developed in Britain, the US and ultimately Germany, mental defectives, criminals, gypsies and Jews – anyone, in fact, not like us) was primarily felt by the middle classes. This can be seen just as clearly now in the desire of the less fertile West to limit the number of children born to poor mothers in the Third World. Masked behind the argument that it is for their own good (more food for fewer babies), it is at least partly an expression of the impatience of Western politicians and civil servants at the thought of having to give aid forever to these fecund, irresponsible, ill-organised people, who could get things so much better in their own countries if they really tried. Germaine Greer's brilliant *Sex and Destiny* is a thoroughly convincing argument along these lines, even though she probably underrates the fear felt by some women in the Third World when things go wrong in childbirth, and medical intervention is unreachable. But that is another battle.

So if the eugenics argument was not going to work, what was? A variety of factors came into play. First there was the view, held remarkably uncritically in the 1960s, that women were entitled to orgasm too. The vaginal orgasm became sought after by every self-respecting woman, and by then the Pill was freely available. But the history goes back longer than that. Wartime had a lot to do with it. There is no doubt that sexual adventures, short-term liaisons for women as well as for men, are a feature of the insecurity about the future prevalent in wartime. If you could not be sure that you were going to survive, what, after all, was the point of normal 'moral' behaviour?

Certainly sexual morals appear to have changed considerably during the Second World War. Women I have spoken to describe the normality, in a time when it was not clear they would survive, of having sex with a comparative stranger, something that would have been unthinkable a decade or so earlier. Many used condoms; some used diaphragms. They made love in the strangest of places, under the pier at Blackpool or in the bushes at the back of the NAAFI. But the sense that the end of the world was nigh, that there might be no future, that the men especially were likely to die in combat, made the girls generous and reckless, and the men demanding and not always careful. Recent TV programmes have shown women in their seventies talking about the backstreet abortions they had during the war and saying that they were sure their friends did the same. It was part of what the war did to people. There was no security and no certainty, but morals – so they said – were easier and looser, and diaphragms easier to get.

Men in the army were constantly being treated for venereal disease, but then they always had been. It was a court-martial offence, but that was rarely carried out. But women in the forces were catching a lot of gonorrhoea too, and being treated for it. A now dead friend, Dame Albertine Winner, had charge of the health of the women troops during the war, and frequently reflected on their sexual activity. There was, she said, a large instance of promiscuity, related to a sense of danger and impermanence, but also to a great desire to experiment sexually, which had never been possible at home. It is very likely that those women formed the beginnings of women's sexual liberation, in the same way that women in the First World War working in men's jobs whilst they were away in the army can be viewed as the beginnings of the liberation of women in a professional sense, despite it taking until after the Second War for the concept of equality in the workplace to establish itself. (I say 'concept' deliberately, since there has not been equality in actual fact in the workplace even now.)

But the obsession of the 1960s with sex, sexual satisfaction and the female orgasm has still not been adequately explained. Living through it, it seemed blindingly obvious. Living through it, the older generation who had themselves, one can only suppose, been fairly sexually liberated during the war, seemed to have prehistoric attitudes. The mothers who asked, 'Darling, are you sure this is sensible?' were seen as stuffy. The fathers who threw boyfriends out of bedrooms came out of the dark ages. As one team of writers put it, 'In the 1960s sexual freedom was widely and confidently accepted as the obvious aim, and, for the first time, efficient birth control seemed to offer a sure means of reaching it. . . . It is striking now to see the confidence with which the liberating feminists of that day accepted both these ideas.'⁴ We had no doubts. It was the day of the commune. One girl I knew well at Cambridge, who now lives a surprisingly sedate suburban life, had a commune in her room in college consisting of a minimum of fourteen people and often very many more. They were big rooms, but even so the crowding was considerable and the degree to which everybody slept with every-body else pretty great.

The dream soon turned into a nightmare. Apart from the obvious virtues of the Pill as an unfeelable, invisible (because hormonal) barrier to prevent conception, and an infallible one (as it seemed), it also made women entirely responsible for contraception and removed at a stroke the obvious excuse for saying no. No wonder women felt that they should always say yes. So they said yes, and believed that they were inadequate if they did not keep saying yes, to different men, all the time. But the main beneficiaries were men, for women became suddenly very available. The slogan was 'Make love, not war,' and the hippy girls made love, and more love, and more love, and cooked his aduki beans and his tofu, and became quite worn out in the process. Indeed, their exploitation was very similar to that of women of an earlier age. Their role was purely for men's pleasure.

Yet they could have said no, and no doubt many did, and often. There were and are always reasons: not fancying someone, not wanting sex at that time, not feeling there was a relationship there, not knowing the man well enough. But that has to be set against a culture where sex itself was adulated, where the philosophy of letting it all hang out, doing what came naturally, was at least in some circles surprisingly dominant.

And 'at about the same time a whole set of new reasons for saying yes appeared in the emphasis laid on the female orgasm as an easy and obligatory experience, a necessary diploma in self-fulfilment, obtainable by consistent practice, enlightened attitudes and reading all the right books.'[5] So much for the Pill's liberation.

It was also going to keep us eternally young and nubile, since it reduced menstrual flow and the anaemia associated with it, and it was suggested that if we kept on taking it, our hormonal balance would be up on the oestrogen side, allowing us a youthful appear-ance, skin-deep at least (which was part of the theory behind hormone replacement therapy some fifteen years later). Allied with that, we threw away our bras, though our breasts were larger as a result of taking the Pill, and the sight of women bouncing along as they ran for buses and trains is still embedded deep in my visual memory as one of the funnier sights of the late '60s and early '70s.

But in fact the Pill may well not have done much for our health, and, although it took us a long time to realise it, it may well have contributed to the degree of depression already often felt by young women when premenstrual. Germaine Greer put the side-effect situation very well in an article she wrote for the *Sunday Times*:

> The Pill is supposed . . . to be the perfect contraceptive, regardless of side effects, short-term and long-term. Somewhere there is a Pill for every woman, specially adapted to her particular hormone balance, a Pill which does not nauseate, bloat or depress her, does not cause breakthrough bleeding, will not activate any disposition to thrombosis. The trouble is that the woman herself has got to find it. She may go on for years experimenting, waiting three months for side effects to settle down and finding they don't, while her doctor finds, in the suggestion that she changes her Pill, a panacea for all ills. . . . In order that one process be inhibited, a multitude of other related processes are disturbed . . . women are distressed by the efflorescence of brown discolouration around their mouth, forehead and eyes, and the upsetting of the hormone balance in the vagina which affects lubrication and sensitivity, and the inhibition of sexual desire itself.[6]

Not to mention the headaches, the tension, the added tendency to thrombosis and the now discovered increase in the number of younger women with breast cancer which, according to some theorists, appears to correlate with taking the contraceptive pill, though that is unproven.

So for many women the Pill has its disadvantages. What, then, are the other possible forms of contraception available? Some feminists still argue boldly for abortion on demand, because it does not mess up women's endocrinal systems, because it is not something that has to be used during every sexual encounter but only when pregnant, and because they feel it should always be the mother who chooses, who decides whether or not that particular foetus lives or dies. That was a very popular argument in the late 1960s and early 1970s. Don't let the men tell us when we can and cannot have our babies. But there is a huge problem here. Abortion is a particularly sensitive issue, and no book which is trying to examine changing patterns of thinking among women over the last twenty years or so can ignore it, even though it still raises extraordinary passions, both among those who oppose it under any circumstances, and those who insist it is a woman's right, to be given her 'upon demand'. Curiously, the latter view now holds sway more among middle-aged and middle-class women in the West than among younger women, who nevertheless have more of the abortions.

The instance of abortions in the UK is still very high, at around 283,000 per annum, but it has become a less generally accepted method of dealing with an unwanted pregnancy in some quarters. Though many women still opt for it, the evidence is mounting that it does cause considerable emotional distress, that most women do not regard it as the easy choice, and that to the surprise of many doctors, who see it as the logical way of dealing with difficulties instead of going ahead and having a baby and wrecking a promising career or relationship, the women concerned shy away and opt for adoption, or simply having, and then keeping, the baby. One of the best results, perhaps, of the changes in family patterns which have had such terrible knock-on effects in other ways, is the extent to which young women choose not to have abortions but go ahead and have the baby, and bring him/her up quite successfully.

But the economic impact of this, with serious poverty in many families headed by a single woman, and particularly amongst those headed by a single very young woman, has not yet been taken into account, yet another feature of the failure of government, and political parties, to regard children as a national asset, and an absolute necessity, particularly as our birth rate fails to match our death rate. In the European Community in 1985, only the Irish Republic had a birthrate above the mean of two, with the population replacing itself, with Great Britain at 1.78, and Italy, West Germany and Denmark below 1.5. Figures as low as these suggest that there will have to be inducements to persuade women to have children, in order to have the labour force necessary for economic growth. All the evidence points to it being in the national interest to think much more corporately, with much better social provision, about the business of having children, and supporting their parents and community structures.

Yet plenty of erstwhile 1960s feminists continue to argue for abortion. This has become easier with the morning-after pill, a form of abortifacient which nevertheless does not always presume a pregnancy, and which does not have the shocking emotional and physical after-effects of abortion itself. Nevertheless, many people, both male and female, feel horror at the thought of deliberately terminating the life of a fertilised ovum, an embryo or even a pre-embryo, as the scientists like to call the pre-fourteen-day creatures. It is undoubtedly true that many of those embryos and foetuses are going to be aborted naturally. It is equally true, as Germaine Greer with her faultless logic points out time and again, that sperm are living organisms which will perish unless they find an ovum to fertilise. But illogical or not, there is for many people a sense that the fertilised ovum, the pre-embryo, is the beginning of the growth of a foetus and ultimately a baby, and that it should not be wilfully destroyed for the convenience of anybody, its mother included.

This is not, let me hasten to add, a total anti-abortion argument. I used to be much more firmly opposed to abortion in all circumstances than I am now. But, like many other women who would describe themselves as feminists, I find the direct association of feminism with the belief in abortion on demand hard to take. It seems to me that there may be situations where an abortion is, sadly, the only right thing to do. Rape victims are one example, but very young girls are often talked into having an abortion more because it suits their families and their families' expectations of them better, than because it is absolutely clearly to the benefit of the girl herself. There also seems to me to be no argument about the hypothetical, but occasionally actual, example of a case where the woman's own life is at risk from giving birth, and the choice lies between the woman and the unborn child. There I think the woman takes precedence every time, in that it must be more important to preserve the life already established than the potential, however near. This view is often put forward by those who hold a utilitarian view of such matters, who argue that the woman's other children need her more than the unborn child needs to be born. But that is specious, since it assumes that all women in this situation are already mothers, and therefore would make it entirely possible to take the opposite view if the child were the first pregnancy.

It cannot be said that an unborn child is equal in value with either a man or a woman. It has hopes, expectations and prayers attached to it. If it is unwanted, it does not even have that. But it does have some status, a status which grows until the point where it is viable and can exist without its mother's support. It acquires its status gradually, and the loss, by miscarriage or abortion, of a foetus of twelve weeks is not as distressing as, say, the loss of one at eighteen weeks, or, even worse, a stillborn child or one that dies after a few hours or days.

This is a very important part of the argument. In many cultures and legal systems, a baby under thirty days old does not have full legal status. In my own religion, Jewish law states that a child who dies under the age of thirty days does not have a full funeral. That in itself presupposes an attitude that such a child, or a miscarried foetus, is not a 'real person', i.e. does not have fully established personhood. That being the case, it is illegitimate to campaign against abortion on the grounds of 'murder' or wilful killing of a person. It can only be argued on the basis of potential, and that the foetus, left uninterrupted, might have grown into a baby, if it had not aborted naturally.

This is not a view that many feminists, certainly of the 1960s vintage, would agree with. As a result of that insistence upon abortion on demand, I believe that many women lost sympathy for that aspect of the women's movement. It was particularly true when it became clear that many women who did have late miscarriages or indeed stillborn children were deeply distressed at the lack of a grave, or a proper service, or some method of grieving over this being with whom they had had some sort of relationship in the womb. In other words, there is a stage at which some women feel that the unborn child – a great deal more advanced than the foetus the campaigns for early abortion on demand are about – is a person due at least some of the respect accorded to other human beings.

This makes it imperative for campaigners for abortion on demand to think about what they are saying. Women who are deeply sympathetic to the view that women's bodies have been taken over by men – doctors and scientists in particular – will find it hard to be sympathetic to the claim that the early foetus has no 'being', because that is not how they feel about it. Indeed, one might argue that precisely the same complaints made by those who write the feminist critiques of medical and scientific practice – that they do not ask women how they themselves feel because that is not objective, ascertainable evidence – could be raised against those same writers, who, for the excellent motive of not wishing to harm women's endocrinal system, argue for early abortion on demand.

Germaine Greer argues that the major and most glaring inconsistency in the abortion debate is the IUD. There is pretty clear evidence that this acts either as an abortifacient (that is to say it causes a twenty-eighth day termination) or at the very least not as a preventor of conception (since the sperm does fertilise the ovum), but as a preventer of implantation, because the uterus lining becomes toxic to the fertilised egg. She puts it very clearly: 'The commonest kind of IUD abortion, the twenty-eighth day termination, is, apart from increased blood loss and perhaps some pain, completely non-traumatic. No theologians, bishops, pro-life groups, psychiatrists or jurists sit on the case of the IUD acceptor, and the manufacturers and promoters of the devices are not at all anxious to attract their attention.'[7] And she attacks with good reason the slipperiness of the birth-control lobby in its discussions about the IUD. They rarely say the IUDs are abortifacients, and still try to keep going the notion that they do not really know how they work (which would seem an excellent reason for arguing that if they do not know, they should not prescribe them), yet they are able to speak as follows: 'Biologically, intrauterine devices may work partly as abortifacients. No doctor is going to stop using them because of this possibility, and no reasonable woman is going to be disturbed by this fact, both of which observations emphasise the very genuine difference between the destruction of a newly fertilised egg and an abortion later in pregnancy.'[8]

This is somewhat cheap. The writer is muddying the waters. Whether he likes it or not, many women *are* going to be bothered precisely about whether it is the destruction of a newly fertilised egg or something which prevents fertilisation altogether. And there will be a variety of reasons for that concern, some good and some less so. But because they know that many women feel this way, the birth-control lobby deliberately pretend that there is doubt about the matter and call IUDs contraceptive, rather than abortifacient, devices. Their concern is not only for the peace of mind of the women (another example of the medical profession and its allies taking the decision out of the hands of the women involved) but also, presumably, to avoid the problem with the law and with the medical profession's own code of ethics, stretching right back to the Hippocratic oath.

That is the evasive account of the situation given by the birth-control professionals, those who see a profound distinction, invisible to anyone else, between the early abortifacient, which may or may not be procuring an abortion depending on whether a pregnancy actually existed at the time, and the later abortion, and who manage to encourage the abortifacient at the same time as denying the abortion. In other words, a physical plastic or copper intrusion into women's bodies on a permanent basis, which certainly prevents implantation is all right, whilst a single intrusion into a woman's body in order to remove the definitely established contents of her womb is not.

But that is only one part of the story, and it is not what the radicals wanted at all. They wanted abortion on demand because it made women more sexually available than ever, without requiring them to take any responsibility, not even for the possible side effects of pills and IUDs. It was the culmination of the sexual revolution to have abortion on demand. As Andrea Dworkin wrote in *Right-Wing Women*:

> It was the brake that pregnancy put on fucking that made abortion a high-priority political issue for men in the 1960s – not only for young men, but also the older Leftist men who were skimming sex off the top of the counterculture, and even for more traditional men who dipped into the pool of hippy girls now and then. The decriminalisation of abortion – for that was the political goal – was seen as the final fillip: it would make women absolutely accessible, absolutely 'free'. The sexual revolution, in order to work, required that abortion be available to women on demand. If it were not, fucking would not be available to men on demand. Getting laid was at stake. Not just getting laid, but getting laid the way great numbers of boys and men had always wanted – lots of girls who wanted it all the time outside marriage, free, giving it away. The male-dominated Left agitated for and fought for and even provided political and economic resources to abortion rights for women. The Left was militant on the issue.

There is undoubtedly a lot of truth in this, though Andrea Dworkin, along with other feminist writers, does not on the whole pay any attention to the willing role that women played, women for whom the sexual revolution was pleasurable too. But I am sure she is right in saying that the abortion-on-demand campaign gained such great support because of men's desire for women's availability.

But more moderate feminists do not appear to see this as the case. Mary Midgley and Judith Hughes, in their otherwise excellent book *Women's Choices*, do not examine the causes for the campaigns on either side at all. They simply state the positions of those on each side: 'One party credits all embryos with an absolute right to life, so that all abortion is mere [mere?] murder. The other has replied (not surprisingly) by crediting women with an absolute right over their own bodies, which results in absolute liberty to abort, and indeed to be given an abortion on demand.' They then point out, correctly, that 'this language of absolute rights is unusable.' They argue that the development of the foetus is a gradual process, so that it cannot be given full human status at conception, and take up the point made by Germaine Greer and others that there is a bizarre quality to the argument about the rights of the implanted embryo when we do not talk about the rights of the ovum or the sperm.

But having said all that, and walked carefully through the marsh of conflicting arguments, including a healthy warning to us all to examine our attitudes to aid for disaster victims, or to killing animals, or to caring for the sick and elderly, they come out with the extraordinary statement that 'our present system is surely right to make it available in principle, but to give the factors surrounding each case very careful consideration.' They neither prove the case (to argue that different people and different groups set different values on human life and pre-life is not to make the case) nor do they address the question of who makes the decision.

The present situation is that the decision is made by doctors, once they have been approached by the women concerned, and that there is huge variation from area to area, let alone from doctor to doctor, as to the availability of abortion. It is simply untenable not to take into account the fact that doctors themselves, both male and female, have very strong views on this issue, and that the decision cannot therefore be left to their 'professional judgement', other than in very extreme and obviously life-threatening cases. There must be a cogent argument which runs along the lines that, if abortion is to be available at all, it must be carried out according to the wishes of the specific woman who requests it and not according to the views of the doctors she consults. Which is the argument that brings even the anti-abortionists (who do not want to remove it altogether because illegal abortion poses even greater risks) back to a philosophical position not very far from those who argue for abortion on demand, but for different reasons.

But it is difficult to make the case for abortion on demand unless contraception simply was not available. In other words, one can argue that responsible people, making their own sensible, responsible, moral choices, will not need abortion since they would not have got pregnant in the first place. One can, in the wake of the AIDS crisis, go one step further and argue that any sensible person having any sexual relationship would be using a barrier method anyway to prevent infection. This is seriously written in responsible journals, advertised widely to the young and firmly believed by theologians, philosophers and teachers alike. On this attitude depends much current sex education in the UK. On this attitude depends the rather punitive attitude to the requests for abortion when they are made to many doctors. 'You should have been more careful. Why didn't you use contraceptives?'

This is a rather strange attitude, because it assumes that the writer or speaker has never been carried away by sexual passion, or simply got drunk at a party and been unable to remember next morning what has taken place. They have never lost control. That just is not the case for a large number of, particularly young, people. One might wish that it were otherwise, but the truth is that a large number of girls get carried away, or are ill-informed, or decide to get pregnant anyway. Germaine Greer reports the 1978 House of Representatives Select Committee on Population in the US as hearing from the chairman that 'over one million teenagers became pregnant last year. At least 30,000 of them were under the age of fifteen. Twenty per cent of our fourteen- and fifteen-year-olds are sexually active. . . . You may be as astonished as I was to find out that the adolescent pregnancy rate in the United States is substantially higher than in any of the developing countries.[9] Contraceptives are available to most of those young people, in a way that they simply do not want or use or understand. With all the publicity about AIDS and the desirability of wearing a condom, the evidence suggests that young people between the ages of sixteen and twenty-five are still not wearing them. Older people are. Older people are also wearing IUDs, taking the Pill and being sterilised.

There is then a difficult debate to have. One can go down Germaine Greer's road and argue for a freely available morning-after pessary or pill for those who want it. Or even for a 'free, fast and non-traumatic abortion service'. She realises the problems: 'The idea that young people should use abortion as a primary method of birth control causes the most extreme disgust, while the phenomenon of a very young woman struggling with powerful and potentially very destructive medications leaves most people unmoved.'[10] The problem is that it is not quite a fair comparison. There are plenty of people who find the idea of using abortion as a primary method of birth control both disgusting and morally wrong. That does not imply that they view with equanimity the use of Pills and IUDs by the very young, and, indeed, it might mean that they were concerned to promote the use of condoms, however unaesthetic they have seemed hitherto, or any other barrier method which is neither invasive endocrinally, nor abortifacient, nor liable to damage tubes and uterus, like the IUD. Indeed, they might feel that there was positive benefit in promoting the condom as both contraceptive and anti-AIDS device, unless one were prepared to take the absurd and most unrealistic view that young people should or would stop having sexual relationships at all.

This would not rule out abortion in all cases, but it might have the benefit of making it less prevalent. If a girl, as well as a boy, knew that she needed to carry condoms, and they were thought of as perfectly acceptable and indeed fun, then there might be a change in thinking about the whole subject. But as yet we are a long way from that point. Indeed, the reactions to condoms from those who are beginning to use them more frequently, the over-twenty-fives, on an anecdotal basis, is that they inhibit sensation, that they are hard to get on, that women find them hard to put on their menfolk, and that the Pill or the IUD is far better for regular lovers.

This, of course, takes no account of AIDS at all, nor the clear indication that the numbers of heterosexuals who are HIV positive in the UK is growing rapidly, and is significantly high in some areas of London and other big cities. This was demonstrated by a survey of women in ante-natal clinics throughout the UK, who were known, obviously, to be sexually active, and whose blood was tested anonymously for the HIV virus. The figures, published in April 1991, made depressing reading. What the doctors had warned us about, what the government had warned us about, was coming true. AIDS was a serious danger for the entire population, not just for those high-risk groups everyone had been happy to ignore, male homosexuals (whose incidence of AIDS is now going down, because of their more responsible sexual behaviour), and intravenous drug users. The implications of this are enormous, yet questions of contraception/abortion continue to take precedence over a counter-culture which demands the wearing of condoms by all men, except in absolutely faithful monogamous relations – and those are hard to guarantee.

A relatively recent development in the abortion debate is the question of who owns the foetus? Does anyone have rights over it? It has been suggested that the foetus is not the mother's, but is either itself, as an independent being with rights, or a joint 'possession' with the father. There was, for instance, in 1989, the celebrated case of the Oxford student who got pregnant and decided to have an abortion. The father tried to stop her, bringing a case arguing that he had 'father's rights' which would allow him to prevent her from having his child aborted.

At the time I argued, in the *Sunday Times*, that the question of who owned the foetus was not the one we should be considering. The question was whether or not he had any particular commitment to the girl concerned. If he had, then he had some paternal rights, as he was part of a relationship which could be presumed ultimately to be the parents of the child. If, however, it was simply an issue of principle – in other words, he was passionately opposed to abortion – but had no relationship with the girl, he could make no claim. Ultimately, and unsurprisingly, he lost his case, though the girl did in the end have the baby and the father is now looking after the child as a single parent. This was a clear case of the 'father's rights' argument being used, and we are likely to see more and more of it, in questions of abortion and contraception, and ultimately in the way medical thinking about obstetrics and gynaecology operates.

This is for a variety of reasons, but one factor may be the greater medical involvement in childbirth, and, significantly, antenatal care. Doctors, and parents, can now literally see things at a very early stage – ultrasound has transformed people's picture of early human life in the womb and is now beloved of the medical establishment – and one can see how the view that fathers have rights over these unborn children, and that the unborn children have rights as well, has come about. If you can see a very recognisable human shape in the twelve-week embryo and you regularly look at babies *in utero* in this way, it changes your perceptions. The fact that women have always been able to feel and sense the baby's presence is immaterial – this is clear scientific evidence that the baby is there!

Rosalind Pollack Petchesky argues this case very strongly in her superb paper on *Foetal Images*.[11] She says that the ability to see the foetus via ultra-sound, through the mother's uterine wall, enables the doctors to view the foetus separately, as a patient, rather than as irretrievably tied to the mother who gives it home and hearth and food. This leads to the most extraordinary acts, such as the deliberate keeping alive on life-support machines of women who are brain dead but pregnant, so that their unborn child can be born. The birth of Nicola Bell in October 1986 to a twenty-four-year-old woman thought to be brain dead but not tested for brain death until after the birth was considered by many to be a completely positive event.

The father, Ian Bell, asked for her to be kept alive on the machine until the baby was born, and he cared for the baby alone. But in the USA there have been similar cases where the mother was kept alive on a life-support machine against the wishes of the next of kin, but 'at the instigation of male lovers who claimed to be the fathers of the foetuses that the women were carrying.'[12] The lack of debate about the woman's body and its integrity, let alone the ethics of causing the birth of a baby to a dead woman without her previous consent, is very disturbing. And it does reflect what the same writer calls a 'worrying tendency to privilege the foetus or the baby over the woman in whose body it is carried.'

So to whom does a foetus belong? Its mother, its father, both parents jointly, to the mother more than the father? Or is it a distinct being, with its own rights as a would-be independent person capable of making moral choices? The confusion about this is enormous, and though there is no final way of settling it, there is some truth in Midgley and Hughes' assertion[13] that all this is 'only a specially awkward corner of a larger problem, that of the rights of children', such as the rights of children to take part in medical research, or, indeed, not to do so. The question, however, of whether children have a right to be born goes beyond that, and the question of infanticide remains to be discussed. What is clear is that there is something absurd in the notion that both parents have equal rights in an unborn child when the mother is doing the caring and nurturing, but there is something equally absurd in the idea that a father has no rights or duties in a relationship where he has a commitment to its mother. That very commitment presupposes a commitment to the child she is carrying, which is also his. Beyond that, it is hard to draw clear lines. But it is impossible to support the call for abortion on demand simply on the basis of women defending their reproductive rights. Even if the foetus does not have human status, it might well have if it continues to term, and there are other ways of controlling one's own reproductivity than abortion. Perhaps the next campaign run by feminists for the benefit of women at large, in these days of AIDS which should have transformed people's thinking about sexual relationships, should be for the non-invasive, non-threatening, life-preserving, life-enhancing, cheap, fun condom. The only question that then remains is: 'Will he wear it?'

5

Pain in Childbirth

Damascus is waxed feeble, she turneth herself to flee, and trembling hath seized on her; anguish and pangs have taken hold of her, as of a woman in travail.

Jeremiah 49:24

'I WOULDN'T DO it; I really wouldn't do it. . . .' the midwife said as she brought us tea after the birth of our first child, Harriet. She had seen me through a difficult labour, with quite a lot of pain. I had just completed natural childbirth by default. All those times at the antenatal classes we had been asked what kind of pain relief we wanted. I was always the first one to put up my hand amidst all the other elderly primagravida mothers-to-be (that means we were too old for the job of giving birth, but they did not like to tell us so). I knew what I wanted. Never one to experience unnecessary pain, I had said I wanted an epidural. I was absolutely certain, and could not be shaken. 'Aren't you worried about the risk of paralysis?' 'Not very – it's pretty unlikely and I'd rather do without the pain, thank you.' End of conversation. I was somewhat fed up with the whole business, as all I wanted to do was get it over as quickly as possible, having already had a frightful pregnancy.

The waters broke and I found myself in hospital, being ignominiously induced after labour failed to happen naturally. Another sign that natural childbirth was not for me – my body could not even manage it! I asked for my epidural. Contractions were coming hard and fast as the induction got under way. The anaesthetist came and put it in. No anaethesia. I called again, as it was becoming painful. He returned and did it again. No result, and I was gradually going into agony. The midwife, looking glum, called him again. This time it worked, up to a point. My feet were successfully anaesthetised and freezing cold for the rest of what was to be a long and painful natural delivery.

And there's supposed to be virtue in it? The natural childbirth movement encourages us all to give birth naturally. Breathe properly and learn to relax and you won't have a problem. Yet it could be argued that their advocacy of natural childbirth expresses at least partially the old sense that women should have to endure pain. After all, the woman, Eve, lured the man, Adam, into sin. Doesn't she always? The punishment for that was pain in childbirth, which is therefore perceived to be the natural order of things. It says so in the book of Genesis. One can take it a stage further, and look at the attitude – in Christianity particularly, but pervading many of the world's other religions to some extent – that sex is sinful, that the woman lures the man into sex (as into sin), and that giving birth to children is the fruit or wages of sin. There you have a picture of childbirth as a deservedly painful experience.

Now it has to be said, *pace* all the good birth experts, that it is still a painful experience. Few people would deny this totally, quite apart from the fact that the teachings and quotations about 'women in travail' are legion. Edward Shorter, in his magnificent book *A History of Women's Bodies*, makes it clear that 'the typical woman before 1900 faced her approaching delivery with foreboding.' The actual statistics suggest that roughly one in ten deliveries before 1900 had considerable complications. Shorter quotes a Massachusetts woman, Sarah Stearns, facing birth for the first time in 1813, writing in her diary after taking communion with relatives: 'Perhaps this is the last time I shall be permitted to join with my earthly friends.' The fear was there, of dying in childbirth, of infection (which frequently led to death in the first few days after delivery) and of incredible pain.

Accounts given of the actual births, particularly if there were complications, are quite terrible. The number of times that the uterus was ruptured by unskilled doctors and midwives was horrifying. 'If a woman knew ten or fifteen other women, she probably knew someone who had died giving birth, or who would later die.'[1] She would also have known of women who had difficult labours (the average was probably five hours longer before 1900 than it is now) in which the baby had to be turned (what we would now call 'version'); the treatment at that point was unbelievably painful, so much so that women frequently said that they would rather die than go through it. It also has to be admitted that few doctors and midwives were sufficiently skilled to perform version with any degree of success, and the common treatment in a difficult birth was to pull at anything available, so that an arm might come off, or a head, or indeed a polyp or a fibroid, leaving the unhappy woman to die in a pool of blood. Fear and pain were the two prime factors in the contemplation of childbirth for women before 1900, and the fear was presumably in equal parts fear of pain and fear of death, with the two very often inextricably confused.

This history of 'natural childbirth' makes it all the stranger to read the National Childbirth Trust's book *Pregnancy and Parenthood*. It has a number of virtues, and is clear and informative in many ways, even if it does appear to be geared to the middle-class reader and have a somewhat patronising tone. So, after all, do most books on the subject. But it includes a most extraordinary passage about pain in childbirth:

> You may find it helpful to recall that pain is often associated with extra effort which people demand from themselves: the even further stretch made by the ballet dancer; the even greater pace achieved by the sprinter in order to beat his own record; the extra effort we've all put in at some time, when our muscles were telling us to stop digging/polishing/decorating, but we pushed ourselves to complete the task to our satisfaction.[2]

The problem is that most of us do not find it helpful to compare ourselves in labour to a sprinter or a ballet dancer, and even the comparison with gardening or decorating or, terrible thought, housework seems less than appropriate at the time! It just is not always a question of making the 'one last, supreme effort'. Quite a lot of the time, and for quite a large number of the people concerned, the women and their menfolk who watch anxious and then appalled, it is very painful. What the natural childbirth movement has succeeded in doing is picking up the attitude that childbirth is painful, without the attendant moral element that the pain is the just desert of the sin of sex, and it has almost glorified that pain.

Sheila Kitzinger, high priestess of the natural childbirth movement, is on record as describing birth as 'ecstasy – the perineum is
stretched to its utmost – that ring of fire as the baby is born, yes,
ecstasy!' She gestured graphically. 'It is a sexual pleasure.' When
asked about pain she continued: 'Ah, but pain and pleasure are so
very close.' For some of us, maybe. There is, however, a reminiscent
ring here of the 'burn' described by many women at the height of
the fashion for aerobics. The idea was that you exercised to get fit
and the really pleasurable sensation was the 'burn' as you felt your
muscles burning, yourself going over the top. Is that what the NCT
regards as the exertion of the extra stretch for the ballet dancer, or
the extra effort for the long-distance runner? Maybe there is an
important tie-up here, for what the advocates of the burn sensation
are implying is that there is a rare and special pleasure to be derived
from the over-exertion – be it from childbirth, running or ballet
dancing – which is ecstatic. The problem is that it does not work for
everybody. The number of injuries from over-exertion at aerobics
is apparently considerable. Most of us are not athletes or ballet
dancers. That sense of 'burn' may elude us. But the pain on a lower,
more humdrum but inescapable level, does not.

Even Sheila Kitzinger admits that 'pain in labour is real enough.'
She adds a story recounted to her about a woman who gritted her
teeth so hard during the second stage of labour that she had a
chipped tooth at the end. So did I, and it seemed unnecessary at the
time and does so now. But, more interestingly, Sheila Kitzinger also
suggests that different women feel pain differently, and that this is
probably affected 'as much by social factors as by sheer physiology
or by anything which might be uncovered by psychoanalytic
techniques. Pain is always interpreted and placed within a predeter-
mined scheme of things.'[3] Her examples include the West Indian
woman in Jamaica who does not usually feel any discomfort in the
perineum, but has excruciating backache because she believes the
back has to 'open up' for the baby to be born. Kitzinger suggests
that the worry Western women have about the perineum as the
baby descends and puts pressure on bladder and rectum, is that
they will soil the sheets, whilst West Indian women would mind
that less.

While it is no doubt true to say that there are great cultural
variations in the experience of pain and ideas of dirt and soiling, it
is also true to say that there may be Western women who would

not worry desperately about soiling the sheets and no doubt West Indian women who would mind terribly. One of the important lessons I learned a couple of years ago when working on a book for nurses about caring for dying people of different faiths[4] was that the variation *within* each religious and cultural group was often greater than that *between* them. Precisely on this issue of pain, more nonsense has been written than one would have dreamed conceivable, about how primitive people do not feel pain, about how women complaining of severe pain with ovarian cancers are probably neurotic, about how Buddhists will always want to meditate to overcome pain. One of the lessons the hospice movement has taught the general population is that if a patient says the pain is acute, then it is acute for them. If a patient says that she has very little pain, then that is true in that situation. There are no generalisations, nor are there clear objective measures of pain. All that there is is increasing evidence that the body releases its own pain-reducing hormones, endorphins, which give great relief to some people in some circumstances. This may, incidentally, tell us a bit about how acupuncture works, in stimulating the production of the hormone concerned.

But the control of pain in childbirth by acupuncture is not widely practised in the West, whilst the idea that by 'doing it right' one can avoid pain is growing in popularity. There are undoubtedly ways of rising above the pain. There are breathing exercises and meditation exercises and different positions in which to give birth. There are romantic ideas about old-fashioned methods. Birth stools are coming back into fashion. In many London teaching hospitals, the midwives, taking the antenatal class on a tour of the delivery rooms, will proudly point to a collection of stools and low chairs and tell you that these are their birth stools. One hardly dares ask whether they are ever used, though the one time I plucked up the courage recently I was told that, sadly, no-one had asked for them yet. I bit back a retort about whether it had been sensible to waste health service money on buying them, if that was the case, and examined them more closely. There were two low chairs with quite high backs, reminding me curiously of some of the traditional low chairs used by mourners in the Jewish faith, and there were several low stools, kidney-shaped, made of what appeared to be plywood. I was told that they used to use plastic stools which were in fact steps

made for toddlers to climb on to reach things, but that the shape
had been changed to oval or rectangular, which was of no use.

Birth stools have an interesting history themselves, well
recounted by Edward Shorter.[5] They may have existed in ancient
Egypt, if the Hebrew Bible is to be believed; they certainly occurred
at Ephesus and were generally adopted for use in the medieval cities
of Europe from about the fifteenth century. In England, as on the
continent, birth stools appear to have been used in the cities while
standing or squatting were the norm in rural areas. It is not clear
whether the women themselves wanted birth stools, or whether
the new professionalised associations of midwives thought that
they were 'proper', or whether they were simply used from habit.
Nor is it clear whether they went into disuse as a result of male
intervention in women's business of giving birth and the gradual
medicalisation of the birthing process, or because women became
less worried than they had been about soiling the sheets (linen was
very valuable in the Middle Ages and Renaissance, and one did not
want to bleed or excrete all over it), or for some other reason.

One also cannot help wondering whether the prevalence of birth
stools in cities, and their relative absence in rural areas, may not
have something to do with class or status: birth stools may have
distinguished 'ladies' from country women and animals.

As with so many other ideas in our society, what happened in the
past is seen as infinitely preferable and much less invasive. Those
who believe this barely address the counterview seriously. The
politics of the home birth and natural childbirth movement are such
that it is almost a sin to mention that the UK has the highest
perinatal mortality rate in Europe, and that home birth is still
practised in the UK, though many obstetricians would like to see it
stopped totally. But Holland has a high ratio of home births to
hospital, too, and a very low perinatal mortality rate, so our high
perinatal mortality rate is likely to be more to do with what goes on
in all our births than with home births alone. But obstetricians
argue that home births involve a greater risk to mother and child,
and also suggest increasingly that the newly fashionable, amongst
the moneyed classes, tendency to have babies in clinics and nursing
homes without the vital support of special baby units and hi-tech
obstetric monitoring may have its risks too.

So there is a desire on the part of the obstetricians to 'medicalise'
childbirth, and an understandable resistance on the part of many

women to being hospitalised for what should, in the normal course of events, be a healthy experience. Why should this resistance have come about? On one level it is to do with a romantic view of the past, when things were undoubtedly better, where mothers gave birth naturally and were surrounded by willing female helpers in the shape of trained or untrained midwives.

Much dispute has surrounded the vexed question of the role of midwives in childbirth. They have been praised for the role they played, where doctors were interventionist. Yet, historically speaking, for the majority of women, it was remarkably rare for a doctor to be called upon at all to attend a woman in childbirth, and urban midwives in some European countries were highly thought of. In Germany, for instance, they became minor city officials, were signed in once a year and then celebrated with a feast of wine, bread and cookies. They were a self-governing body who provided a relatively high standard of service, including the ability to perform 'version' to correct the baby's position, although it was an extremely painful procedure if carried out, as it was, without any anaesthetic. According to Shorter,[6] these groups of midwives organised into an independent corps stretch right back to the Middle Ages. But they became subjugated to the *collegio medico* in Nuremberg in 1755, and in other cities at around the same period.

Until that point, however, they had had stringent professional standards imposed upon them by other women. And there is little doubt that they knew more techniques for dealing with difficult births than their contemporary doctors. Indeed, the science of obstetrics had gone into abeyance from Roman times on, and though the doctors knew little, the guilds of midwives, by their experience, discovered helpful tricks, such as the use of ergot, which they consistently refused to pass on to the doctors. By the early eighteenth century, however, the concept of medical supervision for midwives had carried the day, and the desire for a publicly stated policy on midwifery provision had been expressed. So we get examples such as this from Schwäbisch-Hall in Germany, dated 1706: 'Every Christian authority should attempt to see that women are cared for as well as possible before, during and after giving birth. Therefore intelligent, conscientious and experienced persons are to be appointed [to the office of midwife].'[7]

These welcome signs failed to appear in England, or in rural areas anywhere. Jean Donison,[8] who has written absolutely brilliantly about the depressing history, records that, despite the English bishops getting the right in 1512 to examine midwives along with other medical personnel, most midwives remained outside any official network, and that no national regulation came about until 1902. This was a century later than in France, and, in some states at least, nearly two hundred years later than in Germany.

But not only were the English midwives ill regulated. They were also probably a frequent source of life-threatening infection to the mother. For they did not only use their fingernails, grown specially long for the purpose of feeling the baby's head, to rupture the amniotic sac, or pull on any extruding part to hasten the birth, but went in for all kinds of fruitless exploration. They pushed heads back up the birth canal, they massaged the area between the thighs, they dilated the vagina manually (with enormous attendant risk of infection), and tried to 'steer' the infant's head with one hand. Indeed, they had a reputation for terrible impatience, which meant that they could not bear to sit for hours with hands folded, waiting for something to happen. They did not know anything about infection, so they cannot be blamed for spreading it, but they must have added enormously to the depth of human misery, implanting the source of infection into a woman's womb as they came direct from the stables or, even worse, another birth. The degree of hygiene was minimal. And they can be blamed for furious intervention, the tearing of women's uteri and vaginal walls (the incidence of fistulas was enormous, and must have been very embarrassing as well as painful to the poor sufferers) and for putting the poor mothers on the birth stool at the onset of labour, exhorting them to 'bear down' for hour after totally useless hour.

All this somewhat explodes the myth that there was a golden age of midwifery. In no way can one support the assertion made by one American chronicler that 'the midwife's role was confined primarily to offering comfort and reassurance to her patient, encouraging and supporting her without interfering in the normal process of parturition.'[9] Alas, that is a highly unlikely scenario, and its use in history books is deliberately partisan, to show that things were fine before doctors became involved, when natural childbirth was the norm and women took charge, when women were not bullied or treated as lumps of meat and there was no interference in the beautiful, natural process of giving birth. Things were not really quite like that. It is a highly romantic view of getting back to nature, also associated with other romantic historical aspirations, such as, for instance, the quite extraordinary adulation by American Jewish writers of Der Heym, the Pale of Settlement in Russia and Poland where Jews lived before the pogroms of 1881 to 1905. This, through rose-coloured spectacles, is seen as a beautiful place, with wonderful values, where life was good. And the honest facts that it was dirty, smelly, frightening and dangerous – and very poor – seem to have no impact on the romantic scene. It is a desire to go back home – whether to Poland or to nature seems immaterial.

Certainly the natural childbirth movement seems to have some of its roots in the 'back to nature' hippy philosophy of the 1960s. Yet the stark evidence of what happened to the women who went along with that philosophy all the way down the line shows that they are weary and exhausted, with too many babies and too little medical help and support; that natural though such a life may be, it is not always pleasant. Nor does something that is natural necessarily have to be good for you. The unnatural facets of civilisation, such as heating and lighting, freezers and antibiotics, can be good for you too. In West Cork, in the Irish Republic, where we live for part of the year, the women in the old hippy colony look washed out before their time, thin, stooped and put upon. There is also a high incidence of perinatal mortality because of their frequent refusal to travel to Cork to give birth.

Though feminism took up some of the ideas of the hippy movement, it did not advocate what has turned out to be near slavery for the women involved. But it did, mistakenly, take the line that as obstetricians and technicians were largely male and the medical establishment was largely male, it was somehow wrong for that medical (and male) establishment to tell women how to give birth. Pregnancy is not, after all, a disease, so there should be no earthly reason why, when pregnant, one should put oneself in the hands of doctors.

That attitude was undoubtedly fuelled by two things. One was the sense that (male) doctors were pretty patronising anyway, and did not appear to achieve anything very significant that a (female) midwife could not. The other factor, which is infinitely more serious and has a grain of truth in it, is that women began to feel that much of what had gone wrong with women's health was in itself the fault of the doctors.

Classically cited was the Pill, the contraceptive that revolutionised people's sex lives in the 1960s. The scares in the early '70s about high-dosage pills, and the overnight changes of prescriptions to low dose, suggested to women that the (male) doctors did not know what they were doing, and that they were prepared to take appalling risks with women's health in order that they (men) might have their sexual pleasures. Now if these same doctors were telling women how to give birth, with monitors and epidurals rather than walking around or under water, then they were plainly not to be trusted.

Those were some of the reasons why some women began to move away from the medical establishment when it came to childbirth. But there were others. There was undoubtedly a great deal of very bad practice. The prevalence of episiotomies, dealt with brilliantly in Sheila Kitzinger's *Good Birth Guide*, was undoubtedly one incentive to women not to have a hi-tech, hospital delivery. This practice of cutting to prevent tearing often leads to acute discomfort after too-tight stitching, when many women would not have torn anyway. The bad habit continues in many places, and it is hard to encourage a woman who is wavering between giving birth in hospital or at home to go to a hospital where you know that episiotomies are pretty well routine and she will therefore feel as if she is sitting on barbed wire for a week, without good cause. And with the present parlous state of the National Health Service in Britain, she probably will not even be given one of those elegant rubber rings to sit on, to protect the most tender parts of her anatomy.

There were also the undoubtedly degrading antenatal examinations by a different doctor on every occasion, only partly overcome by shared care with general practitioners. And there was always the sense, by no means restricted to obstetrics, that the doctor's time was infinitely more valuable than the patient's, so that until the time the mother-to-be could not wait because the baby was on its way, the hanging about and the different doctors and the unavailability of information made the whole process a misery.

All these things are still true. There is still much wrong with the way babies are delivered in hospitals and with the way pregnant women are cared for in the antenatal clinics. When Ann Oakley reviewed antenatal care in the UK,[10] she commented (after the publication of the Short report of 1979–80 that had suggested that one of the reasons for the high perinatal mortality rate was linked to antenatal care, even though it could not be shown exactly why or how),[11] that the question was not: 'Why do some women fail to attend for antenatal care?' but 'Why *do* women attend antenatal clinics?' This was as a result of seeing crowded, unfriendly clinics with hugely long waiting times.

When I had my first baby on the NHS in 1979, waiting three hours was not unusual, and then one would never see the same doctor twice (except for nephrological care, which was excellent, and where we always saw the same consultant without undue delay). If one challenged the midwife on duty as to exactly why it was that we were all in at the same time and waiting so long so pointlessly, she would answer that the problem lay in the fact that so many women failed to turn up for their appointments that they had to book a lot of us in at the same time to avoid wasting the doctors' time.

The massive arrogance and illogicality of this response almost took one's breath away. Firstly, it was hardly surprising that women failed to turn up if they thought that it was likely that they would have to wait for three hours. Secondly, the fact that it was so crowded made it perfectly clear that the non-attendance was not colossal, or that they had over-compensated for it in a monstrous way. Thirdly, they seemed to feel that the doctors' time was valuable, but to have no conception of the value or otherwise of the patients' time or whether the patient had other children to look after (sometimes they brought them to the antenatal clinic, but this was not encouraged), or dependent adults, or possibly a job to go to.

On this subject, the natural childbirth campaign has done sterling work, and has suggested, in some of its publications, that women should band together to complain about the services. Beverley Lawrence Beech's *Who's Having Your Baby?*, a health rights handbook for maternity care, even suggests a draft form of letter of complaint to the supervisor of midwives in the hospital concerned, and she then suggests contacting the Community Health Council. Sheila Kitzinger, too, has helped to improve treatment in antenatal care via her *New Good Birth Guide*, and the National Childbirth Trust's handbook *Pregnancy and Parenthood* sounds a healthy warning note to new mothers:

Antenatal care, unfortunately, easily becomes a mechanical and impersonal process for many doctors and midwives, unless you are prepared to question them and make it necessary for them to treat you as an individual. Make them aware tactfully that it is your baby, and that your fears and doubts may be as important as the results of any tests that are carried out.

Sensible advice indeed, and a point that needs constantly re-emphasising, as the production-line philosophy of childbirth shows no sign of disappearing.

Some of the more radical material on maternity rights, advocating natural (they call it 'normal', which begs a lot of questions) birth, illustrates only too well the difficulty, even now, of ensuring that the mother gets what she wants in the busy maternity unit of a big hospital. In *Who's Having Your Baby?*, there is a wonderful description of how an unwilling mother is persuaded to have a foetal monitor attached to her unborn baby's head:

> 'Well, of course, Mrs Smith, I respect your wish not to have foetal monitoring, but I do feel I should draw your attention to the fact that babies sometimes become distressed in labour and that can happen very quickly. When it does happen the brain can be deprived of oxygen and if that were to happen for any length of time then you could have a brain-damaged baby. Or worse, the baby could die. Of course, the decision is yours, but I must warn you that you will have to take full responsibility for your decision, which will be against medical advice. And, of course, I do have the best interests of your baby at heart, we never do anything routinely at this hospital.'

Now one might have thought that this was a joke, or indeed a piece of such propagandist writing on the part of the natural childbirth lobby that it was not worth taking seriously. I always feel forewarned when I read the description 'normal' for what is usually referred to as natural, since the implication that births using epidurals or foetal monitors are abnormal is pretty clear. But the truth of the matter is that even now, with all the publicity that has been given to the matter of women's choice in the whole business of childbirth, with major hospital obstetric departments still falling over themselves to get into Sheila Kitzinger's *Good Birth Guide*, this kind of persuasion is far too frequently used.

It also has to be added that unless the business of what a woman wants is sorted out before she actually goes into labour, it is very hard for her to fight a battle between contractions. The natural childbirth movement has done sterling work in waking up obstetricians to the need to consult women about their desires, and to the necessity of offering choice in childbirth methods, but they have not been successful in establishing either that the choice should be available to all women, irrespective of whether they want natural childbirth or not, nor in explaining that pressure to conform to a hospital's norm should not be applied to women who are already in labour. Yet they have done well in alerting the medical profession to the appalling way women were, and sometimes still are, treated – waiting on a conveyor belt to be processed impersonally through hi-tech foetal monitoring which does not appear significantly to reduce our high perinatal mortality rate, but does make a woman feel as if she is attached to a piece of equipment very much more important than she is herself, and allows endless electricians and technicians to come into the delivery room to make sure the monitor is working all right, not whether she, the mother, is in pain.

That in itself is not a justification for natural childbirth, for throwing out much of the good advice and help that is available in favour of some other theory, the idea that you can avoid pain by discipline and training, by breathing and relaxing, and that this is somehow nobler, better, braver, than screaming because it hurts, or having anaesthesia. There is an element of dogma here. Prunella Briance, founder of the National Childbirth Trust, wrote a book called *Childbirth with Confidence* in which she said: 'Expectant mothers should realise how important it is to learn to accomplish the birth of a baby. One cannot expect any theory to work if one disobeys the rules.' Consider also the wonderful passage in the NCT's *Pregnancy and Parenthood* which states categorically: 'Without suggesting that there is any merit in suffering for suffering's sake, we believe that many mothers would rather suffer some discomfort or pain than risk affecting their baby by consuming drugs, and some will accept a certain amount of pain in order to experience also the sensations of giving birth.' The degree to which there is any risk in the drugs involved has become a major battlefield, since many doctors argue that the NCT and other campaigners are simply inaccurate about that fact. But the theme song here is not about risk – it is about rules, discomfort and pain. That it hurts, they do not deny. But they insist that pain has a value, and leads to a fulfilling experience of childbirth.

Is the idea that it should hurt in fact connected with the Biblical story of Eve? 'Unto the woman he said, I will greatly multiply thy pain and thy travail; in pain thou shalt bring forth children; and thy desire shall be to thy husband and he shall rule over thee.' (Genesis 3:16).

Jewish tradition takes a wholly different view from the Christian one, where this story is about the Fall of Man (and Woman) from Grace. It is about sin, and about punishment. That, in association with a strong prejudice against the sex act in the early Church, as well as adulation of physical suffering, may explain something of the acceptance of the idea of pain and suffering in childbirth. But even so, it is odd that it should have raised its head again in the modern natural childbirth movement. Their defence would be that natural childbirth can be painless. The truth of the matter is, however, that it very rarely is. A conversation with an experienced midwife is enough to clarify one's ideas on that point, though most midwives would say that painful births are particularly prevalent for first babies. But even if it were painless, which is allowing a lot, there is something of a puzzle underlying the idea that it is better to go through childbirth without pain because you are relaxing than because you are given a drug. The usual argument against drugs, that one becomes used to and dependent upon them, does not apply in this case, since it is hard to become dependent on a drug one would only use at most once a year. Nor is there any proof of a long-term effect on the baby, whilst the long-term effect on a mother giving birth painlessly is that she feels better.

It is extraordinary that feeling against these drugs should run so high. Beverley Beech, author of *Who's Having Your Baby?*, chairs the ultra-pro-natural-childbirth Association for Improvements in the Maternity Services (AIMS), which put out a leaflet recently listing 'routine procedures that British women have been subjected to in the name of safety'. Within that list were 'routine ultrasound, routine pain-killing drugs, epidural anaesthesia on demand'. Ultrasound clearly sparks off great ill feeling in some sections of the natural childbirth lobby, who compare it with the use of foetal X-rays, which continued for twenty years, in some cases, after they were known to increase the chances of childhood cancers.[12]

But ultrasound is different from drugs. Ill feeling against pain-killing drugs is different and to my mind peculiar. In Michelle Stanworth's anthology on reproductive technologies, pain does not even merit a mention in the index. It is as if it were irrelevant. In *The*

Experience of Childbirth there are at least twenty-seven entries under pain and a further seven under pain relief. Yet although Sheila Kitzinger allows that pain in labour is very real for some women, she also argues that 'all drugs given to the mother enter the blood stream and cross the placenta, in varying proportions, to the baby. Many, especially given in large doses, lead to "flat" babies who are floppy and limp, lie inert instead of looking around alertly as does a healthy new-born, who do not wake to feed or suck vigorously when put to the breast, and who may also be slow to breathe at delivery. . . .' She continues by saying that 'many women who are offered drugs for pain in labour would think twice about taking medication which is offered so freely as part of the accepted routines for managing labour, if they knew that what is a moderate drug dose for them can be a very large one for the baby, which its immature liver cannot excrete.'

She then quotes Professor Kieran O'Driscoll writing in the *British Journal of Anaesthetics*[13] as saying that 'no effective drug exists which both has no unpleasant side effects and is 100% safe for the mother and her child.' He argues, as quoted by Kitzinger, that pethidene causes 'nausea, vomiting, disorientation and mental confusion which leads to failure to co-operate, especially in the second stage of labour. . . .' and that 'many of the discomforts attributed to labour are, in practice, the result of pethidene. . . . Labour can be transformed easily into a nightmare experience by pethidene, after which a mother may remain unaware that her baby is born and may suffer a profound sense of depression which continues into the next day.' Kitzinger's research then shows that those women who were forced to take pethidene found its effects unpleasant. But it has to be added here that it is unusual to force a woman to take pethidene, though in most cases it is readily available on demand. Even in Kitzinger's researches (and she is not sympathetic to the use of analgesia in childbirth at all) she has to admit that the conclusion was that 'when they had the choice as to when and if to accept pain relief, the effects were much more likely to be good. . . .' Of course. That is what one would reasonably expect. And it suggests that Professor O'Driscoll's worries may be somewhat over the top, or that, secretly, he believes that a woman needs to suffer in labour!

As for epidurals, Kitzinger cites evidence that the baby's heart rate changes (she does not say whether this is significant, and a number of obstetricians and pediatricians I have spoken to seem to think that it is not) and that there is some association between epidurals and babies who, though in good condition at delivery, are unresponsive, with slack muscles, a few hours afterwards. But her real objection appears later in the section where she argues, correctly, that there is a link between the use of epidurals and a higher rate of the use of forceps for delivery, because of the lack of sensation enabling the mother to bear down. What she does not admit, however, is that her figure of five times more likely is probably inflated, because she does not take into account the very difficult births where epidural is used and forceps would have been essential anyway. Nor does she justify O'Driscoll's urging of doctors to avoid offering forceps deliveries as a 'bonus given to women who accept a package deal of induction and an epidural' (which is now far less often offered as a package than it used to be, anyway) except by the bald comment that 'anything that interferes with the natural process produces an element of risk, however slight, which could have been avoided.' In other words, her view is that the natural thing to do is go along with the pain, for the pain is also pleasure, and is the way that nature intended it to be.

The opposition to this thinking is just beginning to emerge. This time it comes not from the obstetricians, who have accepted at least part of the natural childbirth philosophy. It comes from a small group called the Association for the Advancement of Maternity Care, organised by a woman called Maureen Treadwell. She set it up after an appalling experience giving birth naturally, with no pain relief of any kind, having asked for an epidural but been refused because there was no anaesthetist available. 'The pain had been so unbearable that it left her with recurring nightmares,' Polly Toynbee reported in the *Guardian* in 1986. She complained and went to the Community Health Council, which arranged for her to meet the consultant. The consultant said dismissively, 'You're not the first and you won't be the last to suffer in childbirth. What are you complaining about?' But she carried on complaining, and eventually the regional medical officer agreed that she was right and that she should not have been made to suffer so greatly against her will. Six months later another obstetric anaesthetist was appointed at the hospital concerned.

When she was expecting her second baby, she searched around for a hospital and a team that promised proper pain relief. She had an epidural: she did not feel a thing, and went home a few hours later. It was that joyful experience which made her start campaigning for epidurals for all women who want them. For women are not, in her view, given a balanced view about pain relief. The reasons against are as Sheila Kitzinger has them, or sometimes a simple lack of available anaesthetist, or one who is too busy (as happened to me, so he was too tired to get it right). Sometimes – but increasingly rarely – staff (including midwives) tell women to stop complaining and not to act like babies.

Maureen Treadwell's first action was to write to local newspapers around the country, soliciting views from women. She was deluged with correspondence, telling her terrible stories of how women were treated 'in the name of the natural childbirth game'. 'Many of the letters, while angry, are still full of guilt at having "failed" to give birth naturally. Many said how wonderful it was to hear someone for the first time say there was nothing special of mystical about childbirth. But a large number of letters contained terrifying stories, where babies had died or suffered irreversible brain damage because the mother had been left in labour for long hours when a quick caesarean would have saved them.'

As her campaign gathered members and momentum, Maureen Treadwell realised it was a far broader issue then mere pain relief. The safety of mothers and children was in some cases being put at risk by the 'natural' fad. 'Until now there has been only one voice speaking for women to the medical establishment and that was the natural childbirth lobby. Now there is a more moderate view available.'

The question here is why mothers are not given a choice of what takes place. The choices are made largely by male obstetricians and female midwives, on behalf of the women giving birth. Pressure against intervention has come from the natural childbirth lobby, but it seems strange that in this country the feminist and the progressive view is to inflict as much pain as possible on women in labour. In Sweden, feminists took entirely the opposite line. They even got the right to pain relief embodied in the constitution.

It is a strange business, and there seems to be a quite different idea lurking in the background, which is that there is a better relationship with the new-born baby and a 'more meaningful' experience for the mother herself, if she is aware of everything that happens during the birth. Whilst this may be an argument against gas and air, because of the knock-out effect, or even arguably pethidene, it seems strange in relation to epidurals, where the only experience which is lost is the pain – one is fully aware of everything else. Perhaps there is another idea underlying this, too, that there is a mystical experience to be gained in childbirth, which is wholly or partly lost if there is any interference whatsoever in the process. The bonding of mother and child will be disturbed, and that delicate pink glow of content on the face of the new mother will not be quite the same if she has not just got over the pain and effort of the last stage of labour.

There is much romantic writing by both women and men on the subject of the bliss of having just given birth. Sheila Kitzinger particularly has some wonderful descriptions. For her, giving birth is less controlled than the ordered, self-disciplined, easy, natural birth of the NCT books. It is wilder, more romantic, and quite unlike anything I ever experienced. For instance, she describes 'the gradual opening up, like a bud into full flower, a strange experience. . . .' But although these images are rather floral, her own preferred imagery is that relating to the movement of water:

> The wave surges toward me, rises in crescendo as I am enveloped by the walls of its pressure, and then sweeps back and away, leaving my body bounded by the little space . . . between contractions . . . the muscle fibres [of the uterus] contract and contract – feel as if they must grind and pulp, like a ripe peach pressed till all its juice pours out, and everything in the deep well of the pelvis is squeezed and trodden as if in a wine press.

Picturesque, idealised and romantic, it is not a description that many women would recognise. Indeed, some of the writing has a flavour of a particular group of earth-mother women of a particular period. Are these the women in dirndl skirts and open-toed sandals of Posy Simmonds' wicked cartoons? Are they what Polly Toynbee has described as 'a noisy group of lentil-eating earth goddesses'? Or are they carried away on a wave of pseudo-psychology, able to describe the 'feelings of childbirth as encouraged by a somewhat indulgent psychotherapist'?[14]

The extent to which childbirth really is some mystical, intensely personal and important spiritual moment obviously varies from individual to individual, but it would not be surprising to discover that the sense of bliss and relief on many women's faces has nothing to do with mystical experience but is rather an expression of exhaustion, and pleasure that it is all over and that both mother and baby are well. Were that to be the case, the natural childbirth movement would have to think about the scientific evidence which suggests that monitoring babies can save them from distress, and that hi-tech births may look and feel less attractive than low-tech, but they have considerable advantages for the peace of mind of the mother.

Natural childbirth is not always wrong, however irritating its prophetesses and proselytisers may sometimes be. The movement has changed the way many obstetric departments operate, by teaching them that factors other than the health and welfare of the mother and child have to enter into the treatment. That can only be a bonus. The negative side is the one that feels you should experience the pain, that it is not real pain, that the experience itself is meaningless without full sensation. That is the dangerous philosophy, for it leads on to the idea that pain is good for us, and that suffering is right and ennobling.

Sheila Kitzinger's curiously masochistic view of pleasure may nevertheless have a considerable following amongst a wide variety of people. There are many beyond the strictly 'perverted' (if that word is allowable at all) or 'abnormal' who receive immense sexual pleasure from different forms of beating, which is certainly not to say that all people who are beaten gain any form of pleasure from it at all. But the strand that does not allow the pleasure element to enter into the event at all is a different one, and has its roots, I would argue, deep within the Christian tradition in connection with women, sex and the relationship with holiness. This is delicate ground for a Jewess to tread, but there is undoubtedly something very peculiar indeed about the early Church Fathers' view of sexuality, and of women in general. Women were already being exhorted by St Paul to keep silence in the churches, to learn with all subjection, but it is the writing of the early saints that displays a mortification of the flesh, shared with fantasies about women, though not real ones:

Oh, how often when I was living in the desert in that lonely waste, scorched by the burning sun ... how often did I fancy myself surrounded by the pleasures of Rome. . . . My unkempt limbs were covered in shapeless sackcloth; my skin through long neglect had become as rough and black as an Ethiopian's. . . . But through my fear in hell I had condemned myself to this prison house where my only companions were scorpions and wild beasts. My face was pale with fasting, but though my limbs were cold as ice my mind was burning with desire and the fires of lust kept bubbling up before me when my flesh was as good as dead. . . .[15]

This was the stuff of fantasy about women, but real women had to be dirty in order to gain respect, to make themselves revolting, as Karen Armstrong records so well in *The Gospel According to Woman*. These ideas were profoundly tied in with the thought of pain in childbirth as a punishment for the sin of Eve. No sympathy is therefore normally expressed for the woman in acute pain; it was seen as her just deserts, a form of thinking that is exactly comparable to that of the persecution of medieval Jews, who were treated as if they had killed Jesus. So women were regarded as if they were Eve, the temptress, and bound for this punishment.

What is remarkable about that view is that it allowed for uncontrolled, unhelped pain in childbirth, and it is the natural childbirthers who have made an unholy alliance with that strand of thinking in brooking no interference in the pain and discomfort of giving birth, because this is how Mother Nature (and the medieval Church who saw childbirth as partly the wages of the sin of sex) intended it to be.

That belief is not shared by all women, nor by all men. Yet saying that suffering might be bad for people, or that stoic biting of the lip may not be the only, or even the best, way to give birth to children, requires considerable courage, even now. Battalions of women are massed on either side. How they fight it out remains up to them, as long as they do not put other people's views into the heresy category, or make belief in the childbirth methods even more like an article of faith than it already is. Yet the analogy with attitudes to be found deeply embedded within religious traditions, particularly those concerned with pain and pleasure, suggest there is a genuine debate of faith taking place here, which needs to be recognised as such.

6

Infertility and Surrogacy

O Lord of Hosts, if thou wilt deign to take notice of my trouble
and remember me, if thou wilt not forget me but grant me
offspring, then I will give the child to the Lord for his whole
life, and no razor shall ever touch his head.

Hannah praying in the Temple, I Samuel, 1:11

THE POLITICS OF birth are such that the infertile woman is thought
to be seriously at fault. Mind you, this has its origins in the Bible,
where a woman who remained childless could in fact be divorced
for her barrenness. It was, of course, never the man's fault. Only
women were barren. The facts about low sperm counts were not
known, though presumably in the days of polygamy there must
have been some men who had no children, unless their wives were
unfaithful to them, because they were in fact the infertile parties.
But it was clearly a source of immense sorrow to women that they
could not have children. Think, for instance, of the stories in the
Hebrew Bible of Sarah or Hannah, both childless and both deeply
distressed as a result. Hannah was found by the priest Eli in the
Temple weeping to such an extent that he thought that she was
drunk. (Shades of the usual 'hysterical woman' description in
I Samuel I:10ff). Her co-wife, or perhaps more accurately rival wife,
Peninah, had been taunting her because of her childlessness.
Hannah, of course, prayed, her wish was granted and her son went
to serve the Lord in the Temple as she had promised.

The case of Sarah is rather different. For Sarah can reasonably be argued to have been involved in the first surrogacy case in history. Having failed to get pregnant for many years (she was apparently in her nineties at the time of the eventual birth of her son Isaac), she gave her handmaid Hagar to Abraham as a concubine 'that he may be builded up through her' (Genesis 16:3), so that any child that Hagar might have was in fact to be regarded as belonging to Abraham and Sarah. Nevertheless, Sarah's barrenness distressed her considerably, and she was reduced to helpless giggles when the three messengers (or angels, since the Hebrew word means either) came to the trees at Mamre and told Abraham whilst she was eavesdropping at the tent opening that she was going to give birth. The son she produced was called Isaac – 'he will laugh' – because of her mirth, but the story is based round the terrible tragedy of remaining childless (Genesis 17).

That legacy of the shame of childlessness has continued throughout history. Women have been embarrassed and distressed by their inability to produce a son and heir, or, even, if needs must, a daughter. At least a daughter proved that a woman was not infertile. In Jewish law it was legitimate to divorce a wife after ten years of childlessness, even if a man still loved her. Heirs were more important. In the early Christian era the sole purpose of sex was for procreation, so, to a man affected strongly by the advocacy of celibacy and the horror of sex as a debasing human activity, what use was a woman who could not conceive? Later attitudes concern the production of boys rather than girls, but the elements of the idea of a woman's usefulness being defined by her childbearing are there, and very strong. It is no surprise, therefore, to find that the idea has left its legacies, that many women regard themselves as failures if they do not produce children.

The criticism which abounds of women who go to extreme lengths to have fertility treatments always describes them as essentially selfish. 'Aren't there enough unloved and unwanted children in the world already without her going to all these lengths to produce her own when clearly God, or nature, or destiny, did not intend that she should?' She should adopt, or spend her spare time (which she obviously has if she has not got any children) doing voluntary work for the underprivileged children already in our midst. It is a deeply judgemental attitude which fails to take account either of this pervading sense of failure or of the unaccountable but nevertheless enormously strong desire of human beings to reproduce themselves. The critics of the women who go to these lengths might not personally feel those longings, but they need to have some understanding of the emotions which bring about the obsession and the sense of urgency.

Nor is it only women who feel that they are failures if they are unable to reproduce. The accounts by men with very low sperm counts of their distress at their apparent lack of virility make depressing and painful hearing. Several friends have told me that they felt 'unmanned' by the experience of being told that their sperm counts were low, and that the advice to wear loose underpants or boxer shorts and to keep the testicles cool was laughable in its apparent simplicity and almost total uselessness. Two friends said they felt that somehow they were not proper husbands because they could not be fathers, and the offer of *in vitro* fertilisation combined with donor insemination because their sperm was inadequate made them feel even worse. The desire to reproduce themselves became stronger and more upsetting the longer the inability to become a parent manifested itself, and although artificial insemination was a possible answer, it did not go all the way in providing a sense of parenthood, any more than adoption would. This is not 'flesh of my flesh', not somehow natural.

Part of this is about producing heirs, about replicating ourselves, be we male or female. Part is the age-old sense of wanting someone to look after us in old age, precisely the reason adduced in many Third World countries, where infant mortality is high, for having large numbers of children: at least some of them will survive into adult life and be there to look after aged and needy parents. But part of it is simply beyond rational explanation. It is a deep-seated urge to have children, to mother them or father them, to be with them and to see them. It is not a sign necessarily that those who feel these strong emotions will be good parents. It is as primitive, according to one male friend, as the rutting instinct, of going out and looking for a girl when one is very young, or as the itch of sexual desire.

For most men it is so simple. When one cannot 'perform', however delicious the sex act itself, it is as if an essential part of one's being has suddenly been kicked in the groin; the proof of sexuality, of manliness, of virility, is just not possible, and it cannot be blamed, as it always was in the ancient world, on the 'barrenness' of the woman.

The problem for women is more complex than that. Gena Corea describes the attitude to women as mothers very well in her book *The Mother Machine*: 'A cow's function is to produce calves. One of woman's main functions has been to produce children: children to carry on the names of men and inherit their property; children to become soldiers, workers and consumers; children to populate the lands of states seeking "national greatness".

'Argentina has been one of those states. In March 1974, its Ministry of Health issued a decree restricting the sales of contraceptive pills and accusing "non-Argentine interests" of encouraging birth control and "perverting the fundamental maternal role of women".... Commenting on the population issue, *Las Bases*, a magazine considered the official publication of the Peronist movement, wrote: "We must start from the basis that the principal work of a woman is to have children."'[1]

Women are under enormous pressure to have babies. Some people argue that this is partly internal, because it is really what they want to do. Many of the critiques of early feminist literature, particularly that originating in the US, focus on this issue. It is natural for women to want to have children. It is in the nature of their biology. Germaine Greer has very much come to the view that women want children, and that the problems lie more in the provision of food and education for them than in their being unwanted.[2]

But some of the evidence is against this theory. There are plenty of women who batter their children, though it has become fashionable to ascribe all child abuse to men. Recent horrifying child abuse cases show that even when women themselves have not sexually abused their children, they have aided and abetted. In the Congleton case reported in early August 1988, three men and a woman were found guilty of child sexual abuse. The woman pleaded guilty to aiding and abetting her former husband to rape their daughter, aged four. She had held her down while he did it.

Similarly, there are those who kill their children at birth, rather than face the consequences of having them. The celebrated case of the Kerry baby, or indeed babies as it became, is a good example. It started with one baby being found washed up on a beach in County Kerry in the Irish Republic. Then it became two babies. Then there was a discussion as to whether they were, in fact, twins. In the end, journalists writing in the *Irish Times* and in the English national press began to feel that there was a certain amount of deliberate fabrication by all parties; that it had, perhaps, been common practice for girls in that area to drown their newly born babies in the sea; and that this was by no means an isolated case of a young girl getting rid of unwanted, illegitimate twins. Certainly the total clamming-up of members of the local community on the subject suggested that it was well known in the area that this went on. What was never clear from police investigations was whether it was the norm for other people actually to drown the babies, or whether it was the mothers themselves. But it is very little different from the practice of exposing babies on hillsides in ancient Greece, or killing female children at birth as still occurs in some parts of the world. Although it is undoubtedly true that one of the reasons for killing babies is that they are conceived out of wedlock and the shame, in some societies, would be hard to bear, nevertheless the truth of the matter is that those babies are unwanted.

The history of the foundling hospitals, superbly recorded in *The Kindness of Strangers* by John Boswell, shows that there was deliberate collusion between the women who abandoned children and the organisations that took them in, to ensure that many of them did not survive; the wet-nurse baby farms of much of the seventeenth and eighteenth centuries appear to have operated in the same way.

Nor is it likely that all child abuse perpetrated by mothers is solely the result of social deprivation or poor education, though those are clearly factors to be taken into account. There have been recent cases where women have simply killed their children. Some, like Maria Bechook, a mother living in a close-knit community in south-east London where normally there would be little willingness to talk to the police, pretended that her own daughter and a friend had been abducted. In that case local people had their suspicions, fuelled by prejudice against her as a South-East Asian immigrant, and talked to the police, which led ultimately to her conviction.

Others kill their children and themselves as well, leaving no clue as to why they have done so, so that fathers come back to find scenes of devastation and horror for no reason that they know of. Nor is this so infrequent as to be of little significance. If both fathers and mothers are taken into account in the pattern of killing children and then themselves, it is reported in the press at least once a month, and sometimes more. Nor is it always to do with an estrangement in the marriage, though there often seem to be underlying tensions within the relationship which may account for the desperate suicide, spiked by the desire to prevent one parent having the children after the death of the other. The violence of emotion and the desire to take revenge, even on the children, beggar belief, but this is a well-established pattern.

The very fact of these cases makes one wonder whether the maternal instinct is all it is cracked up to be in every woman. Perhaps women vary as much as men do in their feelings about when, or indeed whether, to have children, but it is less admissible for them to say it now, particularly since the strident '60s and '70s feminist voice which suggested that all women should be in the workplace and not at home has gone out of fashion. The proper thing to believe now is that all women do have a maternal instinct, even though they may put off its expression for a number of years whilst they get themselves established in a career.

Indeed, the numbers of women having a baby at forty-something is clearly on the increase, and women having first babies at a later age is now a pronounced trend throughout Europe. Talking to childless friends of forty-ish, it is clear that some of them, at least, have felt in recent years what they describe as an 'unaccountable' yearning to produce a child, that well-known biological time-clock ticking away. But there are also those who have no such desires, who simply, and deliberately, do not want children. They do not share that maternal instinct. I myself had no desire to have children, but had agreed with my husband that I would have at least two, which I did. Nor can I say that I had a close relationship with my tiny babies, such that after awful pregnancies I suddenly felt it was all worthwhile. I felt closer and closer to my children from the time they began to respond, at about four or five months, and I enjoyed them more and more over the years. But in the early stages the maternal instinct eluded me. The same is true with many friends and acquaintances, especially those for whom their career was the first priority, and for whom having babies meant at least a career break, if not a complete change of life's pattern.

Along with later childbirth come some increased infertility problems. This is partly due to use of contraception for a long period earlier in life, particularly the coil or other type of IUD, and affects women who were in the forefront of the sexual revolution of the '60s most acutely, since many of them were taking the high-dosage pill or using an IUD for years without a break, before the dangers became generally known. But it is also due to lower fertility rates in older women.

The result of this has been desperation on the part of many 'last chancers'. They are sometimes single, feeling that if they do not have a child now, husband or no husband, they never will. (Nevertheless, the numbers of single 'lone' mothers in this age group is very small. By far the majority of lone mothers are very young women. It is just that the older group has been surprisingly vocal.) These older women are frequently married or in a stable relationship, and feel that the years are going by and that they must have a child. They are not necessarily influenced by the feeling that a woman's main role is to have children. But many of them would admit privately, and have done, that they feel something of a failure if they cannot produce a child. One woman I spoke to recently confessed that as she was approaching her fortieth birthday childless she felt that all her other achievements paled into insignificance beside this failure to produce 'what was natural', a baby. She is a bright, sparky woman with a great career, a splendid marriage and much that is apparently fulfilling in her life. And yet she does not feel it. Another acquaintance had one child three years ago, when she was well into her forties, and is trying desperately to have more. Miscarriage after miscarriage goes by, as she becomes more and more tense, more and more disturbed. She cannot bear it, and cannot bear to speak of it. Fifty is looming. The menopause is not far away. And will she be more than the mother of one much adored child?

There is a problem in the 1960s feminist analysis that argues that it is all due to men that women want children. Women want other things in life, the same things as men want, career, life in the workplace, an absence of domestic responsibilities. Women who want life outside the home are plainly not consciously influenced by men's pressure. They may, of course, be influenced subconsciously. But they do have what they would describe as a strong physical urge, as Germaine Greer remarks in *Sex and Destiny*, where she argues that to some extent it is contraception which men are inflicting on women who only wish to produce children.

It is not as simple as this. Nor is it totally amenable to a feminist analysis that argues that it is all men's conditioning that has produced these desires in women. Although the view that women are only for child production is familiar in many societies, particularly in some that are strongly influenced by the early Christian Church, many of those who desire children so strongly are deeply sophisticated Western women with no religious affiliations over generations, for whom contraception was a liberation, who are angry that they were not told the risks (where they were known), but who nevertheless themselves have regrets that they did not decide earlier in life to forgo the delights of a burgeoning career for the sake of having babies. They do not regard themselves as the victims of men's desires. Rather, they regard themselves as the victims of their time. In the 1960s they were sexually liberated, taking the Pill and sleeping with whoever they chose (or chose them), but in the 1990s they are, many of them, less interested in sex, but desperate to have a baby.

Hence the infertility industry. Just over eleven years ago, the first test-tube baby was born in Britain, a cause of enormous celebration. Since then, Mr Patrick Steptoe's work has gone from strength to strength. All over the UK there are now clinics working in *in vitro* fertilisation and other forms of assisted reproduction. Many of them are private. Treatments of the first instance – some sorts of surgery to correct problems in the fallopian tubes, for example, and some super-ovulatory drugs – are normally part of the NHS infertility provision, but the more hi-tech services are not widely available on the NHS. Only a very few practitioners are continuing to be able to provide a free service for IVF and GIFT (Gamete Intra-Fallopian Transfer, a commonly practised technique not at present subject to the control of the Human Fertility and Embryology Authority, which supervises IVF and donor insemination), and even those that do usually ask for a donation to the department if the couple has enough money.

Some NHS services run on an at-cost basis, providing treatment at the actual cost to the hospital and where possible asking GPs to prescribe the very expensive fertility drugs required. If the GP refuses, the couple have to pay for them themselves, which can be extremely difficult, since the likelihood is that there will be several attempts, in several menstrual cycles, requiring the expensive drugs each time. As the new NHS reforms take effect, with GPs becoming budget holders and Family Health Service Authorities watching their drugs budgets more and more carefully, it is likely that fewer and fewer GPs will be able or willing to prescribe expensive drugs for women having infertility treatments, throwing the cost back on the individuals concerned.

There is a crying need for questions to be asked about why there should be plenty of infertility clinics around the country which cannot provide the most sophisticated services. Then, too, there should be questions about the prescribing of the Pill and the IUD. In the early days, there was all too little reporting of the serious long-term risks of the Pill and the IUD, particularly of increased risk of pelvic inflammatory disease with the IUD, leading in some cases to blocked fallopian tubes. Yet there was a scare in the early '70s about the high-dosage Pill which led to low-dose oestrogen and progesterone-only Pills being prescribed.

But doctors under contract to the NHS were giving the Pill and IUDs freely on prescription – in many cases literally giving, since local authorities often bore the cost of the dispensing of contraceptives rather than face the prospective cost of social service provision to care for all the putative unwanted children. It could be claimed, therefore, that part of the blame for the infertility of many women who were young in the '60s lies precisely with the health services and social planners. And even where the Pill was not given away free, in some areas of the UK and almost everywhere in the US, there was so much encouragement to take it that few women would have doubted it for any reason.

All this makes it peculiar that the infertility services of the highest technical difficulty and expense should not be available within the same health service that arguably, at least partially, caused the problem in the first place.

But attitudes to infertility services are themselves very odd. In the UK in 1986 the Warnock Committee reported on the whole area of IVF and surrogacy, emerging with the apparently inconsistent view that IVF was to be allowed, that disposal of pre-embryos was allowable up to fourteen days of development, but that surrogacy should be outlawed, or, at least, declared illegal on any kind of commercial basis.[3] The government has now chosen to legislate, and has set up the Human Fertilisation and Embryology Authority to license centres providing some of these hi-tech services and those that carry out research on the human embryo. But there is no debate about the question of IVF itself. The doubts are about the vexed issue of 'research'. Should research be allowed on 'spare' embryos – that is, the additional fertilised eggs that do not get replaced in the woman during the IVF procedures? Is 'observation' the same as research? In other words, is there any suggestion that simply observing a 'spare' embryo in a dish but in no way interfering with it is wrong? And what constitutes the sort of 'invasive' research which clearly concerns a large area of the public? Is this the abortion issue all over again, raising the ire of the Roman Catholic lobby in particular but also of other religious groups and some members of the public, or is it wider than that?

The immediate question of the pre-embryo, or embryo, is the same as that of the foetus in the discussions on abortion. In that area, the debate is clearly the one in which the Catholic Church has played a major role: it concerns the vital question of the beginning of life. There are those who are opposed to embryo research on the basis that it has no proven benefit to a particular woman in the way that it can be argued that an abortion does, and there are those who consider it quite acceptable to treat very experimentally a specific embryo on the basis that somehow one may improve its welfare and try to give it life by implanting it within the womb. The issue is a utilitarian one – the divide lies essentially between those who regard it as legitimate to conduct research and experiments on human embryos for the possible future benefit of mankind, and those who regard that as illegitimate, because it gives no direct benefit to the embryo concerned nor its parents, and therefore it is an abuse of the human person, however early a stage of development it has reached. To a large extent, that divide is irreconcilable.

To add to that, in IVF practice and particularly in GIFT, there are some clinicians who take a large number of fertilised eggs (in Britain, under the Interim Licensing Authority guidelines, the limit is three, or in exceptional circumstances four, and it will be reduced to three by the new Human Fertilisation and Embryology Authority) and reimplant them in the womb, on the basis that some can be removed later in a process known as 'selective reduction', a form of partial abortion. There are those who regard this as a waste of embryos and a deliberate destruction of human life, who would sanction the replacement of only one at a time. But others who do not take such a purist line nevertheless find the process of selective reduction distasteful, whilst seeing the enormous distress caused to parents by multiple births, let alone the cost to the NHS of the intensive use of neonatal units for these very tiny babies, usually born prematurely. Scientific opinion, however, is moving towards the view that with good quality embryos, there may be no need to implant more than two in many cases, and that implantation of three has serious consequences in terms of multiple births and the resulting handicaps and use of scarce and expensive neonatal care resources.

But there is a far wider issue here than meets the eye initially. It is the question of who controls fertility. The hi-tech methods of IVF require doctors and scientists. The low-tech methods of surrogacy and artificial insemination do not. Yet curiously they too are being 'medicalised', in order to prevent people, largely women, from taking the law into their own hands. The classic example lies in the area of artificial insemination. In 1974, the American Medical Association declared that 'because human artificial insemination is a medical procedure, the medical profession should exert its influence and efforts to the fullest extent necessary to ensure that the procedure is performed only by individuals licensed to practise medicine or osteopathy.'[4] Yet artificial insemination is easy to achieve, and there is no reason whatsoever, at first consideration, why doctors as a professional group should have a particular involvement with it – unless what they are concerned about is controlling the procedure.

There might, however, be reasons why society would be concerned to prevent donors becoming too enthusiastic and trying to people the earth, or even their own country, with their children. These reasons are both epidemiological, with the need to screen donors for HIV and AIDS, a genuine medical argument, and scientific, because of the danger, small though it might be, of the children of anonymous donors meeting and forming half-incestuous relationships, and the attendant risks of congenital disorders and other problems of the children of close relatives.

This becomes more serious when we learn that there are growing numbers of agencies in the USA where one can obtain the sperm of a Nobel prize winner or some other such genius for payment. The risks of congenital disorders if numerous children are in fact each other's cousins become much higher. The messianic desires of those who wish to give large numbers of sperm donations become more and more suspicious. Add to that the desire of many donors to remain anonymous, and one wonders why they are doing it at all. Is it purely altruistic, or is it because they receive payment, however small, which is welcome to the average

impoverished medical student? There are clear arguments for
control of some kind, but that might well be conducted by nurses
and counsellors as much as by doctors, and the important feature of
the new legislation in Britain is that a register of donors is to be
kept.

But questions are still raised. In early 1991 in Britain, we had the
'virgin birth' scandal, a complete misnomer if ever there was one,
and a source of instant delight to certain sections of the press, which
had a field day discussing the horrors of a woman being given
artificial insemination by donor so that a virgin, never having had
sex with a man – a true rejection of the male species, in the eyes of
some of the journalists – could have a baby.

The agency concerned was the Birmingham Pregnancy Advisory
Service, a registered charity. They had counselled the woman, and
concluded that she knew what she was doing. The question that
arose was whether she should have been allowed to have the
treatment irrespective of her desire not to have sexual intercourse.
One has to presume that she could have got pregnant by having
intercourse with a friend, or a comparative stranger, but that was
not her choice. Is this decent? Does it reject men? Will it make men
feel that they now have no use at all in a world increasingly
controlled by women? Such were the concerns of some of the press.
Yet the truth of the matter is that the woman could not have
become pregnant if some man had not donated his sperm, and that
men are not going out of business in the human reproductive area.

As for the worry that she was sexually a virgin, that is surely no
concern of anyone else's, unless we take the view that the wages of
sin, in terms of sex, are children! In which case the idea that sex is
immoral except for the procreation of children is being turned on its
head – we are saying that one cannot have procreation without the
essential forerunner of quasi-sinful intercourse: a somewhat
curious view. One can only be left with the real question of how
moral it is for women to have children without fathers, where that
can be prevented. Virginity is irrelevant, but the fact of it, in this
case, was certainly enough to make many men very angry and to
make them feel increasingly that this kind of practice must be
controlled, and at least in part by men.

Similarly with surrogacy, where it can be the oldest trick in the
book. A man has intercourse with another woman, who bears a
child and gives it to the man and his wife to nurture and cherish. It

is not the 'mother's' child, but then in the case of artificial insemination by donor, it is not the father's child either. Curiously, although there was a considerable public hue and cry when donor insemination (DI) became common practice in the 1950s and '60s, earlier thinking (mostly in the 1940s) having maintained that DI constituted adultery and that the children so conceived were illegitimate, it was surrogacy that was the cause of most of the controversy in the 1980s.

There are, of course, a variety of ways of practising surrogacy. There is the most old-fashioned of all, where a man simply has intercourse with another woman and then the child is 'given' to the man and his wife. There is a similar process where no actual intercourse takes place but where the woman who is to be the surrogate mother is inseminated artificially with the father's sperm. And there is the more difficult method of implanting within the surrogate mother the already fertilised egg of the 'real' mother and her husband, using the techniques of *in vitro* fertilisation, because the 'real' mother is unable to carry a baby to term. This is frequently called womb-leasing.

The Warnock Committee found forcefully against any of these options. There was a minority opinion which allowed for very limited cases as long as they were controlled by doctors at infertility clinics and women did not earn money for being surrogate mothers. Yet objections were rife, particularly in the areas of legitimacy and inheritance, as well as the question of whose child it would be if it turned out to be handicapped. The debate was profoundly depressing. Hackneyed ideas about inheritance were trotted out, as though human beings could not make their own choices about who should inherit their goods. Illegitimacy was cited as a problem when practically 25% of all live births in the UK are technically illegitimate. And the age-old canard was raised, that this would be exploitation of women's bodies.

Oddly enough, the radical feminists and the opponents of surrogacy agree wholeheartedly about the exploitation. The Warnock Committee wrote that 'a woman should not be put in the position of selling the use of her body.' Yet the religious traditions of Judaism and Christianity, as well as many others, extol the virtues of hard physical labour and the dignity of the sweat of the brow, and one cannot help asking whether there is really any difference between a woman going through labour and birth for

someone else and a male labourer building a road or a house
for someone else, with good, honest, sweaty toil. That is equally
the sweat of one's brow. The truth is that the debate has little to do
with the nature of exploitation, but far more to do with the desire
of society at large to control fertility. Nor is that wholly without
good reason, which complicates the issue.

To add to this, the general public, particularly its female
members, have been curiously unable to see what is going on. The
very same women who have constantly complained about the over-
medicalisation of childbirth, and hated the use of foetal monitors
and episiotomies, have objected to surrogacy; they do not seem to
see that, at least in some cases, it is a woman's answer to female
infertility. It is just as legitimate intellectually and morally to praise
the woman who is prepared to be a surrogate mother for someone
else, on the basis that she is involved in what Richard Titmuss, the
great social scientist of the 1950s and '60s, called, in connection with
blood donors, 'the gift relationship', as it is to condemn her because
she is allowing herself to be used for breeding, and is disregarding
her body like a prostitute. Indeed, the radical feminists who argue
that women are being used as 'breeding machines' need to examine
their opposition very carefully, for surrogacy is one of the very few
of the so-called modern reproductive technologies which are very
largely in the hands of women to control.

But, as a result of considerable opposition, particularly to its
commercialisation, it is on the way to becoming wholly unacceptable, and in most cases outlawed, unless it is carried out purely out
of love. And even then there is a view that it is harder for the child
to accept being the natural child of another mother who is known
to him or her, such as an aunt or close family friend, than for the
surrogate to be a total stranger. Yet if money is not to change
hands, it is more likely that only those who know the woman who
cannot carry her baby to term will be willing to act as surrogates,
out of love. It is a greater example of a 'gift', in the 'gift relationship'
sense, to carry a baby for someone else, unknown, for nine months,
than to give a pint of blood. The question of payment ought also to
address the real costs of pregnancy, such as maternity leave and
extra food and clothes, rather than necessarily the profit motive.

And although the American experience thus far suggests that
the majority of women who come forward to be surrogates are
fairly badly off, that may be to do with the fact that money is

already part of the relationship. If it were clear, as it is in the UK in relation to the giving of blood, that no money changed hands other than that needed for the actual costs of having a baby, then a different kind of person might well consent to be a surrogate mother. It is the fact of women having babies for one another, out of love, which gives the lie to the feminist critique that surrogacy is yet another method whereby women are merely used as receptacles of men's sperm, and that because only poorer women come forward to have babies for others for money, the process is plainly exploitative.

In fact, there is a need for very careful intellectual and moral analysis here. The first question which has to be asked is whether it is a good or bad thing for a women to be prepared to have a baby for someone else. Then, if it is a good thing, should she be paid for it? The question there, however, is less whether or not it is moral for her to be paid for it (since what she would be paid for is the effort put into the pregnancy and the labour, rather than for the baby itself), than whether or not it is distasteful for her to be paid for it. And the truth of the matter is that in Europe it would probably be thought distasteful, but it could hardly be described as morally wrong, any more than it would be possible to describe as morally wrong paying a man for the sweat of his brow on hard manual labour.

Another issue raised by the radical feminist critique is that the renting of a womb, or the act of surrogacy, is not comparable to the use of donor sperm. Corea quotes Andrea Dworkin arguing that the sperm is to be compared with the tears, whilst the renting of the womb is to be compared with the taking out of the eye itself. But that, of course, is not an apt comparison, since the womb is not removed, merely used for a period of nine months. Though the relationship of a woman to her womb, and the fruit of it in the shape of the baby she produces, is infinitely more intimate than that of a man to his sperm, nevertheless it is possible to consider using it for the benefit of others, if that seems to the individual woman concerned to be a good thing. And then it can be either for cash, which we may or may not find distasteful, or for love, of a friend or a sister, or, like the gift of blood, for a total stranger, out of love of humanity at large. Given the strain being pregnant can be, this last is not a likely activity for many women. But it is perfectly possible, and its value in the sense of the gift relationship should not be overlooked.

Corea quotes Margaret Adams talking about the 'compassion trap', arguing that there is such huge pressure upon women to be nurturing and caring that the appeal to a woman's sense of compassion for her childless sister is somehow unfair. She also quotes a friend of hers, arguing that 'the worst thing you can do to someone is mess with the core of her in some way and I think that is what is going on in the appeal to surrogate mothers. . . . You violate or exploit a person's sense of herself.' And yet there are those women who do enjoy being pregnant. There may not be many of them, and I am certainly not one of their number. But many of my friends have said that they never felt better than when pregnant, that they blossomed or glowed, and they might be the sort of women who would consent to have a baby for someone else.

The feminist critique argues that they are being exploited because their compassion for the childless is being wound up. But I fail to see why this is so. It was entirely correct to argue like this for those women who were persuaded into parting with their illegitimate babies for adoption, on the grounds that there were all those respectably married women unable to have children, and here was an unwanted little surprise. But this is a different scenario, where no pressure is being applied, but where some women feel strongly that they are prepared to help others, particularly if they are able to have babies without difficulty. The feminist argument that women should have the right to do as they wish with their own bodies should surely include letting them have a baby for someone else. Why should it be acceptable, in feminist terms, to get rid of an unwanted baby because one is in control of one's own body, and not acceptable to use that body to have a baby and give it away to someone else, be it by surrogacy or by adoption?

The main questions to be asked of doctors in this area are not, in fact, about surrogacy. Doctors should not normally be involved in surrogacy cases at all unless they involve embryo transfer and 'womb-leasing', both of which require great medical and scientific skills. Where a serious feminist or any other kind of moral analysis is vastly overdue, is in the area of DI, IVF and the decision-making process on the part of the doctors and other professionals involved.

There is amusing anecdotal evidence about the number of

medical students who give their sperm for use in DI, as though to say that it would be a better world if it were all entirely populated by doctors. There is no doubt that many professional groups try to perpetuate themselves and regard themselves as the acme of human development. Less amusingly, there is evidence to show that sperm from very bright males has been collected in the US, by a sperm bank called the Hermann Muller Repository for Germinal Choice in California. It was the idea of a businessman called Robert K. Graham, who wrote a book called *The Future of Man*, in which he described the middle and upper classes as 'the repositories of every nation's intelligence and wisdom' and described those people living on welfare benefits as 'indolent people of low intelligence'. They are the ones who produce 'deficient offspring'. He regarded those who were of superior intelligence but who chose only to produce one or no children as 'reproductive malingerers', and wanted huge birth-control programmes for the less intelligent. He felt that there was no such thing as the right to reproduce, and wrote that 'to assert that people should be free to pass on their deficiencies is like arguing that a leper should be free to infect his own offspring.'[5]

This is the real stuff of eugenics. I do not for one moment think that there is much eugenic thinking going on amongst those who are experimenting with IVF and embryo transfer, but subconsciously there may be a feeling that medical students are the best donors of sperm (they are certainly the easiest to get hold of in a hospital setting!), and that it is legitimate, where fertility services are in very short supply, for doctors to find out about the stability of a person's marital or cohabiting relationship, to ask all sorts of questions about criminal records, to decide whether these people or those should be helped to have a baby.

This is worrying not necessarily because the doctors concerned have particularly wrong or undesirable moral standards and views about where a baby will best be cared for, but because they will tend to have quite a *uniform* view, and those who do not agree with their views are less likely to get help. Since this kind of attitude cannot prevail amongst those who have no fertility problems, unless we envisage a system of massive and enforced birth control, it is unfair, to put it mildly, that it should happen with those who do have difficulties in conceiving. There have been, for instance, doctors in IVF clinics who refuse to treat those who are not married. There are doctors who refuse to treat lesbians. There are even more who regard a criminal record as a contra-indication for suitability for IVF. The Code of Practice from the new Human Fertilisation Authority will have to take all these issues into account when licensing centres.

In vitro fertilisation is an area where treatment is very limited (and success rates relatively low but rising). It is understandable that the practitioners should want to have a say in how to allocate scarce resources, particularly within the NHS. But there are problems, and the moral questions will need to be answered, by practitioners, by counsellors, by the Human Fertilisation Authority itself, and by public debate; women have a key role to play here, particularly if decisions are to be made about who is treated and who is not.

The eugenics element is not a serious threat, in the way it was understood in the 1920s and 1930s. There is no suggestion that we breed mental defectives, or Jews, or homosexuals, out of the population. Yet there is, rightly to my mind, a desire to be able to breed out the genetically transmitted diseases which are later killers, the cystic fibrosis, Down's Syndrome and haemophilia in our midst. That can be considered a form of eugenics. So too can the ability, probably not all that far off, to determine the sex or eye colour of a child. If this becomes possible, should it be allowed? Should mothers be able to choose the fathers, or types of fathers, of their children by DI? Should a woman be able to choose Nobel prizewinning sperm? Or brilliant acting sperm? Or the sperm of a best-selling writer? Is it right that donors of sperm for DI should be unknown, as they are in Britain, or should a child have the right to know her or his father, genetically and biologically speaking? Is there a halfway position, where donors can be encouraged to give some details about themselves, without their names, so that the child can have some idea of what their biological father was like?

The situation at the moment is still haphazard. Although the Interim Licensing Authority (on which I had the honour to serve) controlled IVF, it did not police all the centres where donor insemination was carried out. There is no means of knowing, for instance, if DI is carried out by a doctor or indeed a woman herself with a known donor's sperm because the woman wanted to have a particular kind of child. Nor, despite recommendations that donors should not give too much sperm (more than ten donations in a lifetime), is it at all easy to police this. The result, of course, is that there could be large amounts of sperm from particular individuals or families cluttering up the gene pool and destroying any attempt at eugenics that might be being made.

But the desire to have the 'perfect' child should not be underestimated. The 1960s liberated women, who were not going to have children at all and who now yearn for them, do not want a less than perfect child. That is wholly understandable. The agonies of looking after a desperately handicapped child are considerable, and watching a sick child as he or she moves inexorably towards death from an incurable, genetically transmitted disease is unbearable. So on one level, and in one area, the scientists' concern to try to rid the gene pool of some of the worst horrors by genetic engineering is totally worthy.

Other areas of concern are less happy. Those who worry desperately about the intelligence of their children, their gender or their colouring should not necessarily be helped in their endeavours. I have watched friends who have large estates at stake struggle womanfully to produce a boy, because of the male entail. Yet I cannot help wondering whether it would not be better simply to change the system which so discriminates against first-born daughters. Should it be legal to allow families, be they royal or noble or simply conservative in their organisation, to leave titles and lands and money to the first-born sons? Should this not be examined by the Equal Opportunities Commission as a matter which affects very few girls in fact, but where the acceptance of the practice colours the perceptions of many, many more?

Britain places relatively little emphasis on the gender of a child. But in many societies girls are exposed or murdered at birth, because they are considered useless. In China, for example, where families are only allowed to have one child because there is such concern about the population explosion, girl babies are very often mysteriously 'stillborn'. Where food supplies are scarce, boys are fed rather than girls. If choice of gender for children were totally possible, in many societies there would be no doubt. All too many stories circulate about those women who have amniocentesis apparently to determine whether the child is healthy or suffering from Down's Syndrome or some other disorder, but at the same time they can be told the gender of the child. In many cases, so legend has it (there is apparently no proof that this has occurred), they opt for an abortion on the social grounds of overcrowding, poverty and the intolerable strain of a large family, if the unborn child turns out to be a girl.

This is beginning to be a serious problem for those involved in obstetrics and gynaecology, who are being asked the gender for precisely those kinds of reasons, and have to decide whether it is legitimate for them to disclose the information or not. There are all too many instances of feelings of preference for boys, even at a time when in the West the number of boys being born exceeds the number of girls. Up to age twenty-five, there are roughly 102 boys/ men in the population to every hundred girls. Taken to its logical conclusion, this kind of choice-making about the gender of babies could bring about a world in which girls and women are in very short supply. Would the cynics then say that justice might prevail and that girls would be treated more equally? Such a dream, or rather nightmare, is a long way off. But the abortion of girls, the stillbirth of girls and their lack of inheritance are all very near.

In discussions about infertility, questions of adoption are rarely raised except in the context of counselling couples opting for infertility treatments. Yet one option would be to adopt a child, if it were not so incredibly difficult. One has to remove from this debate those who desperately want their 'own' child, not someone else's, and take into account the fact that those seeking infertility treatment are often older than those normally encouraged to apply to adopt, particularly because there is such a shortage of children for adoption. But there are punishing and difficult interviews to be gone through for prospective adoptive parents – and rightly, since the desire to care for someone else's child as one's own needs to be tested out. And despite huge numbers of unwanted children in orphanages around the world, and pitiful pictures of deprived and starving children in countries as diverse as Roumania and Ethiopia, Brazil and the Sudan, trans-national adoptions are extremely difficult to arrange, and therefore tend to be carried out illegally, an issue which the British government has promised to try to rectify.

Nor, were it easy to adopt, were young pregnant girls to be encouraged to put up their babies for adoption, would it be any easier, since the requirement that adopted children should know their history is often a cause of considerable disturbance amongst the family, and adopting and caring for children is no easy option.

Nevertheless, it is a reasonable option, much impeded at present by practical difficulties.

All these are issues of paramount importance for women. Interestingly, it has been a woman minister, Mrs Virginia Bottomley at the Department of Health, who has taken on many of these matters in a practical way. This is where women's organisations have much to contribute, much to say. The difficulty is that the established orthodoxies, of a women's right to choose, of 'exploitation', and of a right to all sorts of infertility treatment, do not look as clear cut once the issues are examined closely; there are many groups representing different interests, all with a strong claim for their views to be heard.

7
Fashion, Beauty and Health

Professor Albert Kligman of the university of Pennsylvania . . . [is] the developer of Retin-A, the one substance that does seem to do something [to alleviate the signs of ageing], including subjecting the skin to inflammation, sunlight intolerance and continuous heavy peeling. 'In the industry today,' he wrote presciently, 'fakery is replacing puffery . . . Some of my colleagues . . . tell me, "Women are so dumb! How can they buy all that grease and stuff? Educated women who've been to Radcliffe and Cambridge and Oxford and the Sorbonne – what gets into them? Why do they go to Bloomingdale's and pay $250 for that hokum?"'

Quoted by Naomi Wolf in *The Beauty Myth*

WHEN SUSIE ORBACH wrote *Fat is a Feminist Issue*, many men and women thought she was completely crazy. But her main thesis, that the perception of what women should look like has been conditioned by men rather than women, and that women are not sufficiently in control of the situation to say that they do not care how fat or large they are, is absolutely correct. The 1960s was the era of the first of the stick-like women, Twiggy, Jean Shrimpton (the Shrimp) and Faye Dunaway as Bonnie in *Bonnie and Clyde*. But the history of women's shape as an indication of attitudes is fascinating. Though it is legitimate to go back to the beginning of time, to examine the steatopygous figurines of early near-eastern goddesses and reach the conclusions Jung and his disciple Erich Neumann reached about 'The Great Mother',[1] for our purposes looking back to the Second World War and the lean, fit women of the land army contrasted with the New Look women of 1947, with their padded hips and breasts and their nipped-in waists, is probably sufficient. For fashion, and the way it manipulates the female shape, has been of exceptional variety since then.

Wartime women wore short skirts, were out at work and had clothing coupons which were always in short supply, so that lavishness was far from easy. But the New Look, as commented upon by the leading London fashion designer of his time, Hardy Amies, was 'part of a plan to emphasise women's best characteristics . . . curved shoulders, high busts, small waists, full hips and a good carriage . . . Speaking very personally, I feel that this must lead to more satisfactory relations between men and women in general, to what the Americans call a more "gracious" way of living . . . I hope [the new clothes] mean order, peace and plenty: order because everything is in its place, peace because they want to avoid the sharp cutting off of the line at the knee, and plenty because they are not skimpy.'[2]

What does this reflect but a wish to return women to the home, to a more 'feminine' way of life? Enough of women in the land army and the factories. It was time to make way for the men, leaving the jobs to them and becoming the Little Woman again, at home, getting everything ready for the ideal husband when he came home from work. These were the clothes of the return to the old values, and it was quite possible, even legitimate, for Hardy Amies to talk about them making relationships between the sexes easier. For to many people, both men and women, the short skirts and trousers of wartime had spelled something of a real change for women.

The New Look did not last long, but the '50s followed, with bouffant hairdos, polka-dot skirts and cool elegance – the Grace Kelly look with the hint of sex about her, though she always looked like the perfect, understated English lady who married her prince. There were hats, gloves and proper handbags. It was only at the end of that decade that a rather naughtier look, pert and pretty, came about, and Ann Shearer suggests in *Women: Her Changing Image* that this was because women now wanted to get away from the calm, the poise, the control that the '50s had so adulated. She mentions that the first tranquilisers were marketed in 1951, and assumes that the calm and poise had been bought at a price.

Then came the '60s with the mini-skirts, white faces, Courrèges boots with no toes, moon-boots, which we all saved up for and wore in the snow so that we got chilblains. We were lanky and curveless, or at least we tried to be. We ironed our hair so that it would be totally straight. Mine was a frizzy mop, which I spent hours with on the ironing board to little effect, though my mother still remembers the smell of singeing hair permeating the kitchen. We were 'unfeminine' in the terms of the New Look, but we thought we were the acme of desirability. Yet this was beginning to be the hippy generation. Before we knew it, we were into droopy Indian clothes or, at best, romantic new Laura Ashley long dresses in the summer. We still had our long hair, though some of us had progressed to our natural curls by then, and we had open sandals and long, dangling earrings, and we burned joss-sticks. The image was theoretically that of being back to nature, but in fact it was far from that. It was, however, the sign of the so-called 'permissive' society which, according to Anna Coote and Beatrix Campbell in *Sweet Freedom*, 'far from permitting women to do anything, had kidnapped them and carried them off as trophies, in the name of sexual freedom. In the era of flower-power and love-ins, of doing-your-own-thing and not being hung up (especially about sex), girls were expected to do it, and impose no conditions. The more they did it, the more "liberated" they were deemed to be.'

The clothes, first the mini-skirts which made us obviously available in the sense of very little of us being covered, and then the droopy 'natural' look of the late '60s, were an indication of our role. The later clothes particularly, with their emphasis on being back to nature, flower power and all of that, made it increasingly clear that we were there for sex, that we would have sex when asked, that we were somehow liberated by that, and that we had been trapped by the clothes, the attitudes we had previously worn. And this is the origin of the bra-burning myth. For no bras were ever burned, insofar as anyone can remember or tell, at the great demonstration in Atlantic City, USA, in 1968.

What happened was this. The Miss America pageant took place in Atlantic City. For a couple of years before that, small groups of women had been meeting up and down the country in the US (and in Britain), partly inspired by Betty Friedan's book *The Feminine Mystique*, which had been published in 1963. Friedan had pointed out the suburban imprisonment of American womanhood, the search for an unattainable dream of domestic perfection and the trap away from other satisfactions, other fulfilments women might have wanted, all in order to promote this delicious to men, but distressing to women, feminine mystique. Her readers had discussed the problems of women's role in the US, and were developing their own political theory of feminism, though they would not yet have described it as such.

They decided that the Miss America pageant degraded all women, both the contestants and the viewers, and that women were being forced to pull and tug and push their bodies into quite strange and alien shapes, in order to fulfil the fantasies and desires of men, but in no way for their own ends. So they decided to stage a protest, and to illustrate that particular point they threw their bras and girdles into what they described as a 'freedom trash bucket'. The flames were presumably later added by a news agency reporter and the media loved it. Reports went coursing round the world of the 'bra-burning' escapades of these mad American women's libbers, and it became, as Coote and Campbell put it, 'sexy and absurd, it neatly disposed of a phenomenon which would otherwise have proved rather awkward to explain.'

Yet the bra-burning scenario became a by-word on both sides of the Atlantic for women's liberation (at that time mostly referred to as women's lib). It seemed so extraordinary to most people that no-one asked the serious questions about why women did wear bras, or, at least, the types of bras that they were wearing at the time, and 'the smokescreen of the "burning bra" helped to obscure the real nature of the women's liberation movement. It wasn't the result of a deliberate conspiracy; it was simply an example of what happened as the dominant sex went about its daily business of managing information and opinion.'[3]

What then was the point of the bra-burning? To what extent did the women's libbers of the late '60s and early '70s take the clothes and fashion arguments seriously? We certainly began to at Cambridge. There was a ceremonial bra-burning, which I remember very well, in the garden of friends in Jericho in Oxford one spring. We threw our bras on the flames, but since most of them were padded and underwired, indicating exactly the point that the original demonstrators had wished to make, they smelled dreadful and did not make a dramatic blaze. They merely smouldered and fumigated the neighbourhood. For us, it was the beginning of a women's lib identity, but we failed to see the real significance of the issue of fashion, dress and bodies at that point, or, indeed, until much later.

Yet plainly the issue of dress and fashion infuriated many men. Nicholas Davidson, in his critique of feminism entitled *The Failure of Feminism*, describes the feminist attitude to fashion and looks like this:

> Anything that emphasised the physical dichotomy between the sexes was frowned upon: high heels, which emphasise the swaying gait caused by the female pelvis; smooth-shaven legs, which emphasise the difference in hair distribution between men and women; and any garment that seems to emphasise the relative helplessness and vulnerability of the female before the male. Many women who continued to shave their legs, use cosmetics and wear pretty dresses felt that they somehow weren't quite up to snuff. They acknowledged that their behaviour was wrong in principle, even though they persisted in it.

The language he uses is precisely that which infuriated the early women's libbers of the late '60s and early '70s. Yet to some extent he has a point, if only he did not put it in quite such an unpleasant way. For there was and is a view that women should make themselves spare and lean, fit and athletic. Part of that is undoubtedly a feature of the fitness craze which has taken over the Western world, leading business men, and women, to have workouts before they go to their offices or in the lunch hour, should they have the luxury of having a lunch break in the first place.

But there is more to it than that with feminist attitudes to the female body. Although many feminists have followed the Orbach line and allowed themselves to become fat and remain that way, though exercised, there is a significant number of women who have followed a different line, who, by exercise and eating less, have emphasised leanness and fitness as the proper way for a woman's body to be.

> On both sides of the Atlantic women are running, jumping, stretching, dancing, seeking fitness for the rigours ahead. Some are building their bodies too: pumping iron, flexing muscle. When Jane Fonda promises women a workout for today's life, 10,000 a week go to the workshops. . . .[4]

This, then, was the proper way to be. No longer the large-bottomed fertility figure of the Victorian woman with the bustle, women were to be lithe and slim, and wear trousers and tracksuits rather than skirts. Susan Brownmiller, in *Femininity*, describes the '70s as a decade when 'suddenly it was all right to wear pants. Then it became a feminist statement to wear pants. Never again would most women wear skirts, I thought, in the way that friends of mine have thought that the revolution is just around the corner. And here it is, well into the '80s, and the woman who wears nothing but pants is a hold-out, a stick in the mud, a fashion reactionary with no sense of style.'

This is the Brownmiller who is peculiarly unpleasantly ridiculed by Nicholas Davidson:

> For Brownmiller is making a fashion statement in this picture, despite her disparagement of fashion. She is wearing a dress, not the trousers of which she approves, but what a dress! Formless, sacklike, it gives no clue to what lies beneath. One cannot tell if she has a bust, where her waist is, whether she has hips, or even whether her arms are plump or thin, slack or muscular. It is the body desexualised. Even the fabric, a dull linen, is without pattern or colour. No patterns for the woman freed from the patterns of conditioning; no colour for the woman who fears to excite men's attention. This nondescript smock is belted with a man's belt: not too wide, with the plainest of buckles. Brownmiller's assumption of the belt, an archetypal symbol of masculinity, shows her determination to assume the masculine qualities it represents: in her case, presumably intellectualism and the search for identity through extrafamilial activities.[5]

The hatred Davidson expresses, and the extent to which he, too, has been caught up in the symbolism of various types of clothes, notably in this case the belt, makes one grieve for the emphasis put on the issue of clothes and undergarments by the 1960s and 1970s feminists. Utterly understandable though it was, it gives such a weapon to the men who oppose the whole philosophy, without doing very much to improve the lot of women. The marriage of Sarah Ferguson to the Duke of York evoked terrible cries from the popular press that she was too fat, particularly in comparison with her sister-in-law, the extra-slim fairy-tale princess, Diana, Princess of Wales (the rumours were, of course, that Diana was anorexic). But Sarah Ferguson was not having any of this nonsense. She answered her critics with a fairly terse comment: 'I do not diet. I do not have a problem. . . . A woman should have a trim waist, a good "up top" and enough down the bottom, but not too big. A good womanly figure.' That received an enthusiastic response from the wedding-day crowd, as recorded by Ann Shearer: 'She has struck a blow for the normal women of this country who are size sixteen with large hips and not afraid to say "I obey."' This kind of comment, whether a woman is too fat or too slim, whether she should emphasise her large backside or not, is very much the stuff of men's pictures of women, as well as women's images of themselves, and it does no good to the real debate to spend time worrying about dress and shape in quite such a way.

Suffice it to say that the Duchess of York was not allowed to get away with it in the end, and dieted and exercised her way to a three-stone weight loss via Callan Pinckney's 'Callanetics' after giving birth to her first child. Only recently has it been possible to talk again of the glory of fat women, in the extraordinary embryonic work by literally larger-than-life thirty-five-year-old film camera-woman Cathy Greenhalgh, in her *Fat Women Celebrate*.[6]

Brownmiller, Orbach and the others may unwittingly have done great damage to the cause of most women by their excessive emphasis on attitudes to body and to dress, and they probably have not succeeded, other than in the fitness campaign, which was part of an international craze anyway, in dramatically affecting women's lives. Indeed, where in a sense they ought to be pleased is in the rush of young women executives to buy masculine city suits. (This too is a fashion that looks as if it is going to be very short-lived.) Many young women wore masculine-style shirts and even ties in the very late '70s and early '80s, and the emphasis on suits and neat, uncluttered, 'unfeminine' dress continued well into the '80s. Women wore jackets with padded shoulders, sometimes to excess, *Dynasty* style, and they wore neat shoes, often with low heels.

This should have been a victory for the Brownmiller school of feminism, but in fact it was not, because during the late 1980s skirts once more became shorter and shorter. This has either to be explained as a concession to men's desire to see women's legs again, a return to the availability of the mini-skirted 1960s, or a desire on the part of women themselves to have some fun with fashion, which had become rather staid with its city-slicker suits. What might suggest that this was so was the fact recorded on both sides of the Atlantic that interest in so-called 'sexy' underwear had rocketed, that sales of frilly knickers, French knickers, silk camisoles and slips were enormous, and that men were not buying these expensive items for their wives and mistresses, but women were buying them for themselves, to wear under the formal city suits.

Why should this be so? Did it make them feel more feminine? Or was it for fun? Were the city uniforms, not all that different from the men's, so dull that the women had to branch out into some other kinds of clothes, or was it simply that women, once again, were becoming interested in precisely the kind of 'feminity' the early feminists had found so obnoxious? Or could it be, as it was for me, the sheer delight of wearing expensive, smooth, delicious silks and satins next to the skin, however dull the clothes above them? It is not clear which is the case, and there is undoubtedly quite a lot of confusion about the role that women are supposed to be playing in the late 1980s and early 1990s, which is partly the reason, no doubt, that there are all sorts of conflicts in the way women dress and the shape that they try to attain.

But there is more to this than merely a fashion issue. There is a serious question of health. It exists in the first analysis in the question of anorexia, the disease largely of young girls, though, interestingly, increasingly affecting older women and some men too. It is a condition in which the victim first starts dieting and then continues to see herself as desperately fat even when she is painfully thin and fading away. The old maxim, last quoted to me by an aristocratic lady who died shortly afterwards, horribly painfully of cancer that she was keen that I should try to avoid, that 'you can never be too rich or too thin', is in fact completely untrue. You can be both, and the number of young women who are too thin, in the wake perhaps of the obsession with fitness and slimness that the women's movement has done nothing to alleviate, is rising. These are young women in the affluent, possibly 'too rich' West who literally starve themselves. If they are allowed to, they starve themselves to death. If they are stopped, and treated by therapy or counselling, they recover all too rarely, and they tend to have considerable mental and eating problems for the rest of their lives.

Why do they do it, and why are older women and men joining them? People try to analyse what it is that has gone wrong. Is it that these young women are frightened to leave their childhood behind them, that they do not wish to grow up and become mothers in their own right? An extraordinary number of them, by strenuous dieting, lose their periods and become amenorrhoeic, and are then pleased that they have regressed from the 'womanly' state of bleeding every month to the childlike state of not bleeding at all. Older women may be seeking a real time-reversal, losing their womanhood in search of a long-forgotten girlhood. Both men and women may feel they are following medical advice to get slim and fit, for as health professionals increasingly tell us that our health is our own responsibility, even though there is clear evidence that poverty is a major contributory force in ill-health, people believe it is in their hands to be slim, and fit, and well.

Still others are merely trying to capture the fashion of the moment: girls who are designed to be big and plump, with wide hips and large breasts, try to lose these qualities because they are not fashionable. But who says they are not fashionable? Fashion magazines have always tended to go for very slim models, because clothes tend to look their best on thin women. But men have traditionally preferred women to be a little fatter, a little 'cuddlier'. Nothing, however, can evoke the contempt of some of the feminist lobby of the early and mid 1970s more than the suggestion that women should be cuddly for men's delight. Scorn is poured upon the Page Three girls both for the fact that they are there to titillate men, and because they are flaunting their 'cuddlier' parts.

Yet breasts themselves have in fact become bigger, even though women have been trying to reduce their size by dieting and exercising. To many women, that can be a cause of personal disgust, as I remember myself from being pregnant, and going from my normal 36B to a 38D in two weeks, and then reaching a horrific 46D for my nursing bras, just before the baby was born. I felt gross, cow-like, unfeminine (as though I was anything else!) and distinctly unsexy. Yet increased breast size may be something to do with the hormone content in the Pill and with Hormone Replacement Therapy, and many argue that it may, in fact, be responsible for a higher incidence of breast cancer in younger women. However, that is as yet unproven, and there is no reason to suppose that the huge increase in the incidence of breast cancer, now killing a shocking 13,000 women a year in the UK, is in fact linked to the contraceptive pill. Yet some want to believe it, whilst others are clear that Hormone Replacement Therapy is some protection against brittle bone disease in later life, as bone mass shrinks and bones crack and fragment.

There is something very peculiar in the emphasis that the women's movement has, rightly, placed upon the rise of anorexia, whilst it has analysed so little the obsession with weight and shape and style and fashion. There is urgent need for analysis of anorexia and the reason that girls should wish not to grow into young women with all the choices that young womanhood might imply, and also of the whole obsession with shape and dress. To be able to say to young women, and mean it, that it does not matter if you are plump and chubby as long as you are reasonably fit and healthy is no bad thing. Indeed, since the majority of young women wish to be attractive to men, there is also no reason to avoid saying that many men prefer a woman not to be too thin, so that she is 'cuddlier'. There is nothing wrong with being cuddly, unless it is bad for your health, just as there is nothing wrong with being interested in fashion for fashion's sake, or wanting to look feminine. The Duchess of York really did do some good for other young women. So did her style of dress with a bow worn over her backside, bustle-style, for she was emphasising her femininity and her female shape.

It is a mistake to assume that because a woman wants to look feminine and to follow fashion, she is somehow unliberated and cannot be a feminist. One might well ask what it is she has not been liberated from, and if the reply were to be that she is not liberated from men's pictures of what she should look like, she might well reply that she dresses to please herself, as indeed, very many women do. The woman who wears a skirt or frills at a gathering of feminists knows that she is not conforming to a fashion – she has made that particular choice. Janet Radcliffe Richards wrote in *The Sceptical Feminist* that 'anyone who has tried looking feminine in a gathering of extreme feminists knows that the pressures against that sort of appearance are every bit as strong as any pressure about dress in the wider world: in fact at the moment they are probably stronger.' Ann Shearer analyses what she said very effectively:

> To suggest that what feminism needs is women who are desirable to men but will have nothing to do with any man who does not treat them properly seems like rather a good point to me, but she knew it would be unpopular. To go further and suggest that some women might actually enjoy, without compromising their feminism, making themselves beautiful simply because they love beauty, or that women's adornment might be seen as a central part of 'women's culture' seemed to her more risky still.[7]

Yet in the light of what happened in the 1980s, that is an

appropriate response. Many of the women who have done so well in the business world, who for years have been wearing slick little business suits, ostentatiously dressing for success, have become transformed in the evenings into butterflies with magnificent jewels and colours. Opulence is back in fashion, worn by women newly rich in their own right, and wealth is on display whether as the result of a wealthy husband or lover, or as a result of a woman's own earnings or inheritance.

Of all the misplaced emphases of the women's movement of the late 1960s and early 1970s this one on clothes and shape and fashion, not to mention cosmetics which were not to be worn, has been the worst to my mind. It has been all too easy to turn into a laughing stock as far as men who are opposed to the serious side of the movement are concerned; it benefits very few women; it is meaningless to many of those very poor women whose lives have barely improved, indeed, have often become even worse, over the years that the women's movement has existed; and has only succeeded in making life drabber for those whom it did affect. (The huge incidence of women going for beauty treatments at great expense in deprived, poor and drab Roumania is an indication of how important the ability to give oneself a physical fillip must be to the female psyche.) A philosophy which gave women more choices in appearances, on the basis that women should dress to please themselves as much as to please men, would be a different matter, but that is much more the way that recent fashion has gone in the mainstream of the fashion press, than it has among feminists.

The real issues should be about women being forced to look a certain way for particular jobs, or fired for getting too fat or not being sufficiently glamorous. Naomi Wolf writes eloquently in *The Beauty Myth* about the case of Christine Craft, American TV anchorwoman, who filed suit against her ex-employer, Metromedia Inc, on the charge of sex discrimination. She lost. She had claimed that the company made unreasonable demands on her time and her money, subjecting her to hours of fittings and beauty treatments, and 'set a day-by-day chart of clothing that she would not have chosen herself and for which she was then asked to pay.' Other women covered the trial. Craft was humiliated by her colleagues on camera. Diane Sawyer (who, six years later, when she won a six-figure salary, would have her appearance evaluated on *Time*'s cover with the headline IS SHE WORTH IT?) asked Craft on national news if she really was 'unique among women in [her] lack of appearance skills.'

This is the stuff of real sex discrimination, and this is where men's views of what women should be like, particularly for so-called glamorous jobs, come to the fore. No-one who has spent hours having their hair done for a television programme to look as male executive producers want them to look can have any doubt that this is a male dream of female perfectability, and that if women tried harder, they could always improve themselves, keep themselves in check, diet, stop drinking, be fit and elegant and well groomed and excellently – but not too showily – dressed. In other words, they could be in all ways physically perfect. It simply does not occur to these men that women may not *want* to look like that, even though they wish to be fit and fashionable and comfortable. They may nevertheless wish to be more original, or less sleek, or even possibly less covered in make-up and hairspray.

That thinking is also an essential part of the philosophy that all our problems – being too fat or too thin, having terrible legs or terrible teeth – are changeable, that somehow our appearance is all in our own hands. If we are made responsible, we can always get better. And that leads to the cosmetics industry's huge profits, to magazine articles that tell us how to get thin and fit in thirty days – a guaranteed way of selling papers – and to the idea that one should somehow never be satisfied with what one has, but always, constantly, be trying to be thinner, fitter, smarter. It says nothing about the other values of life, like being nicer, kinder, more caring, more compassionate, and realising that when someone's appearance is not perfect, or their health is terrible, that it might not always be their fault – or that important.

8
Breast Cancer and Medical Research

I feared they imagined the whole breast infected – feared it too
justly – for, again through the cambric, I saw the hand of
M. Dubois held up, while his forefinger first described a straight
line from top to bottom of the breast, secondly a cross, and
thirdly a circle; intimating that the whole was to be taken off.

Fanny Burney, letter, early nineteenth century.

IT IS NOT only in the area of contraception that health issues for
women have been so important, and so subject to medical expert
disagreement. A classic example of this, useful because it shows the
way thinking has changed since the 1960s, is breast cancer. Some
13,000 women die of breast cancer, or rather its attendant
secondary growths, every year in Britain, and the rate is mirrored
in deaths per thousand females throughout the Western world, and
in much of the developing world as well, with odd blips such as a
relatively low incidence in Japanese women, other than those who
eat a totally Western diet, such as Japanese Americans; curiously,
there is a very high incidence of breast cancer in parts of Egypt,
where a peculiarly virulent brand of the disease appears to be locally
endemic.

But breast cancer has all the qualities that make it worth looking
at in the light of the inherent 'no change' argument of this book. For
in the 1960s, a period of great optimism and fair wealth in terms of
medical research funds, it was believed that some drugs were going
to be discovered which would 'beat cancer', and more particularly

that would 'cure' breast cancer. There were grounds for this optimism then. The new platinum-based drugs were just beginning to be tried on animals; work was being done on viruses which seemed to have a link to cancers; proof was emerging that the treatment of women with cell changes in the cervix was preventing their later death from cervical cancer. Things were changing, and the picture of being unable to do anything to help the thousands of women with primary breast cancer who presented themselves to doctors each year, other than the most obvious, and often most disfiguring surgery, seemed likely to fade.

This has not in fact proved to be the case. Indeed, there are those who say that the prognosis for women with primary breast cancer has not changed dramatically in the last 130 years. That assertion is unfair, although until the 1970s it was reasonable to argue that the treatment for primary breast cancer had not changed much over the previous century. Women were still being subjected to what was known as Halstead's mastectomy, a fairly radical operation which entailed removing the offending breast, part of the lymph nodes from under the arm and the pectoral muscle to the bone wall. It was massive, major surgery and the result tended to look pretty awful, but was felt to be all that could be done. (And the view that with cancer the best thing is to cut it out is still astonishingly prevalent, despite evidence that many cancers are some form of a systemic disease.)

But change did come about in the 1970s, as a result of considerable work on randomised controlled trials conducted by a number of British surgeons. Other trials had gone on elsewhere in the world, notably in Italy, but there is still a remarkable reluctance within the British medical profession to accept international evidence unless it has also been tried here. This view may seem puzzling to the outsider, but has some justification because of the clear differences in patterns of disease, and reactions to disease, in different countries and even in different regions within countries.

Doctors in Britain piloted the idea of trying to compare the life expectancy, and, to some extent, the quality of life, of women who were treated with the conventional mastectomy and those who were given a lumpectomy, in which the lump in the breast, plus some of the surrounding tissue, was removed, and the breast then subjected to radiotherapy in an attempt to kill off any remaining malignant cells. The interesting result was that the life expectancy for women in either group was the same, and therefore it became fashionable, particularly in the late 1970s and early 1980s, to advocate lumpectomy instead of mastectomy. It remained true, however, that depending where a woman was in the UK she might be offered very different kinds of treatment, being largely subject to the whims of a general surgeon, rather than a breast specialist, who might not have read the latest literature, and therefore be unaware that there was any viable alternative to mastectomy.

Even more interestingly, evidence is beginning to emerge, out of a trial looking at psychological attitudes to breast cancer, that many women prefer to have a mastectomy, however disfiguring, rather than a lumpectomy. When they are asked why, replies vary, but centre round a belief that with a mastectomy, one has somehow got rid of it for ever, whereas if the breast was left with only a lump being removed from it, another cancerous growth might well appear in the same breast. Women are obviously depressed and frightened by this prospect, and it is undoubtedly the case that there is a significant incidence of a second primary tumour occurring in the breast if only a lump was removed the first time.

All this work on what is best for women who have breast cancer, or indeed, other forms of disease, is done by means of what is considered to be the only respectable way of conducting a trial in the UK, the randomised controlled trial. In this, the woman does not know which group she is being placed into, so that she can only give her consent to the *idea* of a trial, but not to a particular procedure which is to be carried out on her body. This has caused considerable disquiet amongst many patients, although the principle of trials, and of randomisation where necessary, is accepted by most patient groups – albeit with reservations. The problem comes about when the area of investigation is as sensitive as the breast, which is such a symbol, for both men and women, of female sexuality. Most breast surgeons, indeed surgeons in general, are men, yet almost all breast cancer patients are women. The sexual politics in this are considerable, and there is an understandable, though probably unfair, view that if men suffered more from breast cancer, they would have found some better way of dealing with it by now. The result has been to produce a very articulate group of patients, who do not simply accept what the medical profession tell them.

This is in part due to the work of some superb TV journalists, mostly women, who have made popular programmes about the doubts and fears of the doctors who treat breast cancer, making it perfectly clear to women that the doctors themselves do not know all the answers, which tends to suggest that the patients might as well choose for themselves what they want to do. It is also due to the work over the last twenty years or so of the 'agony aunts' in women's magazines, that much scorned source of sensible advice and information, due to whom hundreds of thousands of women have written about things they are not prepared to talk about to their husbands, sons, GPs (even female ones) and women friends. And the letters those magnificent women have received and answered would make fascinating social history, telling us a great deal about women's lives and fears in late twentieth-century Britain.

But the problems are considerable. To the doctors, the obvious thing to do when there is no clear evidence about what is best is to run a series of randomised controlled trials, possibly internationally, on a multi-centre basis. The problem with an articulate, educated patient group, as far as the doctors are concerned, is that they are liable to say, 'If you do not know what the right things to do are, tell me the alternatives and I'll make my own decision.' But women making their own choices about their treatment removes the validity of the evidence in a trial. The whole point about randomisation is that there is no element of choice, because neither doctor or patient is supposed to have any say in the matter.

The result of all this is that it has been almost impossible to recruit sufficient women into these studies. The problem has not been as extreme as it was with the AIDS patients in the US trying a new drug for those intolerant of AZT, the usual treatment, where they simply pooled the pills and rerandomised because they felt it was unfair that some of them were being given a placebo. Nevertheless, women have been reluctant to enter the normal randomised study, and recruiting women to new studies, such as in the use of Tamoxifen for women whose mothers or sisters have had breast cancer, but who have no symptoms themselves, has been difficult and required carefully orchestrated publicity.

The reaction of the medical profession to this has been mixed. The standard response is to say that patients should keep out of this, that they will not understand the science, that there is no point in women making their own choices if there is no evidence to say what the better choice would be. But there is a different mood as well, much manifested at the King's Fund Consensus Conference on Breast Cancer, chaired by Dame Mary Donaldson, in 1985, where a few doctors spoke up bravely about the lack of knowledge and their desire to do what patients wanted them to do, a view which some participants found hard to take.

On that occasion, the panel, on which I served, six men and six women, were observed listening to descriptions of surgery for breast cancer, with all six women having their arms folded firmly across their breasts! The accounts of the different forms of surgery to which women were automatically subjected in various parts of the country, with no explanation as to why it should be radical mastectomy in one place and lumpectomy in another, no choice given and no trial taking place, were rather hard to hear. Indeed, the consensus statement published shortly afterwards in the *BMJ*, advocating the use of lumpectomy as well as mastectomy, plus the use of particular chemotherapies, especially Tamoxifen for post-menopausal women, seems to have had some effect. There is evidence that its publication, and its massive follow-up in the media and especially in women's magazines, has meant that women are asked more frequently what they would prefer in the way of treatment.

This is just as well, since in recent years screening of women between fifty and sixty-five has become freely available, and, indeed, GPs were given targets for the percentages of their patients in the appropriate age bracket to be screened. This first happened when the redoubtable and impressive, often much maligned Edwina Currie was minister with special responsibility for women's health at the Department of Health. She did great things for women's health, even if screening for breast cancer is one of the least certain of them. Foremost amongst her achievements was the institution of the provision of black and brown nipples for women who had had mastectomies, when hitherto only white had been available; she also brought about a great deal of improvement in screening for cervical cancer, where a reduction in the death rate was clearly proven. Screening for breast cancer, however, has brought many difficulties. Because the evidence of improvement in prognosis of those with primary breast cancer, whatever the treatment, is fairly slight, there was a strong argument against screening, on the basis that primary breast cancers would be discovered but that nothing much could be done for the patients other than worrying them considerably.

That attitude is only partly correct. In fact, in post-menopausal women who have primary breast cancer with minimal nodal involvement, in other words precisely the sort of primary breast cancer that is likely to be picked up by a screening programme, the drug Tamoxifen makes a significant difference to survival rates, and its use is clearly to be encouraged. But along with that are the undoubtedly large numbers of false positives, particularly of lumps detected in women who are around the menopause and have lumpy breasts anyway, which are quite benign and related to the menstrual cycle.

An immense amount of worry is caused by these results and the speed at which women can be dealt with, having biopsies and surgery, is not sufficiently great to assuage concern, though in health prognosis terms it is almost certainly quick enough. The result is undoubtedly a great deal of prolonged distress. The question remains then as to whether screening is worth it. Maureen Roberts, one of the doctors in Edinburgh working with Sir Patrick Forrest on the screening programme, wrote a damning article in the *BMJ* just before her own death from breast cancer. It was in fact published posthumously, and, more in sadness than in anger, questioned the rightness of the screening programme then being put in place.

In his massive and authoritative tome,[1] Sir Patrick Forrest spends little time analysing her arguments. He goes through the pros and cons and comes down firmly in favour of screening, though he would privately, presumably, have preferred to screen a wider tranche of the female population, even though the prognosis for pre-menopausal women is much worse. Nevertheless, the definite, if slight, benefit of a course of CMF (cyclophosphamide, methetrexate and 5-Fluoracil – a decidedly toxic cocktail), probably given at the time of surgery, is something that should not be denied to younger women, and if their cancers are not picked up at an early stage, it will be too late to do anything to help them.

In other words, if early detection is genuinely a life-saver in breast cancer, which is clearly open to some doubt amongst the experts, then it must be of greatest benefit where there is something one can do, however slight, in the group with the least good prognosis, pre-menopausal women. And therefore the policy of screening only those between fifty and sixty-five looks like more of a political than a rational decision, particularly as evidence about the amount of distress caused by the processing of the screening mounts up.

Nevertheless, screening for primary breast cancer is to continue, despite the doubts, as is research on women with breast cancer and on those who do not have breast cancer but whose mothers or sisters have. The research field here is a busy one, partly because the figures of female deaths from breast cancer in the West are so appallingly high.

But women are all too often the victims of research anyway, frequently without their knowledge or consent. Women use medical care more than men do. They tend to live longer, they have babies, their gynaecological problems require greater use of healthcare facilities than male disorders of the genital region, and they are also more likely to attend doctors' surgeries with their children than are their male partners.

Alongside medical care in the United Kingdom goes a considerable amount of research. It is done partly for purely scientific reasons, to establish the best treatments and, increasingly, to test the efficacy of conventional treatments that have been used for generations without ever being measured. Much is also done on behalf of the pharmaceutical industry, testing drugs which may be of enormous benefit to individual patients, but are also likely to be a second or third pharmaceutical company's attempt to establish a 'me-too' drug in an area which has proved very profitable, such as in non-steroidal and anti-inflammatory drugs for arthritis and rheumatism Then there is public health research, largely epidemiological, to draw patterns of the spread of disease in areas of the country or on a nationwide basis. Add to that the fact that, increasingly, medical and nursing students are required to conduct a research project as part of their training, and the conclusion that many of us, women even more than men, will be drawn into medical research at some point is not difficult to draw.

It is now an accepted principle among researchers, after lengthy battles, that patients entering trials should do so only after giving their fully informed consent. Yet in the randomised controlled trial, a number of different treatments are compared, and patients are assigned types of treatment on a random basis; neither the patients nor their doctors know which arm of the trial they will be in, and consent has to be given before the randomisation takes place.

For obvious reasons, it is hard to get patients to agree to being allocated randomly to a menu of treatments, and the rate of refusal is growing. In breast cancer trials, refusal is now very common. This is obviously frustrating to the researchers, who want to conduct the trial, and ultimately may slow down the acquisition of knowledge, which is in no-one's interests.

Breast cancer trials have pointed up these problems. Mastectomy versus lumpectomy plus radiotherapy is only one of the trials. There are the Tamoxifen trials for women with no symptoms, and there was a trial in the early '80s of the benefits of counselling, versus no counselling, in breast cancer cases. That was a trial which Evelyn Thomas, a patient who complained vociferously about her inclusion in trials without her consent, described as 'unkind' at the very least.

'Unkind' is a useful description here. Women are not being entered into trials for immoral motives. Improvements in treatment are genuinely being sought. But the need to gain informed consent slows down the process, and the desire to 'get on with it' is particularly great when medical promotion rests so heavily on a corpus of published research. For female patients, who are demographically in the majority, this is compounded by what the distinguished journalist Carolyn Faulder describes as 'encounters with doctors . . . frequently fraught with sexual prejudice'.[2] Medicine is still a largely paternalistic profession, with few women in its higher echelons. It perceives itself as beneficent and finds it hard to marry that beneficence with patients' autonomy, particularly when patient choices seem irrational.

Many doctors find patients' reluctance to enter randomised controlled trials puzzling, because they do not rate highly the individual's desire to keep control of her own body, even if the choice she makes may turn out to do her less good in the end. There are, too, a few well-publicised cases where patients have not known that they were in a trial at all, or where the full details have not been spelled out to them, which adds to the concern. The worst example, perhaps, was the cervical cancer trial conducted at the New Zealand National Women's Hospital in Auckland, in which no consent was sought.

A doctor there, Associate Professor Herbert Green, was trying to prove his conviction that local cancer of the cervix (carcinoma *in situ*) would not develop into the invasive disease. Women diagnosed at the hospital were monitored, but no further treatment was given – even when abnormal smears continued to give evidence of malignant disease. Amongst the 131 women of whom this was true, twenty-nine (22%) subsequently developed invasive cancer. Most of them did not know they were participants in a medical trial. One woman, 'Ruth', who had carcinoma *in situ* diagnosed in 1964, visited the hospital thirty-four times, had twenty-eight cervical smears, five biopsies, four operations under general anaesthetic and ten colposcopic investigations. Fifteen years later, when she was discharged, she still had carcinoma *in situ*. Some years later, Ruth returned to the National Women's Hospital with invasive cancer, of which she later died. The trial led to a judicial inquiry conducted by Judge Silvia Cartwright (published in August 1988), which recommended a raft of changes, including the disbanding of the ten-year-old ethics committee at the hospital, the obtaining of written consent to participation in a trial on all occasions and a patient advocate being available to protect the interests of patients.

The trial itself was highly unorthodox and went largely unchallenged over twenty years. The inquiry found that the outcome for the majority of the women had in fact been satisfactory, though they had not received standard treatment, but that a minority suffered persistent disease, developed invasive cancer, and in some cases died, quite unnecessarily. The remarkable fact is that none of the women involved ever made a formal complaint!

That is a terrible story, but it is a one-off case. Unfortunately, its implications go much deeper. Charlotte Paul of Otago University was one of three medical advisers to Judge Cartwright and said: 'I believe that the ethical issues raised by the inquiry go beyond the specific difficulties in one institution to the underlying problem of accountability in medicine. Indeed, the study at the centre of the inquiry was well known to gynaecologists beyond New Zealand, yet only one attempted to intervene.' She was particularly concerned by the taking of vaginal swabs from new-born babies without parental consent, by the lack of monitoring of the trial in progress and by the lack of real accountability. She also, significantly, argued that such a situation might not have existed if the research subjects had been men:

Could men have been in exactly the same position? It seems to me
likely that women were more vulnerable at that time to being included
in a trial of treatment without their knowledge and consent and more
likely to endure such a trial without making a formal complaint. . . . I
suggest that women were vulnerable because they were used to
submitting to medical checks without being told their exact purpose. I
consider that they were also vulnerable because they were exposed to
examination of the genital area by male doctors; in this situation, the
assymetry of power between the doctor and the patient is
exaggerated. . . .[3]

But women are always the subjects of more research than men, not
only because they live longer and make greater use of health
services, but also because of the presence of a readily available
group for 'research' purposes in perfectly healthy pregnant women
attending hospitals for antenatal checks. Another view is burgeoning in the USA, however. There is a considerable movement there
complaining that women are excluded from research, particularly
in drugs trials. But the other issue about which US senators are
rightly concerned is the type of research conducted. All too
frequently the research that gets greatest funding is to do with
lifestyle, looking at heart disease and strokes, and at the greatest
killers. (Coronary heart disease is still the biggest killer in the UK.)
Those diseases affect more men than women, and therefore much
medical research has focused on men's life expectancy and men's
lifestyles, neglecting women's illness and women's lifestyles. That
may change with research into Alzheimer's disease, a condition
which affects a disproportionately large number of women; if there
were drugs to counteract its effects, a vast profit would be there to
be made by the pharmaceutical industry. This would mean vast
numbers of women being drawn into drugs trials for long periods,
although many of them would be unable to give their consent in a
meaningful way.

It is still true to say that the main focus of medical research,
where the big money lies, is in men's diseases. In the United States,
the National Institute of Health is insisting that all grant applica-
tions include women in their study protocols, or explain why they
are excluded, but as yet the policy is not working well, largely
because of fears of litigation in drugs trials in the wake of possible
effects on unborn children. The net result, however, is that we
often do not know what the side effects of certain new drugs are for

women, with their different hormonal make-up, or whether we have got the dose right.

The notable exception has been in childbirth, in early pediatric care, and in neonatal units, an area of massive growth in the UK and all over the developed world. There may be other doubts about the advisability of trying to save a baby with a poor chance of a normal life, a situation that yet again impinges more on the mother, who is likely to be the carer, than the father. But the research is being done, and vast strides have been made; what remains is for the techniques to be less exciting to the practitioners, and the social implications of what is technically possible to be taken more into account. This is an area where the input of women is essential, but at present all too infrequent.

A way forward may lie with the research ethics committees in District Health Authorities, or with the American model of institutional review boards which examine the ethical dimensions to issues of clinical practice as well as research. Sadly, preliminary findings of the membership of these committees show an over-whelmingly male membership and a high prevalence of medical domination. At the beginning of 1990 the Royal College of Physicians made it clear that membership of these committees should be drawn from both sexes, with a lay input, as did new Department of Health guidelines. But if women are to be confident that they are not being entered into trials without their knowledge and consent, and that the research itself is worthwhile, then research ethics committees are going to have to be tougher with researchers about how their patients are to be recruited and what they are to be told.

There are also going to have to be more women involved in the decision-making about the sharp end of medical practice, which is often experimental, such as with heart transplants for very tiny babies, or other forms of neonatal care. There may also be some value in fostering public debate about some of the more problematic areas, such as the use of life-support machines and the allocation of resources to different sectors of healthcare. Women, who are more often mentally ill than men (one in six of the female population spends time in a psychiatric unit at some stage in her life), tend to get poor psychiatric services, and the Cinderella services of the NHS have traditionally been those with the majority of women patients. These include geriatric services, with an overwhelmingly predominant female patient group because of the discrepancy of life expectancy between men and women; gynaecological services, with a still high use of hysterectomy compared with the rest of Europe, despite questions as to its wisdom in many cases; and chronic conditions of the elderly, such as rheumatism and arthritis, because of the demographic trends.

Although the consumer movement in health has been going for over twenty years now, it is a sad fact that this kind of discrimination is simply invisible to the bulk of the population, and that the extent to which it has got worse is largely unreported. The prospect that many women still face, therefore, is the gloomy one of being ill with diseases which are under-researched and/or with poor prognoses.

9

Women at Work

The National Health Service is the largest employer of women in this country, but despite this, outdated and traditional attitudes to women are evident. In 1990, we concluded a formal investigation against South Derbyshire Health Authority. The facts of the investigation were as follows:

A woman graduate with young children applied for a position as trainee midwife in Derby, and she was asked to wait five years for an interview. She was told that the SDHA had 'too much trouble with mums with young children', and that children needed their mother when they were ill.

Following publication of our findings in March 1990, the SDHA will have to change its practices (all other health authorities have been advised to review their recruitment practices too) and will be monitored by the EOC for the next five years.

Equal Opportunities Commission Annual Report for 1990

In 1969, ALONG with a largish group of scruffy-looking students, male and female, in Cambridge, I occupied the Seeley History Library. I think we were there for about twenty-four hours, before the whole thing became peaceful, the dons came to talk to us and the delicious picnics and sleeping bags were removed back to our colleges, whilst the domestic staff, tut-tutting under their breath, cleaned up the mess we had made in the library and its environs. In Cambridge terms, that marked the end of the swinging '60s. The university had barely been touched by the unrest felt at Essex, at

Sussex, in Paris in the student riots of 1968. There had been some mild anti-Vietnam war protests, but the majority of students who had been interested in that had gone to London, for the big Grosvenor Square demonstration. All was quiet now. Concessions were given. Students were to be members of faculty boards, and some of us received keys to our colleges' front doors. The student battle was won. We were free.

But we were nothing of the kind. I was at a women's college, Newnham. There we had the key to the front door. We could bring in whom we chose, and some were running communes on the floors of their college rooms. The principal at the time, Ruth Cohen, suddenly got worried about reds under the beds. She took away our keys and instituted night porters instead. We could be watched again, and, provided our private lives were not interfered with, some of us were much relieved that it was no longer possible for people no-one knew to be let into the college by students with keys. Meanwhile the students started campaigning again.

It was 1971. I was secretary of the Junior Common Room. Julia Cleverdon was JCR President. We had achieved a major transformation in the life of the college, in the installation of proper commercial washing machines for our own launderette. Now we were involved in the next great campaign, to get our college mixed, rather than single sex.

The first men's colleges went mixed in the autumn of 1972. Bright young women were to be allowed in as undergraduates. There was even talk of some of them coming in as graduate students, and, in later days, as dons. King's was thought to be the most progressive of the colleges and they felt they were well on the way. There was equality at last. The bastions of male power in the university were crumblilng. This was the time of the Equal Pay Act (1970), even though it was not implemented until 1975. The world was changing. It was opening up to us. There was no need for female institutions any longer. Newnham should go mixed – men should be living with us. It would make sexual relationships so much easier. It would be so natural.

To my shame, I thought all of those things at the time. The warnings from senior members of the college that they themselves had had to fight for their degrees from the university only twenty years earlier failed to impress. The world had changed. We were in the bright future now. The sternly repeated statements of Ruth

Cohen, that she had no objection to whom we slept with or how many, but she wanted to prevent us doing our menfolk's washing, she wanted us to be able to send them home to do their own dirty work, went unheeded. We did not understand. On reflection, I think we did not want to understand. A short walk around the drying rooms of the college would have made it clear to us that even without the men living with us, far too many of the women students were already doing their boyfriends' washing, mending and, indeed, cooking.

Domestication was high on the agenda of those liberated late '60s students. We had not seen the writing on the wall when older contemporaries went straight down from Newnham, married, had children and stopped all their academic work. Some of us had boyfriends who came up from London for the weekend, to a round of lunches and dinners cooked by us, and a chronic shortage of time for academic work or for more lighthearted fun, despite all that Cambridge had to offer. But we failed to understand. We did not want to know. We wanted to be in a mixed college. That was the heady environment we envisaged for ourselves. Concerns about women's achievements simply passed us by.

Yet many of us had been involved, before university, in the beginnings of the campaign to get equal pay for women. Many of us thought that legislation was needed to guarantee it, but that the world was beginning to realise its desperate injustices to women, and that all would now be adjusted by sensible people, men and women, so that there was no need for separation any more. Just at the same time, the influential books of feminist thought were beginning to emerge – *The Feminine Mystique* by Betty Friedan in 1968 (it had first appeared in the US in 1963, but was republished in Britain five years later), *The Female Eunuch* by Germaine Greer, herself a Newnham graduate, in 1971, *Sexual Politics* by Kate Millett in 1972. It was all happening just then. Some of us read their work. But it did not apply to us. It was too extreme, too crazy. The world was not like that really. Men were not deliberately trying to keep women down. As soon as the error of their ways was pointed out to them, they would all move up and make room for us. After all, we were bright and attractive, sexually liberated, full of common sense. We were not going to be discriminated against. And, when we were in positions of authority, we would be making sure that other women, with fewer advantages than we had had as bright young things of the '60s, got a fair deal too.

So went our reasoning. But we were in for a rude surprise. Of all my female contemporaries at Cambridge, unlike the men, very few have become household names, or even reached the distinction of being members of parliament or holding other positions of real or perceived power. There are musicians, teachers, high-flying administrators who have not quite made it to the top; a few journalists, some solicitors, one really well-known and very wealthy writer (Arianna Stassinopoulos Huffington); a recent peeress, Ann Mallalieu, QC; some exceptionally talented media people, one of whom, Patricia Hodgson, has recently become company secretary of the BBC; some brilliant academics, mainly in the arts, with Mary Beard perhaps the best known of them; and rather a lot of disappointed women. Once we got out into the real big bad world, there was discrimination. Newnham had given us protection. Had we used it properly, we could have all the fun we wanted, as well as the quiet and peace and untrammelled atmosphere in which to work and to see other, older women scoring successes as academics in that institution. But we did not see it like that. For us, it had to be equality. Nothing else would do.

So we begged and pleaded and argued with the senior members of the college till all hours. The big break came, as far as they were concerned, when the JCR officials were asked to go and take tea with our counterparts at Trinity, the biggest and most prestigious college in the university. They wanted to discuss with us the question of their college going mixed. The discussion went along extremely pleasantly. It was a time when right-thinking undergraduates wanted all colleges to be mixed, but after an agreeable and easy discussion, two members of the Senior Common Room at Trinity came to join in. Their questions to us were all about how they would manage in the college regarding things like lavatories and baths. The baths, they explained, were all together in the side of one courtyard. But women could not possibly be expected to walk across an open courtyard in order to have a bath. Nor, as far as they saw it, could men possibly be expected to share lavatories with women who might be menstruating. We did not ask what they thought the young men did at home, and whether, in their youth, there had been segregated bathrooms and lavatories in all private houses. It was not worth it. For what we were seeing was a blatant example of sex discrimination. 'We don't want women in this college, and so we will do everything in our power, including raising some ridiculous objections, to make it less and less likely that the college will accept women.'

In fact, Trinity did eventually accept women undergraduates, though it has to be said that all the old men's, now mixed, colleges have an extremely poor record of appointing women to senior posts. Pretty young girls are one thing, although even that did not come without a fair bit of resistance from senior members of the colleges, but senior women members, women with dining rights at High Table, women who will have all the privileges of that rather quaint way of life that is so quintessentially masculine – that would never do. And the resistance has been considerable, so that very few women have reached the height of High Table, where the dons dine splendidly in candlelight, with fine wines and considerable style, at an old men's college, on a permanent basis.

Meanwhile, the objections expressed at Trinity were enough to make us think again. If this was the nature of the prejudice, then maybe we needed to reconsider whether we should be so generous in opening our college out to men. We returned to Newnham to ponder and took a look around us. We were in a relatively poor college which had little in the way of grants and prizes and scholarships to offer its undergraduates. But it had dedicated teaching fellows, and women scholars of incredible distinction. Whilst not wishing to prevent male students from studying with our dons, we saw an argument for keeping Newnham single sex.

Although for those of us who had been at girls' schools this seemed very tame, it served a useful purpose. There were reasons for it. There would be real encouragement to women students and bright young academics. There would be a place where women could work without interruptions. There would be a place where it was considered normal for women to be academics, to study and to swot, where they would not be thought of as bluestockings. And it would give a chance for friendships, and an institution, made by women to grow. It would be in a masculine model, maybe, but done by women. This was all a long way from our feelings just a few weeks earlier, when we had been certain that the college should go mixed. A little discrimination against you is an excellent way of realising that being certain of your own identity is very important – one cannot always merge with the rest.

Those years at Newnham were extremely important to me, in working out my ideas about women's lives in the 1970s and beyond. It all seemed very easy. A great advantage of the college was its assumption that we could all of us achieve anything if we wanted to. That was very much thanks to the senior members of the college. Most of them would have been appalled to have been described as feminists, for that would imply, as they saw it, a political component in their thinking about what women were capable of, but in fact feminists is what they were. They were feminists of an earlier generation. Some of them – though few by our day – had been suffragettes. The names of buildings and libraries in the college evoked that time, with Fawcett figuring strongly, and Strachey. Those were the names of the great campaigners, but, as we saw it, the battle was won and we could get on with our lives.

It was, of course, a very secure environment in which to have our university education, and it was also a time when women were in short supply in Cambridge and one could have a lot of fun. But that hard attitude of some of our teachers was important. They were determined that we had to prove ourselves in the outside world, and, however little we took them seriously, it did rub off on some of us. We became aware that the world would not always be kind to us, even though intellectually we believed that things would improve for women once men realised, by reading the works of the new 'liberation' writers, how badly women had been treated.

For we were beginning to realise that women had been appallingly badly treated over the years. The history of the suffragette movement was familiar to us. There were copies of Ray Strachey's *One Arm Tied Behind Us* in both school and Newnham libraries. The First World War had brought women into jobs where they had never been, to driving the buses and running the factories, but immediately after the war they had all been sent home. What had happened in the years just before we were born, after the Second World War, was that women had been less willing to go back home, and the promise or bribe of the vote was no longer of any use. Women had discovered, many of them, that they liked to have a life outside the home, and they were never persuaded back into their domestic bliss as effectively as they were in the USA. Quite a large number of our mothers worked. Some worked part-time. Some did 'cultural' work – they were pianists or painters. But some ran businesses or were doctors or social workers, and a couple were lawyers. We were a thoroughly middle-class group, largely from the south east, and I do not think that we were atypical in having mothers who had considerable interests outside the home.

But because our mothers were middle class, we were not directly aware of the incredible wage differentials between men and women in other areas. Those of us who were involved politically had become aware from about 1964 that something was very wrong with women being paid so much less than men. The beginnings of pressure from some of the trades unions (the majority were opposed to doing anything about equal pay) and the obvious interest and later campaign spearheaded by Barbara Castle had become Labour Party discussion material in Hampstead by 1966. Something had to be done about the fact that women were earning about 70% of what men were being paid for the same work. More significantly, something had to be done about the fact that very few women reached any kind of seniority within factories, that men were always the bosses and women always subservient. It was, of course, just as much a part of the awakening of a feminist perspective as reading Millett, Greer and Friedan was. It was also, to my mind, then and now, something about which one could propose a series of practical solutions, or at least ameliorations. And so some of us became involved in a campaign to get equal pay for women. Just as we were about to go to university, in 1970, the Equal Pay Act became law, and we thought that the issue which of all issues had most concerned us, had been won.

We should have known better. This issue, more perhaps than all the others, has made me feel that the battle is not won, but that the concentration of radical feminists upon quite different questions, without serious reference to the real difficulties hampering real women in terms of coping with children, elderly or handicapped dependents and work, has been seriously misplaced. Most women are simply not enormously concerned with the maternity rights of lesbian would-be mothers. That may be a serious civil liberties issue, but what concerns most women is how they can cope financially, on their own or with a spouse, and how they can cope in terms of physical endurance when adequate provision for women's needs is not made. And this is where those of us who felt all would be well in the late '60s and early '70s found ourselves horribly wrong. Men did not suddenly decide that they had been monstrously unfair to women, nor did the trades unions, some of whom had been in on the beginning of the campaign, show any serious interest in fighting for women's rights. Indeed, it could be argued that the main reason some of the trades unions are now, finally, in the 1990s, becoming interested in the issue of women's rights at work is that they have declining memberships and want to recruit women to their midst.

Yet according to the Equal Opportunities Commission's report on *Women and Men in Britain 1990*, women are still significantly under-represented in the primary sector of employment, agriculture, energy and water, where, in the latter two at least, there is strong unionisation. They are over-represented in the service industries generally, but specifically in the hotel and catering trades, where unionisation has been very weak; in the retailing field, where the same applies; and in Health Service 'support' jobs, such as cleaning and other menial tasks, as well as nursing, physiotherapy and occupational therapy. The clear evidence of women's over-representation in the worse paid, poorly unionised areas of work suggests that the trades union movement is still not appealing to women, or using the right arguments to get female members. And this is despite such bright lights as Brenda Dean of SOGAT 82, the printers' union, Liz Symons of the First Division Association and a few other women union leaders and officials, who have broken through an essentially male organisational structure.

But the really alarming figures relate to earnings. Equal pay legislation has been in place since 1970, and in force since 1975, yet in the ten years between 1978 and 1988, the latest up-to-date figures available, the relative earnings of female manual workers as against male have actually deteriorated, and there is a sombre warning note in the EOC's publication to say that because of changes in the methods of collecting and collating the data, the actual decline for female workers was probably greater than appeared from the figures. The EOC argues that if the old method of calculation were used, female manual workers would earn only 69.7% rather than 70.8% of the pay of their male equivalents.

At the same time, non-manual female workers received a mere 62.2% of their male co-workers' earnings, a far wider gender differential than in the manual sector, which had been true over the previous decade. Childcare provision was lamentably low, with only 24% of all three- and four-year-olds being in nursery education in England, and a further 21% in infant classes in primary schools. Though proportions were slightly greater in Wales, they were markedly lower in Scotland, leading to real difficulties for women in organising childcare for children of those very ages which could most benefit from group care of a learning nature.

All these factors suggest that despite the rhetoric, there is little impetus to make it easier for women to return to the workforce other than as part-timers, and not necessarily then. Even women who want to play a more traditional domestic role, but do a modicum of public service as well, in a voluntary capacity, have difficulties, because there is no provision for mothers to have their small children taken care of other than by childminders and friends. Yet spending, say, a day a week on some social, child-free activity could add to the personal development of these women, and bring benefit to the community as a whole.

What price active citizenship for women now? The possibilities are very few, but even if they were greater in terms of family organisation and sorting out the working day, there is marked evidence that very few women are given government appointments, some 19% of the total, and even those vary enormously according to department. Scottish women, who fare much worse in childcare provision, do however get more appointments: some 34.1% of government appointments in Scotland are given to women.

The issues to do with equal pay and proper protection from discrimination are fairly clear now. But they need to be effected by a body with greater teeth than the Equal Opportunities Commission has, and with far more money. The EOC has backed cases which have made legal history, and it has succeeded in getting women's economic issues on the public agenda to some extent. But whilst the protection of part-time workers, of temporary workers and of home-workers is still a political mirage, with no force in favour other than those who hold no power, and a lamentable lack of trades union campaigning for them, there will be little change, despite European directives on those subjects and despite the fact that, as the 1990s progress, we will become more and more European.

Indeed, the UK, along with other countries such as Germany, has been keen to block several of the European Community directives, especially those on part-time workers, which would give part-time workers the same rights and benefits, *pro rata*, as full-time workers already have. In his submission to the House of Lords Select Committee on European legislation, Norman Tebbit argued 'for sound economic and commercial reasons' against the draft directive on part-time workers, and said that the disadvantages that part-time workers suffer, if any, were 'a fact that part-time workers are ready to accept'. Within that same House of Lords committee, which was, in fact, broadly in favour of the directive, it was also said that such measures were 'an unnecessary striving for egalitarianism'. In the Department of Employment's own submission to Europe, the argument went along the same lines, reiterating the government's belief in determining remuneration through voluntary agreements and not by the use of legislation: 'Interference in voluntary agreements is not warranted in the case of part-timers, where any "discrimination" is likely to be the result of economic and commercial considerations, rather than irrational prejudice. Thus, while there are clearly disadvantages which some part-time workers suffer in relation to full-time workers, it is possible to see this as the price which part-timers, in particular women, are prepared to pay.'

The tone with which the directives on part-time work, parental leave and temporary work were dismissed suggests a disregard for European initiatives, and a feeling that the old British way of proceeding will do us very nicely. This is in a country where our sixteen-to-nineteen-year-olds are less well educated, and in smaller numbers and proportions, than in all but two other European countries, and where we are becoming less and less competitive. Yet we do not follow Europe on forward-looking, socially responsible employment legislation and practice, because we cannot see the long-term advantage.

This applies equally to the fight over implementing serious remedies for discrimination in equal pay cases, where the UK resisted the 'equal value' part of the equal pay provisions. For in 1975, the same year as the Equal Pay Act became law, the European Community passed a directive on equal pay which included the following words: 'The principle of equal pay for men and women outlined in Article 119 of the Treaty, hereinafter called "principle of equal pay", means, for the same work, or for work to which equal value is attributed, the elimination of all discrimination on grounds of sex with regard to all aspects and conditions of remuneration.'

It was those crucial words 'equal value' which made the difference. For the directive meant that women in segregated jobs, of which there are many in the UK, could claim that the work they were doing was of equal value to their employers as that done by men doing different, and better paid, jobs. In July 1982, the European Court in the Hague found against the British government in not complying fully with the 1975 directive, and started infringement proceedings against them. The government responded by drafting and then introducing regulations under the European Community Act of 1972, which were approved by the House of Commons in 1983.

But those regulations, and the draft procedures required for implementing them, were, to put it mildly, a little strange. They did theoretically enable women to bring equal value claims before an industrial tribunal, but they made it extraordinarily difficult to do so, and it seems as if the procedures were specifically designed to prevent women having the value of their work compared with men's. For the tribunal had to be satisfied at the outset that it was reasonable to refer the matter to an expert at all, and if the applicant could not satisfy the tribunal of that reasonableness, she could take the matter no further. But if she managed to get over this initial hurdle, the original provisions ensured that she could not question the expert or call evidence, and that the tribunal would effectively have to rubber-stamp the expert's conclusion – a state of affairs which seems a far cry from the judicial process and sense of fair play one expects in a court of law.

But the real horror, which made many of us who felt that few battles were left to fight in this area sit up and take notice, was the introduction of a new defence for the employers, which is the defence of 'other determining factors', a defence they can advance before the evaluation of the woman's work is even begun! The then Employment Minister, Alan Clark, suggested that these 'other determining factors' could include 'market forces'. So if an employer could argue that he was paying a woman less because of another determining factor – the market forces in operation at that time and place – then the evaluation could cease. And in a world where it is market forces that ensure that women are paid under 75% of what men earn anyway, this seems a bit unfair on the women!

But to add to that, the regulations themselves are virtually unintelligible, to the extent that leading counsel Anthony Lester

QC described them as 'a highly complicated version of the game of snakes and ladders, with several fierce new snakes and a few shaky ladders – a game for expert lawyers, but not for ordinary men and women.' And these awful regulations, bravely and roundly criticised by many politicians, came into force in 1984, preventing employees from claiming back pay for two years, and thus giving the employers an eighteen-month pay holiday after the UK was found in breach of European law in July 1982.

But the worst thing of all was the way the regulations were introduced into Parliament. Alan Clark presented them to the House of Commons in July 1983, but in such an extraordinary way, and at such breakneck speed as if he found them ridiculous and pointless, that this response came from the distinguished journalist Hugo Young, writing in those days for the *Sunday Times*:

> Whether the minister was drunk at the time was a matter of some debate. It was late on Wednesday night, and others in the House were well away, as they sometimes are. One new MP was so disgusted that she made the allegation in open chamber, at which the minister was instantly protected by his roaring friends. The certain truth is more ominous: that he was, in fact, stone cold sober. [The new MP was Clare Short.]

It was this experience, and the fact that these regulations could be introduced in such a way as to cause those who might want to use the law to gain equality of treatment to be massively discouraged from doing so, that led many women to feel once again that anger and heat needed to be applied to the political process in this area. The issue was by no means won, and the government obviously felt that it had to do the minimum required by Europe, but the minimum was precisely what it would do, and it would not do it seriously. But despite the appalling nature of the legislation, and despite the fact that few changes have taken place in it with all the complaints made by the House of Lords and by Justice (the British section of the International Commission of Jurists) and other bodies, it has now been used significantly and importantly, and there have been a few notable victories for women, as a result of the 'equal value' regulations.

The best known case is probably Julie Hayward's against Cammell Laird. Ms Hayward was a qualified cook at Cammell Laird in Birkenhead. She claimed her work was of equal value with that of a printer, joiner and thermal insulation engineer. She did so on the basis that she had been paid, as they had, as an apprentice at the standard rate for three years, but on qualification she had become a catering assistant, whilst the male craft apprentices, who had finished their apprenticeship at the same time, earned £27 per week more. She was meanwhile paid at the national minimum level for unskilled workers, after a three-year apprenticeship. The expert assessor who dealt with the case on an equal value claim agreed with Ms Hayward and decided against Cammell Laird. The company then fought against his decision and argued that Ms Hayward was being paid according to a national agreement which classified ships' cooks as unskilled whilst the comparators' jobs were skilled. The good news was that the Industrial Tribunal agreed with Ms Hayward and the expert, and she won her case, backed by her union, the General and Municipal Workers' Union.

It was a cause for sadness that just a few months later, the GMWU was taken on by some of its own women secretaries, who alleged they were paid less than a male 'executive assistant' who worked in the same office as they did. The union argued that the man had been in the union for thirty years and had worked in the executive office for years and years, whilst the women were 'merely secretarial'. The same prejudices that afflicted Cammell Laird seem to be remarkably near the surface. In fact the women lost their case, so not all is wonderful in the new age of legislation.

All one can say is that it does make some improvements. There was, for instance, a victory by Lloyds Bank staff at the industrial tribunal in 1989, when seven female typists, secretaries and bank clerks claimed their work was equal in value to that of a male messenger who was paid more. The bank had used the argument that separate collective pay bargaining existed for the different groups, and that that was legal and an explanation for the difference, but the Industrial Tribunal found that it was the result of direct sex discrimination as well. A much more worrying setback occurred in January 1991, when the Employment Appeal Tribunal ruled that separate collective bargaining arrangements which result in unequal pay between men and women were not open to challenge under the equal pay legislation, unless it could be shown that the arrangements are directly discriminatory. That decision is being challenged by the Equal Opportunities Commission along with the union MSF, but if it stands, many, many women will be unable to challenge unequal pay with their male colleagues.

This particular case arose out of the claim brought by speech therapists in 1985 who argued that their work was equal in value to that of clinical psychologists, who were paid a great deal more. The Industrial Tribunal originally dismissed their claim on the grounds that it was the Secretary of State for Health who decided their remuneration, and not their direct employers, the Health Author- ities; judicial review quashed that opinion. However, a later tribunal ruled that there were no grounds for believing that sex discrimina- tion was the reason that separate collective bargaining arrange- ments had resulted in different pay scales for clinical psychologists, mostly male, and speech therapists, mostly women.

But there are more cheerful results, which make the legal process worthwhile as a symbol for other women, and as a warning to employers. There was, for instance, the victory of Mrs Stella James over Barclays Bank. She had joined the bank in 1969, when the staff retirement age was sixty for women and sixty-five for men. In 1973, the bank changed the retirement age to sixty for all staff, but did not backdate the decision, so those who had been employed earlier had to stick to the old rules. In 1986, a European Court decision forced the British government to amend the Sex Discrim- ination Act to ensure all employers provided equal retirement ages. Barclays changed their policy to allow women and men above a certain grade to continue to work to sixty-five.

But Mrs James, and eleven other women, were too junior. Mrs James reached her sixtieth birthday and asked to stay on. She was refused. So she went to the Industrial Tribunal, and, after a great deal of coming and going, was awarded £10,000 and the offer of her job back in November 1990.

Other cases give similar cause for joy, such as Catrina Ander- son's victory over Alexander Pollock Ltd, precision engineers, when she was refused a job as a machine engraver because there were no ladies' toilets on the site. Or the case against Rodney Day Associates of Sudbury in Suffolk, who advertised for a 'rugby-playing marketing executive m/f'. They justified this on the grounds that there were twelve women's rugby clubs in England and Wales, but lost their case, as it was regarded as discriminatory. And there is the current question of a senior policewoman who believes her promotion has been stopped because of her gender.

All these are cases worth fighting, and they gradually work their way through the incredibly expensive and complicated system, largely backed by the unions and the Equal Opportunities Commission, much revived by its present chairman, Joanna Foster, and its wonderful chief executive, Valerie Amos. But it is slow and distressing work, however essential, and many of the women who have won their cases report a sense of Pyrrhic victory, because the personal consequences for them have not been at all good.

Nevertheless, it is these cases, and the signs of sex discrimination that they so clearly reveal, that make it essential for women's groups to realise that the battle is not yet won. Though governments appear to comply, they are often acting with contrary intentions, as the use of the 'market forces' argument makes clear. The paradoxical success of the equality legislation lies not in the inroads it has made into unfairness and into bringing about more equal pay, for the evidence is that it has been largely unsuccessful in that regard. Its achievement is that it has educated women to feel that there are legal processes they can use, however difficult. Even if those cases bring little change in themselves, they clear the ground a bit for the next generation. Without those victories, without those cases, no progress would be made at all. This has to figure large on the agenda of women's organisations, of trades unions who want to attract women, and, in fact, of all people, of either gender, who want to see fair play in the workplace, and an end to unfair discrimination in pay and conditions, 'just because she's female'.

10
Women and Men: the Basic Differences

Women are irrational, that's all there is to that! Their heads are full of cotton, hay and rags. They're nothing but exasperating, irritating, vacillating, calculating, agitating, maddening and infuriating hags!

Why can't a woman be more like a man? Men are so honest, so thoroughly square, eternally noble, historically fair, who, when you win, will always give your back a pat. Why can't a woman be like that?

Why does ev'ry one do what the others do? Can't a woman learn to use her head? Why do they do everything their mothers do? Why don't they grow up like their fathers instead?

Why can't a woman take after a man? Men are so pleasant, so easy to please. Whenever you're with them, you're always at ease.

Would you be slighted if I didn't speak for hours?
Pickering: Of course not.
Would you be livid if I had a drink or two?
Pickering: Nonsense.
Would you be wounded if I never sent you flowers?
Pickering: Never!

Why can't a woman be like you? One man in a million may shout a bit. Now and then there's one with slight defects. One perhaps whose truthfulness you doubt a bit, but by and large we are a marvellous sex.

Why can't a woman behave like a man? Men are so friendly, good-natured and kind. A better companion you never will find. . . . If I were hours late for dinner, would you bellow?
Pickering: Of course not.

If I forgot your silly birthday, would you fuss?
Pickering: Nonsense.
Would you complain if I took out another fellow?
Pickering: Never!
Why can't a woman be like us?

Henry Higgins from *My Fair Lady*, lyrics by Alan Jay Lerner

OFTEN QUOTED BY men in exasperation and women in humour, this tongue-in-cheek acceptance of the essential differences of the genders is something that still has not been wholly accepted either by the women's movement or by the general public. It is not easy to say that one should use the 'equal but different' argument, as has happened all too often. There is a difference, but the differences, as the Dean of Westminster, the Very Reverend Michael Mayne, pointed out in a sermon on the sixtieth anniversary of the founding of the Townswomen's Guilds in 1989, exist within each of us. He quoted Virginia Woolf on male and female elements in certain writers, with her view that there was 'a marvellous androgynous balance in Shakespeare, a little too much of the feminine in Proust, a little too much of the male in Milton', while, she adds dismissively, 'neither Kipling nor Galsworthy has a spark of the feminine in him.'

Many women would agree about Kipling, still hugely enjoyed by boys and men, and hard to begin for many women. But it is really important to get to grips with the extent to which there is a bit of both male and female elements within us.

In Anne Moir and David Jessel's extraordinary and irritating book *Brainsex – the Real Difference between Men and Women*, the authors argue for the biological difference, for brains of different capacities and sizes. The spatial and visual senses controlled by the right side of the brain function better for boys than the verbal skills controlled by the left side, they claim. Women have less clearly defined areas of the brains for different skills, but are noticeably better at 'reading' a personality, whilst men have superior spatial skills and are, for instance, infinitely superior at reading maps. And so on and so on.

There is some evidence along these lines, undoubtedly. The argument that all differences between the genders are caused by social pressures is certainly disproved when one watches a teenage girl become increasingly irritable and tearful in the days before menstruation, and then show elation as the period begins, and again at ovulation. That is biological, not social. Similarly, the naked aggression of the young – and often not so young – male is rarely found in the young female. The marked difference between the genders in response to the Gulf War in its early days in January 1991 is not coincidental. An ICM poll conducted for the *Guardian* when the bombs began to drop found an unusually large differential between the sexes on a political matter. A substantial majority of men – 68% – supported the use of force to evict Iraq from Kuwait, whilst only 41% of women backed a resort to arms. Men do find it easier to settle things by physical fight, by physical means. Women tend to want other options, though many of them also thought there was no serious alternative to war in the Gulf. The real difference lay in the strongly 'gung-ho' attitudes of male broadcasters and male pundits in the early days, whilst women were off the screen and off the air, and in the apparent total fascination of the male sex with the toys of war: as diagram after diagram appeared on the screen or in the newspapers, the boys marvelled at the accuracy of the aim of the bombs, in rather the same way as they wonder at the technical capacity of the computers and hi-fi equipment on a trip up Tottenham Court Road in London, their noses pressed against the glass windows of every electronics shop.

This picture emerged in conversations with women during the Gulf War and applied to the gentlest and mildest of men, to husbands, lovers, sons, male friends. The fact that one cannot generalise, because there are always exceptions and always those who feel both emotional and rational at the same time, or whatever, does not negate the evidence that men and women respond differently to things, that they have different thought-patterns and that women are cyclical, emotionally, until after the menopause, in a way that men are not.

But all those truths do not justify an extraordinary statement in *Brainsex*:

In spite of greater emancipation in terms of education, opportunity and social attitudes, women are not noticeably 'doing better' than they were thirty years ago. Mrs Thatcher is still the exception which proves the rule. There were more women in the British Cabinet in the 1930s than there are at present. There has been no significant increase in the number of female MPs over the past three decades. Some women, seeing how far their sex has fallen short of the supposed ideal of power-sharing, feel that they have failed. But they have only failed to be like men.

This is plainly nonsense. First of all, if women's 'failure to be like men' is due to innate differences of the brain, how does one explain the greater prevalence of women in the Cabinet in the 1930s in comparison with the 1990s? Secondly, women are becoming senior, albeit slowly, in a variety of fields in a way they did not hitherto – such as medicine and the law. What does not correlate properly is not the absence of women, for they are there, but the slowness of their promotion in comparison with men, when most male doctors or lawyers will admit that they are of as good quality. Is that brain sex difference? Or is it male prejudice? Or the 'innate male aggression' Moir and Jessel write about, which means that they fight fiercely to keep women off their patch?

Of course the sexes are different, and life would be much the poorer if they were not. Of course there are generalisations one can make about capacities of boys and girls educationally, such as boys on the whole doing better at maths and sciences and girls at English. But even those generalisations are somewhat thrown by the statistics which show girls doing very well in maths in schools where they are taught separately from the boys. In schools where this is the case, girls' results are close to parity with the boys.[1] And sixteen-year-old school-leaving girls are more likely than the boys to have good results in all subjects, though boys tend to catch up later.

The problem is not whether we are different, as we clearly are, and have different interests and skills. The problem lies in accepting those differences, in dealing with them, in counteracting them when that seems socially useful, and in trying not to confuse biological and hormonal differences with social ones.

It is, for instance, a fact that the menstrual cycle affects some women so that their emotional temperature varies throughout the month. Mild and calm one week, they can be stormy and apparently irrational the next. That is biological and if it becomes too disturbing, it can be regulated by the judicious use of hormonal treatment. It is also biological that some men are intensely aggressive and find it hard to control their aggression. That can be dealt with, though on the whole one would prefer not to, by the use of tranquillisers; it is surely more helpful to encourage social conditioning, so that some forms of behaviour are seen as unacceptable.

The main thesis of this book is that there are whole areas of life that the women's movement has failed to address, noticeably the reality of women's lives, and particularly the requirement on them to do 'the caring', both for children and for the elderly or other dependent adults. Facing the reality of biological differences and trying to come to terms with them, and learn to cope with them in society, is another facet of our lives that the women's movement has not dealt with. Feminism, in its heady '60s and '70s days, was so angry that it failed to establish realities. Everything was men's fault. Nothing was women's fault.

The truth is somewhat different. Women have colluded with men in some pretty awful things, including, horrifyingly, the sexual abuse of their own children. That seems to go entirely against what seems 'biologically' right, the protection by the mother of her young, in this case from the male aggressor. But the mother might also be the victim of the male aggressor, and the structures of families where child abuse and sexual abuse is the norm make for depressing reading, with generations of victims turning into abusers in their own right, and women and children living in fear of the male aggressor/husband/lover/father/stepfather.

But is this male aggression 'natural'? Do all men want to be violent to women, to rape them? In a 1985 survey of men on American university campuses, where rape prevention organisations have been set up by women and are active in seeking evidence and preventive action, 15% of men interviewed said that they might commit rape if they thought there was no chance of being caught. Over half did not regard sexual coercion as rape! It might be hard to tell the difference, though perhaps they thought that coercion of a girl they knew was different from raping a total stranger. The same survey showed that one in seven female students had been the victim of rape and one in four male students had engaged in some form of sexual coercion. Horrifying figures, yet they may be due in part to the astonishing overuse of the terms of sexual abuse and rape, when what happens is nothing of the sort. For instance, late 1990 and early 1991 have seen an apparent orgy of 'date raping' in

American universities. According to a widely circulated figure reported in *The Times*[2] 'one in every four women students is raped at least once at college, and one in three American women is sexually assaulted in her lifetime.'

This has to be questioned. At the University of Santa Barbara, a group of students have filed sexual harassment charges against a professor who made an off-the-cuff joke about *Penthouse* pets in a lecture. In Congress, a senate committee is working on making rape definable as a 'gender-based hate crime', which would make it punishable under federal civil rights statutes as well as state criminal codes. But what is rape? Sexual abuse and rape of children? Or jokes in mildly bad taste? Is kissing a woman at a party, even if she did not particularly want to be kissed, rape? Or does there have to be penetration, or an attempt at it, or at least some real sexual encounter?

Camille Paglia, professor at the University of Philadelphia, has lost patience with the feminist radicals who are trivialising what rape is: 'Feminists have told young women that before they have sex with a man they must give consent as explicit as a legal contract's. . . . In this way, young women have been convinced that they have been the victims of rape.' She is quite right. The old rules apply. A girl should avoid putting herself in a position where she might be 'taken advantage of', and that includes not getting blind drunk at a party. Young men will, biologically, be the aggressors, but that does not mean that they will rape young women in normal social intercourse. Rape is terrible and serious, and is often committed by people who know their victim, but it is not part of normal social life, and to allege that boys 'date rape' on a regular basis is crazy, as crazy in its way as to allege that a woman who says no means yes, because the clothes she is wearing suggested that she 'asked for it'.

Indeed, it was as recently as March 1988 that Mr Justice Rougier made an apparently landmark statement; in sentencing a twenty-seven-year-old would-be rapist called Fallen, who had argued that the young woman who accused him was wearing a short skirt which had encouraged him to try to rape her, break her jaw and threaten to kill her unless she stopped screaming, Mr Rougier said that women 'are entitled to dress attractively, even provocatively if you like, be friendly with casual acquaintances and still say no at the end of the evening without being brutally assaulted.' He sentenced

Fallen to eighteen months and said: 'This sort of brutal violence, particularly to women, has got to be dealt with severely. You broke her jaw just because she wasn't prepared to go to bed with you.' But to many women, although the judge had made it clear that a woman does not 'ask for it', the sentence, compared with sentences for robbery where large amounts of property are involved, seemed ludicrously short.

That was genuine rape, and there are countless other examples where judges alleged that the woman was, at least in part, asking for it. Those are serious cases, unfairly dealt with all too often. And legal opinion is only just beginning to change, so that rapists are getting serious sentences, and women are not, as a general rule, assumed to be to blame. That is why this use of the term rape for aggressive sexual behaviour of any kind devalues its seriousness. It can also suggest that women have no responsibility to look after themselves, and to recognise male aggression. Even veteran feminist campaigner Susan Brownmiller acknowledges that women should look after themselves to some extent, but her reason is that no-one else will do it for them: she thinks that police and law enforcement agencies generally are not interested in the plight of women, a view with which many women sympathise, though they are heartened by the way that policewomen in recent years have helped and supported and encouraged rape victims to speak out.

But the evidence that genuine and violent rape is infrequently reported because of shame and fear makes the casual use of the term particularly disgraceful, when women who are serious victims of rape need to be encouraged to come forward and tell their stories. The defining line is not clear, however, and that is why the issue needs very sensitive handling. If a young man, an ex-lover for instance, tries to force a woman to have sex with him, that is undeniably rape. If, on the other hand, a young woman goes out on a date with a man and he tries hard to get her into bed, without actually forcing her, that is very unpleasant and very reprehensible, but may not actually be rape. But when one hears the words of the character from the American film *Without her Consent* (quoted in *Cosmopolitan* in March 1991, from a film not released in the UK, but presumably to come) who is convicted of date-raping three young women, one wonders what to think and do:

'They were hot for it. These were dates. They knew the score – they come to your house, that means something. Every girl knows that. Have a couple of laughs, a little music. Sometimes they like it a little rough, so you get a little rough. It's a game. They've got it under control. They even have their own language. No means yes; yes means no. It's just the way it is with women. Every guy knows that.'

Is this rape? Genuine rape? Obviously sometimes so, and sometimes not, though the point about language is very starkly made, and the incidents reported to rape crisis centres suggest that the line between rape and aggressive sexual coercion with an ultimate, unwilling consent, is very fine. But women need to be encouraged to talk about these issues without all instances being described as rape. It is essential that the incidents are discussed openly, and the labels of rape, or sexual coercion, or aggression, are left until later, unless it is absolutely clear which one is talking about. For in that area, the decisions to tell about genuine sexual harassment, genuine sexual abuse as a child from close family friends or relations, are very difficult to make. Whilst women who simply went to bed with a man slightly unwillingly, and then regretted it, describe that as rape, those who have had the violence and the hatred, the use of broken bottles or light-bulbs up the vagina or in the anus, the point of a knife pressed against the stomach, will remain silent. It is another world.

That is one area where men and women are different. There is very little of that kind of crime of hatred by women against men. Female crime is rarely violent, unless it is against a lover, particularly a lover who has abandoned or two-timed the woman concerned. Women are more likely to be sentenced to prison than men for the same crime, which perhaps has to do with the difficulty male judges have in believing that a women is a criminal at all in areas other than shoplifting. But here is male hatred of women, which may or may not be part of general male aggression. There is a desire to hurt, to wound women, and it manifests itself in rape and granny-bashing, but also in the wish to humiliate.

There is a good example in the British House of Commons, where women are few and far between except as secretaries. As Silvia Rodgers, anthropologist and wife of ex-MP Bill Rodgers, has said, it feels like 'a men's house':

References by MPs to the precincts of the House as 'a male preserve' were made with a regularity that demands attention. The House is, after all, the central political institution of this complex society, the pivot of the nation's legislation, and the reflector and generator of social changes.[3]

On another occasion, she wrote:

The only place used by all women members across party and *only* by women is the toilet which lies immediately outside the Chamber, off the corridor behind the Speaker's chair. . . . Toilets for men were built into the original design and simply marked 'Members only'. This has never been changed. New women members are told they can go *anywhere*, and occasionally make mistakes. Does this demonstrate the implicit assumption that in the symbolic ordering of the British political system the members of the House are men? Mrs Shirley Williams, MP from 1964–79, writes: '. . . it tells one quite a lot about the House of Commons.'[4]

It certainly does, but it shows a male aggression, manifested as a desire to embarrass, and not to allow for differences. Women need good access to toilets if they are menstruating, for instance, yet they have precious few in the House. The lack of provision for basic sanitary needs is a sign of the unspoken wish that they should not be there, and a feeling that embarrassing them, by telling them they can go anywhere, is, in prep school language, 'a good wheeze'.

These examples of aggression, of distaste, of desire to humiliate, are elements in male behaviour with which women have to come to terms. The feminist anger of the 1960s and 1970s did not pay dividends in terms of change of policy, but it did make people notice the issue, and the women concerned. The next stage is to behave more subtly, acknowledging differences, asking for those biological differences to be taken into account, being polite but firm, monitoring the delivery of equal opportunity, and denying the assertion of Moir and Jessel that it is due to biological brain differences that women have not achieved great advances in the last thirty years. After all, other countries have other records, and other countries make better provision for children, and if we are going to talk biology, then male aggression is up for grabs.

But even if it is up for grabs, do we want to accept, as Joan Smith asks so movingly in her excellent *Misogynies*, that 'flawed though it is, unfortunate as are some of its consequences, the present organisation of society has a "natural" biological basis?. . . Therefore the question I would put to the proponents of the anatomy-is-destiny theory is this: are you happy with this state of affairs? Can you shrug off the fact that women are routinely denigrated, despised, segregated, raped, mutilated and murdered? Are you saying, in fact, that it is *natural* for men to hate and fear women?'

Joan Smith took as the starting point for *Misogynies* the Yorkshire Ripper case, which disturbed her in the way it revealed attitudes to women she, and many of us, had always known were there. It was the police feeling that no decent woman had any business to be out at night that bothered her, that it was somehow natural to hate prostitutes, that Sutcliffe had particular types of women as his victims, women who were alcoholic and promiscuous, which led to the police including a woman who was not his victim on his 'list' and excluding others who were, because they were a 'better type'. The question that Smith asks is whether Sutcliffe was a one-off, a *sui generis*, 'someone who stands outside our culture and has no relation to it? Is he mad, with no responsibility for his actions?' Or was he, in some terrifying way, sane, able only to live with himself when he had destroyed 'those parts of the female body which signal gender. It was not enough for him to know from her general appearance that his victim was a woman; he had to see the proof with his own eyes in the shape of her breasts, her waist, her hips, her pubic hair. A single blow was not enough; he had to strike repeatedly to gain relief.' But Smith suggests that, mad though he was, he was not so very different from many others: 'The world is full of men who beat their wives, destroy their self-respect, treat them like dirt. They do it because they hate and despise women, because they are disgusted by them, because they need to prove to themselves and to their friends that they are real men. Occasionally, for one in a million, it isn't enough. Peter Sutcliffe was one of those. But when the trees are so rotten, who can with certainty pick out the really rotten timber?'

Smith ends with a 'Postscript: Boys will be boys?' In it she argues that the aim of her book is to suggest that the anatomy-is-destiny theory is unconvincing, and that masculine and feminine behaviour patterns, 'far from being natural, are the means of enforcing an *unnatural* separation between men and women in order to maintain an unstable and unjust power structure. The result is a state of covert warfare between the sexes in which, while not all men are rapists, every women is a potential victim.' I do not go that far, though I too challenge the anatomy-is-destiny theory. But there are what Smith describes as optimistic signs of change in the fact that men, many men, recognise that there are problems and are trying to change the way they, and their sons and daughters, think.

Nor is Smith alone. Rosalind Miles wrote her concerns about the way men are reared, about how the world is phallocentric and how violence is a natural part of the way women and men bring up boys, in *The Rites of Man*, her examination of love, sex and death in the making of the male. For her, the nature of being a man, of behaving like a man, being virile and tough, has its consequences in inbred violence, largely against women, from which there is no escape.

But where does all that leave us, with women and men so very different, with social expectations, familial expectations and even some biological expectations so very different? It leaves us with hope, yet the certainty that much of the campaigning has been wrong so far. It leaves us feeling that the Equal Opportunities Commission, with its excellent research record but its relatively poor recent record in terms of formal law enforcement and insistence on carrying out formal investigations, should be strengthened by government and given the money, the position and the clout to carry out its work and continue to point out inequalities and correct them where possible. It leaves us feeling that commitment to gender equality is at best skin deep in many males, but that it is also deeply felt by many others, and that general hatred, or despising, of men is as unhelpful as it is unjust. And it leaves us feeling that there are some magnificent women, and men, around who see that the advances will, paradoxically, be made for women by men and women together, that the heat of the Women's Liberation movement has paradoxically done a great deal of harm, and that the differences in female and male biology could, paradoxically, be used to show that allowances may have to be made for both genders, but compensations and help and awareness of nurture and nature are a prerequisite for a just settlement.

11

Women and Religion

You might as well ordain a pot of anchovy paste as a woman. The action is physically possible in both cases. In neither did he believe it would be efficacious.

Church of England curate, quoted in the *Independent*, 23 February 1987

AT THE BEGINNING of the 1990s, slowly, painfully, women are inching forwards in their struggle for ordination to the priesthood in the Church of England. To the surprise of many dispassionate observers, the Church of Ireland, not historically particularly known as a bastion of progressive thinking on matters to do with women's advancement, ordained women first, and both in the Republic of Ireland and in Northern Ireland, there is now a gradual move of women into the priesthood, and into serving churches hitherto neglected.

Ireland has been interesting in itself. The Republic, in an extraordinary series of political moves and accidents, elected a woman president for the first time, the impressive Mary Robinson, human rights lawyer and defender of women's rights in a country which has often given women a rough time, whilst respecting the role of mother and virgin, in true Roman Catholic fashion. Yet the Church of Ireland claims some 5% of the Irish population, and now has women priests, whilst the Catholic Church, a formidable political force in Ireland, wheeled out its members to vote against divorce in a referendum in 1986, and to make abortion, already illegal, unconstitutional as well.

The Catholic Church, with its strong traditions of women in powerful positions within the convents, with its Poor Clares and Sisters of Mercy, its Sisters of Sion and its Sisters of St Joseph, its nursing and its teaching orders, has never denied women a role. The difficulty has been in women having all the roles, of marriage, family and motherhood, as well as the power and influence of the women in the Church. For women can be nuns, and thereby receive the highest quality training in nursing and teaching and often in medicine and in academic fields, if they forswear the interests of their flesh and become brides of the church. Entry to a convent was a noble path for a Catholic girl in most of Europe throughout the Middle Ages, and although most convent orders are now short of postulants, that way of life, that dedication and professionalism in the chosen vocation, is still viewed with immense respect within the Catholic Church, and should not be underrated.

The same cannot be said for the Protestant Churches. Although in countries other than Britain the Anglican Church has ordained women, including now a bishop in the USA and priests in China and other countries of the Anglican communion for decades, the Church of England in England (different from the disestablished Church of Wales and the Church of Scotland) has held out. Time and again the view has been expressed that the ordination of women would cause great divisions within the Church, that the time is not yet right, that the communion with the Roman Catholic Church would be made much more difficult (not an area of apparent concern in the United States), and that somehow women should know their place.

The opposition has been expressed in a variety of ways, some measured, if irrational, such as the assertion that Jesus's disciples were all male, and therefore it stands to reason that priests should only be male as well, or the view that St Paul's attitude to the women of his time should still apply, of women learning quietly, sitting quietly, being second-class citizens. But there are also the less attractive facets of opposition. In 1987, Peregrine Worsthorne, then editor of the *Sunday Telegraph*, argued in a piece of virulent opposition to women's ordination that it would turn attendance at church from a 'cosy familiar experience' into 'a stressful challenge, a journey into unknown territory'. He suggested that most English people 'would no more welcome a woman at the altar than they would a foreigner on the throne,' and ended with the passionate cry: 'But spare us, O Lord, the female of the species.' John Selwyn Gummer said that he would leave the Church if it ordained women priests, and the circle around the then Bishop of London, Graham Leonard, in fact began to make preparations for secession, even though Dr Leonard himself was probably not prepared to leave.

Dr Leonard had already said he would be tempted to take a preaching woman in his arms, and used arguments about the biological difference between men and women as an explanation of his opposition to women's ordination. 'Biologically man takes the initiative. Woman receives and is feminine. . . .' He was increasingly embarrassed by having quoted back at him such statements as: 'It's not an accident that when God became "Man" he chose to be a male. There's no doubt He could have chosen to be a woman if he'd wanted to.'[1] The sense that women had their proper place, and it was not in the priesthood, is overwhelming, but the reason for it not being their proper place is never given, because there *is* no reason, other than the conservatism of the requirement to retain the *status quo*.

It is now likely that the ordination of women in the Anglican Church in England will go ahead, provided it gets through Synod first, and then legislation to that effect gets through Parliament. But the arguments themselves are worthy of examination, for what they show of the attitudes of women within the Church and the way that women have allowed the debate to be taken away from them. The militancy that we might have expected – women refusing to take communion, women defecting *en masse* to the Methodists or to the United Reformed Church, whose record on women's ordination, in its Congregationalist wing, is remarkably strong – simply has not happened. The most remarkable and radical demonstrations have come from the thoroughly well-behaved Movement for the Ordination of Women. Even the women's movement against the ordination of women, WOW, as opposed to MOW, the movement in favour, has failed really to provoke the ire of the campaigners in favour of women's ordination.

Yet in Anglican theological colleges up and down the country, young and not so young women have been studying towards ordination for over ten years now, much needed to bump up the numbers of a declining student population. They can achieve ordination perfectly well, but only to the diaconate, whilst their male colleagues, not necessarily of any higher stature academically, go straight on from the diaconate to the priesthood, with hardly a backward glance, and fill one of the myriads of jobs open to the young ordained priesthood in the Church of England, as again and again churches have to team up and share a vicar or a curate, because of the desperate shortages.

The Church of England certainly has its own peculiarly slow and measured way of working. Observing it from the outside, with the manifest lack of enthusiasm amongst the general public for any concept of training for the ministry, with its lack of encouragement of women into the ministry, and its unique position as the established Church with its odd Anglo-Catholic wing which does not quite believe that the break ever happened, one cannot help wishing that the women within it who so want ordination would either make more of a fuss and take no notice of the bishops and clergy who tell them they must behave like ladies, or just leave and go to the non-conformist churches which would welcome them with open arms and give them things to do. And this would be all the more suitable in an environment where the idea of the various churches working together in a mood of ecumenism has never been more popular, if somewhat half-baked in its application.

But these issues of the ordination of women within the Church of England or wherever else would not be half so important if we were not entering a time of considerable religious revival, where church-going is distinctly on the up, where even in urban areas, whose average Church of England church attendance has been under 1% of the population, the figure is creeping up to nearer 2%, and where the presence in our midst of communities such as the Muslim one, with its strong basis in religious values, makes us all consider the role of religion all over again.

And yet again this impinges most strongly on women, even if their own advancement within the Churches is still a very slow one. In very orthodox Jewish and Muslim families, it is the father who decides such questions as whether or not the children receive religious education or attend religious schools. At best the parents do it jointly. But in the majority of so-called Christian families in the UK, it is the mother who sets the religious tone, decides whether or not they attend church, what goes and what does not. And in the new-found fashion for 'the family', the view that the family which prays together stays together is increasingly prevalent, with women taking a strong line in encouraging their husbands and children into church. It is all the more surprising, therefore, that the churches have not made a more concerted effort to attract women. Although some of the city churches have made a definite attempt to recruit families into membership, largely by the activities of energetic young clergymen and a team of (mostly female) unpaid parochial assistants who ought really to be training for the priesthood, the majority have made no such effort, and it remains the churches of rural areas, where the church itself and its services act as the centre of a community, which have tried to find a role for women.

But even there, where the centrality of the church is well established, and where the village school is often a church school, there is still little for women to do, and little encouragement for women, and girls, to participate in the services. They can, of course, sing in the choir and teach in the Sunday School, but they read the lessons all too rarely, where by rights, to even up the fact that a male priest does all the rest, it should be women who read most of the lessons and ask most of the intercessions. There is far too little opportunity for women to study in any serious way about Christian theology. They are welcome to arrange the flowers and clean the church, but the degree to which women's hearts and minds are taken into account is still astonishingly slight.

Serious though this is for women, it is much more worrying for young girls. Educational evidence abounds that young girls, roughly between the ages of thirteen and sixteen, have a tendency to go through a seriously spiritual phase, searching for those meanings in life which are of little interest to most of us, most of the time, until we are considerably older. But it is these young girls who are particularly ill-served by what is provided for them within the churches. The Church of England is not alone in this. It is as true of Jewish organisations and Catholic ones (except where the girl is expressing an interest in going into a convent), and Muslim girls receive little in the way of a religious education beyond the knowledge of duties to be performed in the home and the rudiments of the law. Both Judaism and Islam have traditionally tended to undereducate their womenfolk, on the basis that women did not need detailed knowledge of the law, even though it is clear in those particular family structures that it is the women who pass on knowledge of the religion and the way of life to the children more than the men ever do.

Where then are the courses and seminars for young women that explore their spirituality? They are only to be found amongst the avowed feminists, largely in big cities, and in very specialised circles. They are not made widely available to those who might need them or be interested in them, because the needs are simply unrecognised in the majority of religious institutions. In the non-orthodox section of the Jewish community, there has been a very successful series of seminars for women on their role in religion, run largely, but not entirely, as evening classes by a combination of female rabbis and psychotherapists. They have discussed such issues as women wearing the *tallith*, the fringed prayer-shawl traditionally worn by men, and the special rituals for women around menstruation, or for baby girls, because circumcision is only for boys. They have, on the whole, not discussed whether circumcision for boys should be abolished, presumably because the removal of rituals from one section of the community has no appeal to them, though in fact it would, in my view, be a sensible call for a group of committed progressive Jewish women to make. Someone should fight against the taking over of baby boys by their fathers and grandfathers, submitting them to a barbaric ritual, on the basis that this is what Jews do, and have always done, and it was done to them, and, insult above all insults, 'it probably does not hurt'.

The argument that baby boys cry at circumcision because their nappies are removed is one of the silliest ever put forward, as most mothers know. It is as ridiculous as that advanced by largely male pediatricians, that very small babies cannot feel pain, which justifies lack of anaesthesia for painful procedures. Any mother who has ever heard the exhausted, desperate wail of a very tiny baby who has suffered operation after operation, invasive procedure after invasive procedure, simply will not believe that. Neither will the Jewish mother whose tiny baby son, eight days old, is removed from her and circumcised amongst a group of men, to rejoicing and drinking. She is not allowed or, in more progressive circles, not encouraged to be present. If she were, she would object physically or emotionally, removing the unprotected baby from the horde of marauding men, whose own foreskins were dealt with in just such a summary manner all those years ago.

This is an issue it would be good to see Jewish women's groups become concerned with. But as yet they have not got the energy. For them, issues of the language of prayer, the constant reference to God as 'He' or 'Him', the wearing of the *tallith*, the rituals surrounding childbirth and menstruation, are what they can cope with. And they have not, in Britain as yet, got as far as the American women have both in Judaism and Christianity, in providing a serious feminist liturgy, or a critique of much of the traditional texts on which so much of modern custom and practice is based. In the USA, there is a superb feminist interpretation of the Biblical texts and an attempt to re-read the texts from a woman's point of view. In such an attempt, the matriarchs reach stature they do not apparently have in the Genesis texts as we know them, and Sarah's role in dismissing Hagar, her previous servant and now Abraham's concubine who gave birth to a child before she did, takes on different and tribal proportions. Sarah's son Isaac is shown as a weakling, reliant entirely first on his mother and then on his wife Rebekah. He cannot even go and search for a wife for himself; it is his father's servant who has to go out looking on his behalf. He comes across the fair Rebekah, who gives water to his camels and thereby fulfils the prophecy of the kind of girl Isaac should marry.

These are the kinds of interpretations which are essential if the Biblical stories are to be reconsidered from a woman's point of view, if the structure of religious observance, put in place by men for men's convenience, are to be changed to accommodate, include and excite women. Women's studies of the Bible and of the other texts have to be such that there seems to be some point for young girls, inspired by their innate spirituality, to explore that side of themselves and see it not only in terms of religion as hitherto organised by men, but in terms of women's lives, women's experience, women's spirituality, women's capacity to serve God and humanity. Whilst such reinterpretation can be used to denigrate men, and therefore be wholly counter-productive, the idea that there are various ways of reading the Bible or looking at liturgy, without it always being male-dominated, male-centred, is important to excite young women about their role within religion itself, and in religious institutions.

It is there that the formal structures of religious organisations have been a failure. And as religion becomes a more important force in the 1990s, as fundamentalist, deeply conservative religious belief makes itself felt yet again, women are either going to have to make their way into the churches and religious organisations, creating their own practices and singing their own songs, or be caught up in what is in fact a very reactionary force, which has among its desires the return of women to the home, to a secondary place in society, to the veil or the yashmak or the kitchen or whatever, and to the rule of men. Those ideas, those forces, could have been ignored by women if we had not entered what is essentially a renewed religious age, which has both its virtues and its defects. But where religion is once again a force to be reckoned with, where there is an undeniable urge, on the part of both women and men, towards some form of religious expression, where atheism is on the wane and even agnostics have a new, more positive quality to their doubt, women, who have often found comfort in religion and faith, but lack of stature in religious institutions, have to take on board the undoubted discrimination that exists against them in the religious organisations to which they adhere.

For Muslim women, this provides perhaps the most severe problems of all. In Islam, fundamentalism is on the rise more than in any other world faith and its forces seek to relegate women to a role behind the curtain. Orthodox Judaism, also on the increase, has many of the same aims, though on the whole less crudely put. Nevertheless, the outgoing British Chief Rabbi, head of the mainstream rather than the ultra-orthodox community in Britain, Lord Jakobovits, was able to say that women should be the homemakers first and foremost, and to be very negative about women in the workplace. He was able to take this position in a synagogal organisation which, despite representation from many of its members, refused to allow women a place on the boards of those synagogues, although those boards merely took the business decisions and had no religious authority whatsoever.

These signs are to be found the world over. People, frightened by the materialism of the '80s and its lack of meaning for many of them, and by the increasing political insecurity of a rapidly changing world – to put it into two or three nicely turned clichés, which is as it always appears in newspapers – are looking to the old certainties. One of those old certainties was religion. But the search for religion in the structures of the old-established, tried and tested world faiths, is a search for a conservative force in life, and those conservative forces have a habit of discriminating against women, or, at best, not seeing that women have a greater potential than had been thought when the rules and customs and practices of the particular religious group grew up.

It is in the area of marriage that this is perhaps most clear. For it has been the religions which have first and foremost organised the patterns of marriage. In Judaism, women have been a little above possessions of their husbands, and have had to agree to the marriage. But in the traditional marriage service they say nothing, and divorce is easy – for the man. The woman can ask the rabbinical court to get her husband to divorce her in particular, if infrequent, circumstances. He has more cause for divorce than she does, and fundamentally the right to dismiss her lies with him; she cannot just leave.

The same is effectively true in Islam, and in Christianity divorce is not allowed in vast sectors of the Church. This leads to many trapped people, especially women left with children by husbands who go off with someone else and live with them without marriage. Such men have a horrible habit of failing to support their original family, which becomes all the easier when the Church does not recognise divorce and neither, as is the case in one European country, does the State. Insisting on enforcement orders to guarantee support to an abandoned wife and family is less than in tune with the prevailing thought pattern.

In fact dramatic changes have come about in the recognition of divorce over the last twenty years. Ireland is the last remaining country in Europe that does not recognise it; Italy introduced it in 1970. Substantial changes have come about to make it easier in England and Wales, the Netherlands, France and Germany, in the last three of which there is a large Roman Catholic population, where the Church itself still fails to recognise divorce. But the comparison between the UK, with its 12.9 divorces per annum per thousand in the married population and Italy with its 1.1 or even Belgium with its 7.3, France with its 8.5 and the Netherlands with its 8.7 suggests a strong influence from the Catholic community.[2] The question then has to be the extent to which there is moral, as well as legal, pressure upon men to support divorced wives and children, when the Church does not recognise the divorce in the first place. One can begin to see the difficulties.

Christianity has very different views on human sexuality from those of Judaism and Islam, which recognise and enjoy that part of life and think it one of God's greatest gifts, but all three religions, plus Hinduism, represent attitudes to women which reflect an entirely male-designed view of the world. Women are there for men's pleasure, men's service, and the bearing of children (other than in those strands of Christianity where the sex-denying women could achieve high status, such as in the convents). They are expendable, by divorce, or, more frequently, by death in childbirth.

It is these attitudes which colour the views of modern religious leaders towards women. They are of a lower status than men, or as low as chattels, as they were at various points in canon law, or bound by rules of modesty so as not to attract men other than their husbands, or whatever. That very much lower status, designed by the men who made the rules of those religions, who planned dowries and bride prices and compensation for injury to babies in the womb, means that women have great difficulty being taken seriously within those same religious structures, because the whole design is against them. Thus, even though they may claim to have strong religious feelings, the view has traditionally been that they should express those feelings by doing their duty in the home, by husband and children and elderly relatives, and that their spirituality is a very private thing.

The apologists for women's lower status in Judaism argue that God took one aspect of the human personality, translated either as humility or privacy, and wrote it to excess in women. Women are therefore very private beings, with no need of the public arena for the expression of their deepest, innermost spiritual thoughts and desires. Unlike men, they do not need public worship or the communal feel of the synagogue. They are happiest and most spiritually secure if they can be left to pray and think at home. A better justification for the exclusion of women from the requirements of public worship it would be hard to find, and a more clearly apologetic explanation of how it is that women are excluded from the congregation of ten (men) required to conduct a full service in orthodox Judaism it would be hard to create.

In this climate, there are two main options. There is the option of separate development, which has historically been where the radical side of the women's movement has met the deep traditionalists, advocating women's services, women's meetings, women's groups of one sort or another. It has led to women conducting church services for themselves and serving communion for themselves where traditionally they would have had to ask a male priest to come and do it for them, and it has led to groups of ultra-orthodox Jewish women conducting services for themselves, reading from the scroll of the law (which in orthodox circles they would never do if there were men present), and wearing the traditional prayer-shawl. It has led to a resurgence of academies for women to study their religious traditions, and it has led to a form of lay pietism, in Christianity and Islam as well as Judaism, that is passionately spiritual but frequently profoundly unintellectual, where religious feeling is encouraged, speaking in tongues or storytelling or singing in small groups is the norm, but the requirement to put in any rigorous thought about what precisely is being expressed is lacking.

Alongside that, there has been a more intellectual tradition of feminist theology, a feminist critique of religious traditions, and increasingly an involvement in theology departments in universities of a thinker somewhere within the feminist tradition who takes a side-swipe at some of the more absurd tenets of classical, traditional theology of whichever religion. Thus there has been a mushrooming of books reinterpreting Biblical traditions, depatriarchalising the Bible, a re-examination of the role of Jesus or Mohammed in relation to women, a thinking about the rabbis' attitude to women and a replaying, and aggrandising, of the women mentioned in rabbinic texts. Much of this happens separately from men, in specialist departments and specialist groups, though its influence has extended beyond that, into more traditional theology departments, and even into the hallowed portals of some of the theological training colleges for the clergy, be they Jewish, Christian or even, increasingly, Muslim.

But that is an option women seriously concerned about the place of women in religion should be examining much more carefully. It simply is not enough to have separatist groups, to accept the definition of the apologists that women are equal but different, to give up the struggle for being recognised as equal in a mixed environment, at a time when the forces are so arrayed against women being treated as equals in large sectors of religious communities. Women who care that their sisters and daughters should get the opportunity to express their spirituality must try to have women accepted in the mainstream of religious activity, that arena dominated by men. That requires continuing a campaign to have women ordained as priests within the Church of England, to stand firmly against those who argue that the time is not yet right because of those others who threaten to secede if women are ordained. It means making a fuss about women being denied a role in public worship.

More significantly, it requires women to refuse to carry out some of the traditional roles until they get recognition for them, be they as cleaners of churches, embroiderers of hassocks, arrangers of flowers, or as parochial assistants, sent out to do much of the pastoral work of the clergy but without the recognition that that is what they are doing.

The labour of women in religious institutions has long been relied upon, and unthanked, and women's religious devotion has been exploited so that, uncomplaining, they have carried out tasks men have not wanted to do. The only way that a change will come about is if women carry on performing those tasks if that is what they wish to do, but make it clear that these are essential roles, not just the icing on the cake. It means that women will have to be tougher about reckoning up what it is they do and have done within the institutions and expect to be publicly recognised for doing it, and it means that where that is not happening, where women continue to perform pastoral roles without adequate training and support, they should demand it, and complain when they do not get it.

These are unfamiliar tones within religious institutions, but some degree of polite toughness is essential if those in charge of religious institutions are to understand that women mean business, that they require training and support, and that fundamentally they see themselves as equal with the men. That needs to be said in those institutions where women have apparently reached equality, such as, for instance, in that section of the Jewish community, the non-orthodox reform and liberal section, which I serve; in the Church of England where equality is argued yet women cannot yet be ordained to the priesthood; in the Hindu religion in the schools of thought that allow women to be priests; and in those approaches to Islam which allow women some semblance of equality. For even there, women are exploited, and when a significant number of them reaches any degree of seniority, resentment begins.

It became clear that this was so when I was chairing the liberal rabbinic conference between 1983 and 1985, and my colleague Jackie Tabick, the first woman rabbi in the UK, was chairing the reform rabbis' rabbinic assembly at the same time. Suddenly we were both 'senior', and suddenly we were both somehow a threat. Those two sweet young women who had hitherto been tolerated and whom male colleagues had been able to charm were now, however temporarily, in charge, even though it had come about by rotation rather than by some great stature of our own. Neither of us had an easy time chairing our respective groups of rabbis, and neither of us thought it was coincidental that we were female. Tolerated as junior but equal, we were objects of fear and slight derision when in senior positions. The equality we had been promised, and the equality which our progressive Judaism apparently stood for, and which it made great play of in its debates with orthodox Judaism, only went so far.

That is true of other religious organisations as well. Even the United Reformed Church, on its Congregationalist side the earliest to have women ministers in the UK, has not tended to appoint women to very senior positions, to be heads of theological colleges or have very large senior pulpits, and the glass ceiling felt by so many women professionals, when they have got so far but can get no further, but cannot see the block that is stopping them, is more true than ever for those in religious institutions.

But these are women who have gone in with men, as equals. These are women who do not want, or did not feel they needed, separatist women's groups. As a young rabbi, I scorned the women's groups, and I still often believe that they discuss issues of less than fundamental concern. But when it comes to attacks on women's place in Judaism, when it comes to attempts to attract more young men into the rabbinate because now 'we are getting too many women', when it is even suggested that additional grants might be paid to young married men with small children because they cannot afford to study to be rabbis, when, patently and obviously, young women rabbis with children can, then a women's group, with its self-reinforcing anger, is essential. Whether I really care much about the gender of the descriptions of God in the liturgy or not, there are areas of concern here which I may not share, but which are important to other women, and men, and need at least to be viewed seriously.

In a Britain now committed to largely Christian worship in schools, to largely Christian religious education, in an atmosphere increasingly hostile to multi-cultural education, I fear that some religious truths will simply be lost, that the expansion of ideas of all our children will no longer be high on the agenda of religious education teachers, and that religion will be deep conventionality, rather than a search for spirituality and a development of awareness of the numinous. The need to make sure children understand that there are male and female sides to the deity, whatever it is, that there are male and female sides to all of us, that there are different approaches to prayer, and suffering, and lifecycle events, and community life and ritual, still remains, but a gradual shift to conservatism makes that harder to achieve. It is these issues that women need to tackle in the mainstream of religious organisations. If they leave to join groups for women only, the battle is over before it has begun, and the losers will be the children who see only a narrow approach to religious awareness. If religion is to be a major force in the decades ahead, and it is, then the role of women in it has to be wider than purely that of getting women ordained to the priesthood in the Church of England, though that would be a very good start.

12

Nursing and Caring

And Nurse came in with the tea-things
Breast high mid the stands and chairs –
But Nurse was alone with her own little soul
And the things were alone with theirs.

John Betjeman *Death in Leamington*

THE ALMOST OPPOSING models of medicine and nursing have led to
some interesting reflections on differences between male and
female methods of looking at illness and disease, most of which
have little to recommend them. But there is an important debate
beginning to flourish now about the direction of nursing, seen in
many ways as the acme of a female profession, but a profession
which has not quite got its act together to see itself as a proper
profession, rather than as a vocation on the one hand and a job on
the other.

That is blatantly clear from the discussions about nursing
research. Nurses, especially those who are being trained in the new
academic model, are gradually doing a great deal more research
than they ever did, even though many doctors regard their research
as 'soft' and even though most of it is not properly thought
through. The work that they do is to measure pain, or to assess
qualities of dressings for various forms of ulcerating sores and
varicose veins, or to design and use questionnaires about all sorts of
domestic factors that might lead to ill health of either a physical or
a mental nature. Yet despite the fact that nurses are more and more

heavily engaged in research, they are loath to do what real professionals always have to do, which is to design their research, and think about it, in their own free time. In some extraordinary way, demonstrating that to some extent they still see themselves as shift-workers on a job, they want to be paid for the time they put in thinking about possible research projects, let alone actually carrying them out.

That is clearly one problem with nurses and nursing. The other goes the opposite way, and has a bit of the legacy of the magnificent (and now much under-rated) Florence Nightingale about it. It is to see nursing as a vocation rather than a profession. As a result, many nurses fail to act as professionals, and do not require either the standards or the conditions that professionals by right expect for themselves.

The 'vocational' approach is not helped by the very strong influence, in early modern nursing, of the nursing orders of nuns who were carrying out their comparatively high standard of nursing (certainly compared to the drunken women who made up the mainstream of hospital nurses) precisely as a vocation, and who still play a large role in important areas of creative nursing thought, such as in the hospice movement.

Yet it is in the hospice movement that some of the most exciting moves in 'caring' have come about. For there is real inter-disciplinary, cross-disciplinary work in the hospice movement; nurses genuinely carry out the work of doctors, and doctors of nurses, and nurses of cleaners, and cleaners of chaplains, and so on and so on.

The modern hospice movement was founded in Britain by Dame Cicely Saunders OM. She was a nurse who became a doctor and ultimately an institution, and was driven by passionate religious belief and an incapacity to believe that suffering was ennobling.

The thinking that pain is ennobling, that it strengthens the spirit, is, as we have seen, one that has come through Christianity. Yet the adulation of pain in some strands of British society may have something to contribute here. Pain control, in terms of hospice care, is very much a British invention. Theories abound as to why it came about in Britain, but one explanation that appeals is the 'stiff upper lip' syndrome of British men, who cannot bear to scream out in pain. Pain therefore has to be controlled. At the same time, moderate pain is tolerable, so pain control can only really be used to combat the extreme pain of terminal illness.

Of course that can be picked to pieces, but the strands in Christian thought about the nobility of suffering, the alacrity with which children were encouraged to learn about the sufferings of the martyrs, the exaltation of the martyrs themselves, are all signs of some slightly strange attitude to pain. Pain, in this thinking, is good for us. It makes us what we are. For little boys, it toughens them up, hence the need to have corporal punishment. 'Spare the rod and spoil the child. . . .' For little girls, until relatively modern times, corporal punishment was just as appropriate, and girls were whipped and spanked and are still hit in anger by furious parents, though not in a systematic way. But girls have pain at menstruation, and women in childbirth.

Add to this the term for sexual exaltation, passion, which means suffering, as Karen Armstrong has so neatly pointed out, and look at female writers who relate pain and pleasure over and over again, such as Edna O'Brien, Mrs Gaskell and Emily Brontë, and we have a prescription for the adoration of pain, for self-definition by pain, for mortification of the flesh by both men and women, but perhaps particularly, as a result of Christian teaching, amongst women.

But in order to be able to stand the kind of pain that many people suffer with terminal cancer, some kind of pain relief is essential. The oldest tradition was the giving of opiates in an uncontrolled way, massive doses that probably caused addiction, but only relieved the pain for part of the time. The extraordinarily simple thinking about terminal care, as put forward by Cicely Saunders, was that by careful handling, carefully controlled doses of various drugs and other techniques to bring additional comfort, it was possible to take away most if not all the pain and discomfort of the last weeks and months of a person's life, and enable them to live a reasonably normal life, and to think and to feel and to engage in discussion and dispose of what remained of their lives as they wished.

There are those who think that Cicely Saunders' idea was an essentially 'female' one, more to do with care than cure, and more to do with the female desire to cherish and comfort than with the male desire to mend and put together again. That is without doubt oversimplified, in that much medical care is about caring rather than curing, and the number of conditions and diseases it is actually possible to 'cure' outright is very small indeed. But there is an element of truth in it. The desire to nourish and cherish and care has been associated particularly with women, and the modern patterns in Europe of women caring for the elderly more than they do for children bears this out. And there is a different type of thinking to be found amongst those who want to alleviate suffering, to control pain, to make the individual feel better, for whatever further purpose, and those who want to effect a cure, which certainly, in some forms of treatment of cancer, will make the individual feel worse, and iller, and less strong, and less able to cope.

There may also be a frightening realism here. The medical model, as practised in the West, is to believe largely in the power of 'cure'. Some would argue it is a belief system just as much as any religious belief system is. But the actual rate of cure is comparatively low. Most people are not cured of their disease. They get some relief of symptoms, a wholly different thing. They get a delay in the onset of the final stages of the disease. But the nursing model is much more likely to be interested in the individual rather than the statistics, in the relief of individual suffering rather than an improvement in cure rates, and therefore the nursing model, essentially more female than the medical one, is to try to alleviate the individual's suffering, with pain control or skilled physiotherapy or whatever. The interest of the discipline is likely to be more individualistic, and far more concerned with the relief of suffering as presented rather than in possible ultimate cure.

Indeed, if you talk to nurses who work on wards where very unpleasant forms of chemotherapy are given with a fifty-fifty success rate, such as for instance for some leukaemic children, they express great distress at the suffering the children have to go through, despite the knowledge that 50% or more of them will recover, and that indeed the figures are improving all the time. Unlike doctors, nurses do not see these matters in terms of statistics, perhaps not as much as they should. They tend to achieve a relationship with individual patients, and find the statistics of a group of cases irrelevant, for they are only concerned with the one. Doctors often point to this feature of nurses as proving that nursing does not have a proper scientific base, but they fail to realise that it is simply impossible to give proper care, with a full relationship, however professional, with the individual patient, without taking the patient's interests to heart in some way, and that obviously predisposes against being able to look at the patient concerned as part of a set of statistics.

The interesting feature of this thinking is how doctors are often affected by it themselves if they are ill. The classic example of this is Vicky Clement-Jones, a young doctor who contracted ovarian cancer and died aged thirty-seven, having in her last few years of life set up the remarkable and effective British Association of Cancer Patients United, (BACUP), an advisory service for cancer patients telling them some of the facts about their disease, but even more importantly, teaching them how best to live with it, since that is precisely what most patients have to do.

Although there is nothing inherently female about the setting up of such services, it is, in my view, no coincidence that organisations such as BACUP and the hospices, despite now attracting men to work with and for them, were founded by women. It is something to do with the upbringing of women, the conditioning, the learning to cope, the putting up with things, the making the best of a bad job, so different from the education of young males to seek to change things, that inspires some women to look for new and imaginative ways of living with the unlivable, of coping with the most difficult of situations. Men are perfectly capable of this sort of thinking, but it is not as much part of their training and education as it is of young women's, hence the major 'coping' organisations, support groups and provision of respite care for elderly and terminally ill people, to give their carers a break, are the creation or invention of women.

This was brought home to me when I first met Vicky Clement-Jones, once she had started on her serious thinking about an advisory service for patients. Vicky was particularly worried, after her own experience of hair-loss during chemotherapy, about how to advise patients, male and female, to cope with hair falling out by the handful. As a doctor herself, she was appalled by the quality of help she had been given in that sort of area by the doctors, often close colleagues, who were treating her. But she had developed a method of coping for herself, which was to wear, especially in bed when one did not want to wear a hat, several hairnets of different meshes one on top of the other. That, she found, although looking less than beautiful, stopped hair falling out all over the place, and enabled one to gather enough of it to place as an artificial fringe under the hat for the daytime, should one want to.

These are issues with which doctors are less than concerned, on the whole, unless it happens to them, and they are too rushed and overstretched in busy NHS hospitals in a state of flux to take on these issues at the moment. But these are precisely the issues which are the fabric of nursing – working out what it is that most distresses the patients, explaining what one can do and giving support where possible. The two disciplines are complementary, but because of the sexual politics underlying the roles of largely female nurses acting as 'handmaidens' to largely male doctors, that complementariness has not been explored. Even now, with a female president of the Royal College of Physicians and an immediately past male general secretary of the Royal College of Nursing, the remarkable Trevor Clay, attitudes are still too firmly ingrained to allow nurses and doctors to work together as equals except in very rare cases, notably in terminal care.

This is because of their origins, no doubt. All doctors were male until the beginning of this century, and though 50% of students in medical schools up and down the country are now female, the majority of them will never end up as consultants in hospitals (a mere 13% of all consultants in the UK are female). Women are much more likely to end up as general practitioners or community physicians, or in some other field of medicine where it is possible to combine family life and medical practice without the horrors of the hours junior hospital doctors have had to work, hours which cannot be good for anybody, but are impossible for someone who has more than cursory responsibility for a young family.

But the result is that in hospitals, where most acute medical work is done, the bulk of the consultants are male. And in hospitals, as opposed to psychiatric institutions, most of the nurses are female. The assumption, despite all the new designs of nursing process and nursing training, is that nurses will carry out the doctors' orders, and, even more importantly, that they will not in any way tell patients things that the doctors have not already told them. And so, at the end of the twentieth century, in a society which has hospices, where the hospice movement is flourishing and is internationally hailed as a model, we have doctors up and down the country who refuse to tell their patients that they are dying, and nurses, brought up never to argue, unable to challenge the doctors and working in such a way that they can never get the trust of the patients because they will not tell the patients the truth.

These are issues of key importance to women, who are by and large the carers. The influence of good nursing practice, the ideas about caring for the whole person, the emphasis on honesty, the denial of the medical model that allows the doctor's definition of beneficence to take precedence over the patient's autonomy – are all fundamental to women as patients and as carers. But whilst nurses take their orders from doctors without challenging, without regular case conferences, and whilst nursing itself is largely organised on a hierarchical, task-oriented basis, so that individual patients do not know 'their' nurses, and senior nurses tell junior nurses precisely what to do without discussing it, it is hard to see how change will come about.

The good news is that there *are* changes in nursing practice, including a move towards a nursing process which allows a nurse to take twenty-four-hour charge of a patient, even though she is not there for all of the twenty-four-hour period. But the bad news is that this is taking a long time to catch on, that patients are suffering, that those being cared for at home are suffering, and that the shortage of young women wanting to go into nursing, as well as the flood of young women who leave more or less immediately after their training, is continuing apace.

Nursing has been one of the key professions for women, and at its best it is a source of considerable pride, where women, professionally, have made an enormous difference to people's lives. Yet it cannot recruit enough people into it. It needs some 50% of all eighteen-year-old school-leavers simply to keep up the numbers and deal with demographic changes, and it still behaves as if it were subservient to medicine. Yet patients rely more on the ministrations of nurses than on the touch of doctors. One of the things that the women's movement could do in this strange situation where nursing is so important and has done such a poor publicity job on itself, is constantly to sing the praise of nursing, and, when individuals need to care for an elderly relative or spouse, to talk to others about the understanding gained at that point, if not before, of what nursing is really about.

It is then possible that the nurturing, caring role that nurses take on professionally will gain more importance in the wider community, and that the public will understand that this essentially female profession, the largest wage-earning group in the NHS, has enormous amounts to give and is not to be underrated as servile, handmaidens of doctors, a short job for a nice girl to do before she gets married. It must be seen as a serious endeavour, with complicated training and major skills, dedicated to the relief of human suffering, and the bringing of an atmosphere of honesty into healthcare.

Yet nurses are still regarded as 'angels', as if they had wings. In times of industrial unrest with nurses, the public always shows sympathy. The general perception is that nurses are overworked and underpaid. Yet women's organisations have been slow to address the heart of the reason as to why nurses are now so overworked, which is that if patients are increasingly discharged as early as possible, and sometimes before it is at all wise, then the extent to which all the patients in a ward will need major nursing care is much greater. The old pattern in the general hospital medical ward of the less ill patients doing the teas or helping make the beds for their sicker fellow patients is barely seen in this climate, for if the patients were well enough to help in that way, they would already have been sent home.

Nurses remain underpaid, despite significant pay increases and regrading exercises within the last few years. The financial rewards within the NHS are still so small that many nurses opt for the private sector, going for the money and the better and more flexible working conditions. Nurses are probably badly paid because nursing is still seen as an essentially female profession, like social work and some kinds of teaching, resulting in a move towards the bottom of the pay structures. However, the increasing numbers of men in nursing, and the fact of changes in nursing practice should have done much to attract young women into the profession and encouraged them to stay. The problem is that one of the reasons young women leave and do not come back is that nursing, an overwhelmingly female profession, makes it very hard indeed for women with children to work and care for their families at the same time, so that thousands upon thousands of nurses have let their registration lapse, because going back into the profession is so difficult.

And yet the values and patterns of care in nursing are so important to our society. There is an important political message to women's organisations in what has happened to the paramedical professions – nursing, physiotherapy, occupational therapy and so on. They have become professionalised, certainly, and they have become more research orientated, even if not all the research is of a very high standard. (The same can be said of medical research as well, though that is more likely to get peer review. Nevertheless, a great deal of medical research is in fact contract research for the pharmaceutical industry, and of no real benefit to patients in the short term, or even sometimes in the long term.) But they have also become deeply divided, and the capacity for the nursing and other paramedical professions to have great political clout is distinctly limited. Doctors are better organised, with their conference of the medical Royal Colleges, to get a good hearing in the public domain, and to use political skills and influence to bring about changes in policy.

In recent years, nursing has been more effective in this regard. But it would have been better if nurses and midwives, physiotherapists and occupational therapists, could have spoken out together from their different disciplines, rather like the surgeons and the physicians and the GPs. There is a malaise in the political style of nursing and the other allied professions, which may lie in the confusion between being a profession, a vocation or just a job, or which may say something about its having been initially a women's profession, with the attendant low pay and low promotion prospects.

Nevertheless, whatever the reasons, it is time that the weighting of debate was evened up between doctors on the one hand and non-medical healthcare workers on the other. As medicine becomes increasingly hi-tech, it is the nurses and other healthcare professionals who will be left to ask some of the fundamental questions about whether it is right to spend such an enormous proportion of our resources on delicate, difficult and expensive micro-surgery or transplant surgery when so many psycho-geriatric patients are in very poor conditions with very little in the way of resources being ploughed into their care. Although it may well be that what is difficult hi-tech today may be common practice tomorrow, as has happened for instance with coronary artery bypass grafts, there is widespread public concern about those areas of medicine that are unfashionable, where treatment is to do with alleviation rather than cure, where the whole family needs looking after, and the doctors cannot cope.

In real terms, nurses often cannot cope either. They cannot suddenly divert resources from one area of need to another. But they can, and do, look after the whole person, quarrel with the modern wisdom of preserving life without assessing quality, and comfort the patients. It is that role that the public should back. Nurses need to be encouraged to take a tough line on a variety of issues, and allocation of resources and being included in the decision-making about individual patients should be made part of the requirement for toughness. For in a health service short of funds, with depressed doctors all over the UK, the nurses and other healthcare workers may be able to take the debate further. But to do that, they need to ally themselves with women's groups and patient groups up and down the country, perceiving themselves as the patients' advocates and patients' protectors. Such a move on the part of healthcare workers might well be welcomed by the general public. But it ought, before that, to be welcomed by all the national women's organisations, and it ought to be encouraged by campaigning women's organisations, for only that way will interesting things begin to happen.

The question of caring introduces another issue which was ignored by the feminist movement of the 1960s: that of what exactly a woman's role is and should be, and where her limits are. Statistical projections show that by the year 2008 there will be approximately 2,734,000 women of seventy-five and over, and only 1,647,000 men; the differential will increase sharply for people over eighty and again at eighty-five. It is simply unrealistic to imagine that most women, most families for that matter, most men, will leave their elderly relatives to fend for themselves. But it is also true that one in three elderly people has no close relative, and that is more true of the very elderly, over eighty, than the younger ones. Since four out of six of the over eighty-fives are female, that means a large number of single women who are very old and who have no-one to care for them.

The problem then arises as to what should be done in terms of social policy for these people. The NHS provision is likely to be inadequate. How are visitors and inspectors in institutions to be provided? Who are to be the volunteers who keep an eye on isolated elderly people? This is a major social concern, impinging to a great extent on the lives of younger women and on their own expectations.

Women's organisations need to take a long, hard look at who is going to be doing the caring, for whom and how, and begin to think of mobilising the most unlikely political allies to get serious thinking into place on these issues. Almost three-quarters of women in their early eighties are widows, whilst less than a third of men of a similar age are in that situation. Over 60% of women over eighty-five live alone, whilst only 37% of men do. But over 20% of people over eighty-five live with a son or daughter, and elderly women are far more likely than men to be in such households.[1]

These figures have to be examined alongside growing evidence that there simply is no coherent policy of community care, particularly in relation to those sections of the population previously institutionalised or those who would have been institutionalised. That includes a large proportion of the very elderly who cannot perform basic tasks for themselves or who are severely demented. But the whole structure, or perhaps lack of structure, operates under particular assumptions about the role of women. In the early 1970s, as Melanie Henwood points out in her excellent handbook, *Community Care and Elderly People*, the issue of caring was interesting researchers, and much of their research assumed unquestioningly that carers would be women and women would be carers. She writes: 'Moroney, for example, in 1976 developed the concept of the "caretaker ratio" founded solely on "two potential sources of care: married and single women between the ages of forty-five and sixty."'[2] The Equal Opportunities Commission recognised the implications of community care policies as early as 1982 in a report which said:

> A growing body of evidence suggests that 'community care' has, in reality, meant care by individuals on an unpaid and often unaided basis in the home. Since traditional attitudes and practices within society continue to allocate to women the prime responsibility for caring functions, the majority of 'carers' are women. . . . They will often find themselves badly supported by statutory services and without any real choice as to whether they will care or not. Far from the community carrying the costs, the allocation of caring responsibilities has major implications in financial, social and emotional terms for the individuals involved.[3]

Melanie Henwood puts it succinctly:

> This radical perspective on caring argues that women are cast in the caring role because of the patriarchal nature of society and the

consequences which this has for the sexual division of labour both at work and within the home.

The only way forward, in this analysis, is to work towards equal status in the labour market for people of both genders, so that income can be provided collectively for home responsibilities as well as retirement and unemployment.

But that is a long time hence. Recognition of the seriousness of the situation, with community care genuinely providing services to and in the home, is also a long way off, and ensuring the provision of such services without a family member to check and insist and nag and telephone and fill in the inevitable gaps is a pipe-dream. The reality, therefore, is that the chances are women will have to accept a large section of this caring role which has been cast upon them. Many have accepted it willingly and lovingly, but it is still useful to look at how one can improve it, in emotional, career and financial terms, and even at how one might reward it in societal terms, rather than simply arguing it is an individual's duty.

That means taking on the enormity of the issue. For instance, one adult in seven is a carer. Women are more likely than men to be carers, but the gap is not as large as one might have thought, with the figures being 15% of all women, as against 12% of all men. The likelihood of being a carer increases with age, and disproportionately for women, so that between thirty and forty-four 11% of men are carers and 16% of women; between forty-five and sixty-four, it goes up to 16% of men and 24% of women. The caring can be hard and physical. In *It's My Duty, Isn't It?*, Jill Pitkeathley, director of the Carers' National Association, quoted a series of interviews and anecdotes she had heard, including this one: 'Caring has made me a physical and mental wreck, totally unable to relax and without a clue how to even try to think of myself.'

Even more depressing is a study of the amount of time caring takes up. Ninety-two per cent of carers looking after another member of the household were caring seven days a week, and nearly half of the carers looking after someone within the same household were spending fifty hours or more caring.[4] A further revelation from much of the research, though anecdotal experience of watching 'caring' in action might have prepared us for it, is that once one person in a family has been singled out as the 'carer', little practical support is forthcoming from other members of the family.

Only 11% of carers shared the main responsibility with someone else, and such help is most likely to come from another household member. But the most significant factor in all this is perhaps that when help with caring *was* forthcoming, it was more likely to be directed at male carers than at female ones; this lends weight to the feminist critique of the community care policies, that women are *expected* to carry out this work and therefore are less likely to be helped, by the local authority or health services on the one hand and by family members on the other.

Any study of supporting services bears this out. Elderly people who live with married children are least likely to receive any services, irrespective of the children's circumstances, and the support services are used largely to substitute for family care when it is not available, instead of giving support to the carers. The tensions created by all this are immense. Despite unemployment, women are more likely to continue to increase their economic activity rate in the next twenty years, particularly with more skilled part-time employment becoming available. On some projections, by the end of the century female economic activity rates are expected to be only fifteen percentage points behind men's, but how women are to balance that economic activity in the workplace against the expectations being made of them as carers is still unclear.

The government has begun to take account of some of these issues, but largely – because of the political realities of children being more fashionable than the elderly – in relation to childcare, which is gradually becoming a smaller and smaller part of the whole caring package. John Patten, who chaired a working group for the government on women's issues in a cross-departmental attempt to look at these issues in 1988–9 is on record as saying: 'The 1990s, unlike the 1960s, will be a decade in which childcare becomes a substantial part of the pay package of working women, more important than health insurance, mortgages or company cars.' Melanie Henwood quotes this and continues:

> The implications for those with caring responsibilities other than for young children have received less attention, yet there are over three million worker-carers in Britain today. Around one in nine of all full-time employees are also carers, and one in six of those working part-time. About one fifth of married women working part-time are carers.

Even many of the most heavily committed carers are also working –
42% of carers devoting at least twenty hours each week to care are also
in employment – more than half a million people.

These are frightening statistics in a society that tends to talk of 'the
problem of ageing' rather than view ageing as a natural process
which we will all achieve and should enjoy. The US scenario of a
'war between the generations' is not yet a feature of the UK scene,
but that may at least partly be due to a large degree of quiescence
from carers, and a curiously silent opposition on the subject of
constant delays, many of which have no rational justification, in the
implementation of community care proposals. In a tough paper for
the King's Fund Institute, Tessa Jowell, Gerald Wistow and Melanie
Henwood have argued convincingly that the community care
provisions could have been brought in in 1991, and there was no
reason for delaying them until 1992. This would at least have had
the benefit of supporting carers who have been caught in a two- or
three-year time warp, with promises made and no services
delivered, and would have encouraged those authorities which took
the government seriously and developed strategies and plans for
community care to put them into effect.

As it is, the energy put into planning, developing and encouraging services by the authorities themselves and by the voluntary and
private sector has been put on hold with no justification except the
short-term saving of money. The prospect of ironing out the
myriad problems that will occur with a new and patchwork system
has been put off still further, to the detriment of those who wish,
and need, to use the services.

Women's groups have been slow to shout out. It is a little like
'Scream quietly, or the neighbours will hear. . . .' The problems are
undoubtedly there, people are undoubtedly suffering and all the
demographic evidence shows that the situation will get worse. Yet
the people who are suffering most are somehow too proud, or too
exhausted, or too convinced they are merely doing their duty, to
complain, and those best placed to make a fuss on their behalf have
been loath to do so. Opposition political parties have been slow to
react, probably because cynically they have realised that the
problems are huge and expensive, and they would not wish to
engage in such massive public expenditure, locally or nationally,
either. But even they could be criticising more actively the way that

benefit provisions and social security regulations make it likely that people will end up in residential care at a time when it is community care, in the home, that is being encouraged.

But it is the women's groups, cross-party and cross-class and cross-age, that ought to be taking up these issues and running with them, because of the enormous impact they have on women's lives generally, and because these are the issues that define female existence far more than the having and rearing of children has in recent times. Carers at home, mostly female, are now getting some attention at last, largely because of the delays in bringing in new provisions in community care. But the hidden people who are cared for, in old people's homes increasingly run for profit and in the private sector, in mental institutions, in nursing homes, are unknown until appalling abuse comes to light. Those who are abused are frequently female. Those who abuse are all too often female as well. There is no independent, trained inspectorate that examines institutions where patients are resident, be they in the private, voluntary or national health sector, and the situation is a disgrace. Inspecting of nursing homes and homes for the elderly is done by an 'arms-length' team from social services, instead of a wholly independent, properly trained inspectorate able to perform spot checks. Licensing is often carried out without proper inspection, and local authorities are unwilling to close down premises because of their own statutory obligation to provide care for the residents thereafter.

Yet demographically the problem is considerably worse than it was twenty years ago. The women's movement, with all its campaigning for the interests of women at work, and increasingly at home, has simply failed to pick up the significance of these facts. Women are the ones who are in institutions, left widowed or having remained single, caring for elderly parents. They have traditionally been the carers, and they are increasingly the carers again. The NHS and the public purse is simply not going to provide the care needed for all the elderly in our midst. The effects of that will fall disproportionately on women, and are already doing so, and the implications are frightening, as standards of care continue to fall below what most of us require for those we love, and for ourselves.

This is an area which should have been meat and drink to the women's movement of the '70s and early '80s, when the demographic picture was becoming increasingly clear, and when the political will to pay for all the care required by the elderly and mentally ill and handicapped in our society was clearly diminishing. But because these issues were seen by many, particularly the radical feminists, as the stuff of women's former concerns, the domestic, caring, succouring role that women have played, willingly and unwillingly, for millennia, they received scant attention. As a result, women have been unable fully to take on the new political realities which have both encouraged them into the workplace (particularly on a part-time basis, because of shortages in the labour force) and increasingly into 'caring' roles professionally, and made it clear that 'community care' is to a very large extent 'family' care.

The view at the beginning of the 1990s is a bleak one. There are those who say that the care of the very elderly, the Fourth Agers, is liable to become the duty of the slightly younger, the Third Agers. Those who have retired at sixty or sixty-five will then spend ten or fifteen years caring for their elderly parents or relations. Yet again, that burden is likely to fall upon women, but people, particularly of that age, clearly feel that they paid their National Insurance and their taxes on the full assumption that these services were going to be provided on a national basis; they were not expecting to have to care for elderly relatives because the money for state provision could not be found. Nevertheless, it is likely that they will do a considerable amount of the caring in the future, partly because there will be no-one else to do it. For if predictions are right, and over half of eighteen-year-old female school-leavers will be needed for the nursing profession by the middle of the 1990s, then it is clear that whatever anyone feels about their willingness or otherwise to care for the elderly, there simply will not be enough staff to do it. The provision of care for those who are not seriously ill and in need of full-time nursing care will have to come from within the community, and families.

But that begs the question of how able families are to provide that care, for many will not be able to cope under the strain. One issue which is rarely discussed in areas other than that of terminal illness is that of respite care for those who are looked after by families, but whose families and carers need a well-earned break. If women's organisations were to band together to insist on a right to respite care for a certain number of weeks a year for those who are cared for within a family unit, that would take a major load off caring families. It would also enable the person who is being cared for to feel less of a burden. There is more pleasure to be had in caring for someone who is loved and respected, but often difficult and tiring, if occasionally there is a holiday, a break, enabling the family to sleep late in the morning or have uninterrupted nights. The provision of such services as a night hospital where elderly people can sleep from one to four nights a week, to give their carers unbroken nights, is exactly the sort of relieving social provision that ought to be at the forefront of women's organisations' minds, because it is that kind of provision that will make the difference between doing a job with love and devotion, or doing it in desperation, depression and isolation.

13
Careers – and
giving them up

One man on his own can be quite good fun
But don't go drinking with two –
They'll probably have an argument
And take no notice of you.

What makes men so tedious
Is the need to show off and compete.
They'll bore you to death for hours and hours
Before they'll admit defeat.

If often happens at dinner parties
Where brother disputes with brother
And we can't even talk among ourselves
Because we're not next to each other.

Some men like to argue with women –
Don't give them a chance to begin.
You won't be allowed to change the subject
Until you have given in.

A man with the bit between his teeth
Will keep you up half the night
And the only way to get some sleep
Is to say, 'I expect you're right.'

I expect you're right, my dearest love.
I expect you're right, my friend.
Those boring arguments make no difference
To anything in the end.

Wendy Cope *Men and their boring arguments*

IN OCTOBER 1990, a piece appeared in the *Independent* berating the presenter of the BBC's *Question Time* and its editorial team for their failure to put fresh, able women on the screen on their programme. Indeed, Peter Sissons, at the launch of the new series in September, had said, 'There is a big gap, a real shortage, of front-line women.' The truth of the matter is that there was and is a shortage of women to appear on *Question Time* and present themselves in the same way as the men who appear on it, used to the cut and thrust of Parliament and the political posturing that goes with it. There are comparatively few women in Parliament for a variety of reasons, mostly very well rehearsed: among them the hours of Parliament, the customs of the place, the innate discrimination in the selection process and the unattractiveness of the lifestyle to many relatively young women who have families.

In the *Independent*, Sir Robin Day, previous presenter of *Question Time*, was reported as saying that because women were unaccustomed to working with the political cut and thrust of parliament, and therefore put in the position of making their debating debut, in that kind of forum, on *Question Time*, the situation was rather unfair on them, and they were put into the limelight in a way that was hard to handle. In that same article, Maggie Brown commented very wisely that 'the presence of female novices didn't stop us watching the programme during the '80s. Quite the reverse.' Just so. During the '80s there was a widely felt desire to watch women, to include women in debates, to see more women at the top one way or another. To some extent, however limited and however much she can be criticised for not adding to her effect, this was partly due to the presence of Margaret Thatcher as Prime Minister. We were, as a society, simply used to women – or a woman – being at the top, and however little she gave in to feminist arguments, however little she promoted other women, though she gradually relented towards the end of her time, she did make it all possible.

But as soon as John Major came to office, he had a Cabinet with not one single woman member. He offered Lynda Chalker the job of deputy leader of the party, a non-Cabinet post, and she turned it down. The most senior woman became the main political advisor, Sarah Hogg, a backroom job if ever there were one, however important.

There has been a curious turn of events in 1990. It has become acceptable to say, as in the '80s it was not, that the campaigns to have women in senior positions are degrading, somehow unfair and specious and special pleading of an unnecessary variety. After all, goes the argument, women have got to the top. We have just had Mrs Thatcher. There's the Queen, God bless her, and there are all those female millionaires, like Anita Roddick, Jennifer d'Abo, and, though short-lived, Sophie Mirman of Sock Shop fame and. . .

The truth of the matter is that there has been little change, but that the mood is less optimistic about women's advancement than it once was. All the indicators show little progress in women's pay and women's achievement at the very top. Add to that the newish phenomenon manifested by a number of singularly successful middle-class, middle-aged women who hitherto have seemed to combine the roles of cherishing husband and children, whilst retaining career and glamour, public recognition and private calm of mind. Most of them have achieved much of this with the help of a great number of other women, and, to some extent at least, men, especially their husbands. And they have not been short of money, for if they had been, it would simply have been impossible. But they were the new role models, the women pointed out by mothers to daughters as the ones who managed to do it all, and do it with style. They were the women who looked, during the '70s, as if they read Shirley Conran's *Superwoman* every night before dropping off to sleep. They were the women for whom Posy Simmonds drew her inimitable cartoon (shown over the page) of the huffing and puffing superwoman rushing from office to supermarket to kitchen to nursery to hearth and home into sexy underwear to play the strumpet in bed, and all the time she's longing just to go to sleep. . .

What has happened to many of these women, though by no means all, is that they have given up their careers, at around forty. They have not given up to do nothing, but they have decided to stay at home in order to write novels, particularly, if they can manage it, bodice-ripper type novels. It is a type of life they can fit in with children whose demands get greater in time terms as they get older, and busy and successful husbands who need them at their side. It is a rarefied breed, this, but enough other women who can possibly manage it are also changing the pace and pattern of their life and looking somewhat less breathless as a result.

Of my friends, ten have made this type of move in the past three years, and many more have said they would like to. It is a

phenomenon clearly restricted to a particular class, and to a group of women whose husbands are earning very well, or who have themselves made enough money for actual regular income not to be an issue. Admittedly, in global terms this would hardly count as a blip. But in terms of the group that they are, the bright-eyed, bushy-tailed feminists of the late '60s and '70s, convinced it was possible and desirable to do it all, positive that fulfilment at home and in the workplace was the right of every intelligent woman, women whose contribution to the thinking of the less radical, generally respected women's movement has been so great, this is a remarkable phenomenon.

Nor are they unhappy. They are doing what the women novelists between the two world wars, beautifully described by Nicola Beauman in her *A Very Great Profession*, did so effectively, writing their novels on a corner of the dining-room table between lunch and tea, in amongst dealing with the domestic niceties of life, the maids and the cook and the menus and the callers. It was a life hilariously depicted by E.M. Delafield in her *Diary of a Provincial Lady*, and it would appear to have been a life that disappeared with the servant problem so clearly shown as having been a major factor in that existence. And yet, though servants are no longer part of the picture, the same domestic juggling exists, the two houses and the three children at schools which never have the same half-terms or holidays, the social round and the school exams and the security system and the cars that need servicing and the husband's clothes that need to go to the cleaner's and all the thank-you letters to be written. Not to mention the new servant problem, though we would never call it that, of nannies and housekeepers, the domestic support of women helping other women, with all the attendant worries about exploitation. These are issues which take up huge amounts of time, and sometimes, looking at the wreckage of a week when the nanny was ill or the housekeeper on holiday, women sit down and weep and wonder whether it was all worthwhile.

Those things have not changed; only the manner of dealing with them has changed, and even that not as much as we like to think. And for many women, of middle age and middle class, it is a question either of dispensing with the social niceties of life in order to keep up with the career, or simply putting down the folder and the briefcase in exhaustion and admitting to having had enough. It may, of course, even be the case that some men would have liked to do much the same, but it is still not really socially acceptable for a man to give up his career, even though he may have other things he wants to do, even though he too may see his role as more and more involved with the family.

The 'Superwoman' cult of the Shirley Conran book and attitude needs to be examined closely. If the family is to be retained, the assumption that women are going to do it all, be brilliant cooks and wonderful lovers, superb mothers and high-powered executives, has to go. The idea that there is sharing and new arrangements in nanny-sharing or child-minding, the idea that the state has a responsibility towards children, the idea that domestic chores are perfectly able to be performed by people of either sex and by children, all need to be put into the equation. Yet all studies of housework show that women still do 90% of it. All studies of family structure suggest that the new man, who may change the nappies and push the buggy, leaves the organisation of domestic affairs to his wife or lover. Nigella Lawson has, in a number of articles, made the point powerfully that men who are performing child-managing duties always view themselves with a certain amount of pride, and she has never put it better than in her account of a wedding she went to: 'It was the father who slung the baby over his arm and walked briskly towards the vestry. . . . I admire these men their low cunning. Not for one minute do I think that this high level of attentiveness to domestic duty is matched at home. It was carried out with too much panache, too much good humour and too self-conscious a rueful look-at-me shrug for it to convince as unremark-able, quotidian behaviour.'[1]

Children are still a woman's domain. Childcare provision is still pie in the sky in 1990 despite skill shortages in the workplace. In the Equal Opportunities Commission's Annual Report for 1990, they argued that 'good quality, affordable and accessible childcare is vital for the welfare of families in order to enable parents to participate in employment and public life. . . . In England and Scotland, there were day nursery places available for 2% of the estimated population of under-fives in 1988 and in Wales for less than 1%.'[2] Add to that the load of cooking and cleaning and ironing – though shopping, as one looks round supermarkets at weekends and in the late evening, is more shared than it was.

It is the personal burden of taking on the caring, and doing it all, that has made so many of my women friends give up their careers for new ones, or lesser ones, at or around forty. They talk of exhaustion, but look serene once again, having decided to take the plunge and being able to afford it. But what is this exhaustion these women all describe? Is it simply that they have less stamina than they did in their twenties, or that their children are emotionally more demanding than they were as babies, when nannies could cope entirely? Or is it that their husbands, delicious new men in the '70s, turned into the more conventional variety in the '80s, often under the enormous pressures they themselves suffered in their jobs? Or did we ask too much in assuming we could do it all, unless we were women of abnormal strength and energy, or superhuman organisational powers, or with children and spouses of quite remarkable helpfulness and supportiveness?

Why was it that so few men elected to share childcare by staying at home a couple of days a week and working from home? The journalists could have done it, the architects, some of the computer buffs, and though some did a bit, the pattern was always the same, that the women ended up doing the majority of it, and getting less sleep, or reading fewer novels, or simply doing everything at such a speed that there was less pleasure in it.

The answers to these questions are by no means clear, yet it is to these women, exhausted as they are, and content in their semi-retirement as they are, that this book is dedicated. For they are part of the paradox. They are not miserable – far from it. They are not poor, or unhappy, or unfulfilled. But they are doing things very different from what they set out to do, and they may or may not be doing them successfully. What is clear is that for some reason, as yet not wholly explained, they were fed up in their original careers, and felt the pressure was too great. Now the pressure is off, and they are blossoming.

To see this is to see the old-fashioned picture of the young matron, mother of three, contentedly surveying her growing flock of children around her and supporting them and her husband and making sure that she is always there when she is needed. It is a gloriously old-fashioned picture, of domesticity almost overblown, and of a quiet, less public life. And to some extent that is what these women have chosen, though the novelists amongst them hope for Sally Beauman-like success from writing on the kitchen table, just as I am doing now. Yet few of them would quite recognise themselves in that domestic picture. For they see themselves as more exhausted by the struggle against a career system that was often ungenerous, as having failed to obtain the promotion they should have got because they were female, a manifestation of the glass ceiling so many have come to hit. They see themselves as retired from their careers for only a few short years, whilst their children grow up from ten to twenty, yet they admit privately that they know that having been out for five or ten years, as younger women have found to their cost, it is remarkably difficult to get back in again.

The chances are that they will not go back into full-time employment again. If the novels do not work, and obviously for some of these already very successful women they will, then they will go into the voluntary sector in some way, injecting new blood and new life into a world where all too few new people are devoting their time before retirement. They will be much more like their mothers and their grandmothers than they had ever begun to think, and their picture of what life would be like, with job and children and houses and husband and staff around to help with the worst of the chores, will turn out to have been very difficult to maintain.

But many of them are happier than I have seen them for years. A load has been taken off their shoulders. They are able to function again, because they no longer feel that aching sense in the pit of the stomach of just about having managed to do everything on the list (which was made during a meeting, as the chairman spoke rather dully and the mind went: 'Half a pint of cream, eggs, and we desperately need yoghurt for the packed lunches. . .'), but only by dint of having done most of it rather badly. That sense of skating along on the surface, never quite devoting enough attention to the issues as they came up, has gone. They can listen to their children's conversations with ease now, and they can also make sure all the ingredients are there for the packed lunches, even if they do not do the shopping themselves.

But if they are becoming like their mothers and their grandmothers, what has the women's movement really done to affect their lives in any important way? What transformation has it wrought, that makes most of them, one way or another, describe themselves as feminists, and still think of Germaine Greer, Kate Millett and Betty Friedan, as their heroines, let alone the Pankhursts and Josephine Butler and the women of the early women's movement who got us the vote and education and the right to proper medical care, and stopped the persecution of prostitutes?

In terms of their lifestyles, the truth must be said to be very little, other than in allowing them distinguished careers up to this point. But in expectations and in the sense of justice and fair play, the transformation has been enormous. For they do believe women have a right to work, if they want to. They do not believe, though they have largely taken it upon themselves to carry it out, that women are necessarily naturally the carers in the family, and that children necessarily need their mothers more than their fathers. They believe passionately in education for girls and in opportunities for women, and they campaign to get those opportunities wherever they can. They also believe in some separatist things for women, which their mothers might have been part of but would not have seen in that way, such as networking clubs for women, in an old girls' network, in women's colleges, and perhaps most significant of all, in girls' schools.

But they also see the women's movement as having gone badly wrong in its insistence on the fight for equality in the workplace without recognising the role women play, and want to play, in families. It is in this area that the most interesting, if depressing, discussions have taken place. For just as women who were deeply involved in some of the women's groups in the '70s were shocked by the way their 'sisters' treated them as if they did not exist, or were not proper feminists, when they made it clear that they were heterosexual, and did not themselves, personally, wish to be political lesbians or do without men, so these women, talking to feminist 'sisters' whom they had always regarded as fighters for the same causes, the workplace nurseries and crèches, suddenly found themselves being treated as non-people because they had decided to stop work and to take care of their families. For many of the women they had been working with, this was simply not a legitimate option. Once on the treadmill, once launched on the ladder, one owed it to oneself and to other women to stay around and become as senior as possible, in order to promote other women. Whether that made one happy or not, whether it seemed worth it personally or not, was considered entirely irrelevant.

To what extent this was a feature of age is not clear. One of the women concerned had just spent a horrific year chasing round from one hospital to another, visiting both elderly parents who had had, between them, a coronary artery bypass graft, a stroke, breast cancer, a hip replacement and a second hip replacement. She also took entire responsibility for two children whilst her husband was away on a three-month business trip, with only one visit home in the time; and she was filming on location, partly overseas. She pointed out that the combination of parents needing support and succour along with children not having reached independence did make it all the harder, and that younger women often did not quite have that problem.

True though that is, the majority of women who have a heavy load with elderly parents are those in their fifties rather than their forties, although having children later in life has meant that some of these dual dependencies also come upon women in their forties whose mothers had their children relatively late, too, as part of the post-war baby boom.

But all this has become much more serious, as most of the women concerned make clear, as NHS provision has become even more cursory and the desire to discharge patients from hospital at the earliest possible moment has grown. The result is that children are finding themselves caring for parents who would have gone to convalesce somewhere, or simply stayed in the ward a little longer, and these elderly parents really need full-time care, rather than a comforting hand on the brow or hand under the elbow whilst they struggle to walk after the hip replacement. Women who have to spend any significant amount of time caring for elderly parents or handicapped siblings are finding that it is more of a full-time job than they had anticipated, whether or not they can afford to get help.

These are just some of the reasons why women in their late thirties and early forties are apparently saying that they cannot cope, or do not want to cope, any more with all the balls tossed into the air at once, and why they are retreating into a more domestic life, writing, thinking, caring and, increasingly, going into the voluntary sector, sitting on committees and serving on the magistrates' bench. It is an old-fashioned picture, perhaps, but one that the women's movement did not anticipate. It failed to get to the core of most women's lives, their families, and see that that is where, one way or another, most women want to be based, even though they want to see better childcare outside the family, better parent care outside the family, better family support systems, and more freedom of choice.

The women's movement in Britain took far too long to realise that in other countries in the European Community, the situation for women was very different, that childcare was freely available, for instance, in France, that equal pay legislation had had a profound effect in Italy, that maternity provisions were better in Holland, and, outside the community, in Sweden, all the childcare provisions were infinitely superior, making a woman's life, in organisational terms, a comparative picnic.

Sylvia Ann Hewlett recorded these differences with wit and bitterness in equal measure in her *A Lesser Life*, pointing out that the country with the most vocal women's movement, the USA, had in fact by far the worst provisions for women and children, and that Europe – and Sweden in particular – were streets ahead. The problem lies, in her view, in a failure to realise that women's lives are for the most part rooted in heterosexuality, and that ignoring men is impossible; that women do have children, and provision has to be made for them; and that women, whatever the justice of the situation, do care for their elderly relatives, and that is part of their lives, a part it will take major social changes to alter.

Campaigning for change in these matters in the UK, to make us more like France or Sweden, is further complicated by the women's rights issues, insofar as they were taken up at all, being taken up largely by the left in British politics. Ironically, this also led to massive opposition to entry into the European Community, a position wholly opposed to the interests of women, since the EC had had equal pay provisions from its earliest days, as well as a far better record on childcare and maternity provision and part-time workers' benefits and arrangements. But because 'women's issues' were seen to be the stuff of the left, they were allied with Labour politics, and with Labour's implacable opposition to the European Community.

It took some considerable courage on the part of some of the 1960s and 1970s feminists to admit they had been wrong about Europe. It took them even longer to realise that often it was not Labour governments that acted in the best interests of women, and that much of the stuff of women's issues was not party politics at all but the gender politics the feminist analysis had said it was in the first place. Thus one could have Tory women who were just as good solid feminists as Labour ones, and there was a perfectly good critique of Labour's mid-1980s proposal for a Ministry for Women's Affairs which argued that having a special ministry meant that women's issues could come off everyone else's desks and areas of concern, and that therefore women's issues would be severely sidelined.

This sense that these issues were cross-party led to the setting up of the 300 Group by Lesley Abdela at the end of the 1970s, and to a concerted campaign to keep the issue of equal representation of women in politics at the forefront of the public mind. It was very successful at first, and it was largely due to its efforts that the early SDP insisted on having at least one women on every short list for a parliamentary constituency, as well as reserving four nationally elected places on its national committee for women, something which no other party, before or since, had done with such conviction.

As well as that, there were campaigns to get women into public life, on to commissions and boards, to be school governors and magistrates, and to be present loud and clear wherever women of influence could be used. They could exert pressure in the area of women's opportunities, as well as their other interests. Yet

although the number of women selected as parliamentary candi-
dates has almost tripled over the last twenty-seven years (5.1% to
14.2%), it has not resulted in a proportional increase in the number
of women elected. (After the 1964 election, 4.6% of MPs were
women; after the 1987 election the figure was 6.3%.) The Women
into Public Life Campaign, run jointly by the 300 Group and the
Fawcett Society, was remarkably successful in the late 1980s in
drawing to the attention of the Public Appointments Unit the
numbers of very able and willing women who were prepared to
take on public appointments if they were only given the chance, and
certainly the evidence is beginning to suggest that more women are
being appointed, particularly in areas other than the south east of
England. Yet many women will be taking on these roles without
having what they would hitherto have regarded as 'proper' jobs,
because force of circumstances has restricted them to trying to look
after parents and children, and they found they simply could not
manage it all.

For the nurturing side of women is very strong, which is not to
say that no men have it or that all women do. But enough women
have a strong urge to care for their babies physically, and ultimately
for their elderly relatives too, for it to be clear that it is part of how
women see themselves, irrespective of whether it is innate. One of
the major faults of the women's movement of the late 1960s and
1970s was that it tended to see women as individuals only, or in
sisterhood, and somehow removed them from families, from being
daughters, wives, girlfriends, sisters and mothers. The reasons for
that were not hard to find – one of the most oppressive factors in
women's existence hitherto had been their inability to be seen as
individuals in their own right, but always as someone else's sister,
mother or daughter, or, perhaps most significantly, wife. That lack
of individuality was undoubtedly damaging, and tended to hinder
women's own self-fulfilment and prevent the realisation of long-
held ambitions. At the same time, to dissociate women from their
families, any more than to dissociate men, was to deny them a large
part of what they were, and then to say to them that they should
have nothing to do with men, when their sexual desires, and often
their protective instincts, were turned naturally towards them, was
simply to alienate many women who were at heart profoundly
sympathetic to many of the aims of the women's movement.

The answers lie for many individuals in doing what they have done: stopping, and solving their problems by retiring for a while and becoming the carers and cherishers they want to be, however temporarily. But though that may be possible, and indeed desirable, for the few, it cannot be the answer for the majority. Most women cannot afford to stop, because their income is vital to their families. For most women, the answer lies once again in looking at family structures and at who contributes what, and discussing those issues with all family members in the light of the insights into oppression and exploitation of women's work and women's status which the women's movement has given a whole generation, whilst campaigning at the same time for proper provision for community care.

At a time when more women are needed in the workplace because of demographic changes, and government has been trying to encourage middle-aged women back to work, it cannot be sensible to have more and more middle-aged women cooped up at home, providing care in the community, because there is nothing else, for their own elderly and confused; in isolation, unable to get out and enter the job market. Here is an area for real campaigning. If government and employers want women in the workplace on the one hand, but make pretty little provision for children and the elderly, on the other, the situation is clearly inconsistent, not to mention silly. It is that sort of inconsistency, that kind of double-think, which has to be pointed out time and again to policy makers, be they governmental or in the private sector, and it is solving those issues, to provide flexibility and choice for women and their families, that will really transform women's lives.

14
The Joy of
Female Friendship

He [Bernard Shaw] hasn't an enemy in the world, and none of
his friends like him.

Oscar Wilde

WATCHING LITTLE GIRLS with their series of 'best' friends, and
knowing at the back of one's mind that today's enemy is tomorrow's best friend, is a demonstration of the power of female
friendship at a very young age. Little boys tend not to have such
close friendships, but to rush about in gangs, fighting, playing,
learning to share, taking part in team games and burning off an
apparently limitless supply of energy, needing almost literal
refuelling from time to time.

I generalise, yet there is enough truth in it, from observation of
children everywhere, from seeing children in playgrounds at mixed
schools and in single-sex ones, for me to say that there is something
there, that for girls the close, intense, gossipy, intimate relationships are important while for boys they are almost embarrassing,
and the friends they do make are likely, for most of their years at
school, to be fighting companions, sporting companions, games
players and co-explorers, rather than listeners to inner thoughts,
intimate secrets and the affairs of the heart.

All this continues into adult life, where men continue to have the
'boys' they go out drinking with and the 'muckers' (shades of rolling
in the mud at an early age) they still play a bit of rugby with – or at
least go and watch the match with. There are male colleagues with

whom professional issues can be discussed, and there are bar-room friends who will listen to jokes and dirty stories, whilst the women, if there are women there, will tend to stay quiet, hanging attractively on the man's arm, or at least on his every word. Male friendships with men are often very strong, and last over a lifetime. But they lack intimacy. Men are too afraid of showing their emotions naked to another man, though occasionally they will do so to a woman who is not a wife or a lover, but who can be – with immense difficulties – the kind of friend one might have thought a life-long male friend ought to be.

Women are very different, and their friendships, from childhood, matter passionately. There is something of the sexual about many female friendships, though the waters have been muddied in that regard with the radical feminist espousal of lesbianism as a political force, so that those women who are primarily heterosexual feel something akin to fear about the element of sexuality in their friendships for each other. But women do tend to want to be in the company of other women they find attractive, and curious phenomena, such as the 'herd-instinct' that leads to all the women in an all-female institution menstruating at the same time, suggest a close physical bond between women. Indeed, women friends do kiss and hug. There is physical contact where there is no sexual relationship, but much of that, in my adult life, has come about as a result of one very positive element in the women's movement, the exaltation of female friendship.

Even those women who have no real idea that there is a strong strand in the feminist philosophy about female friendship, about the support women can find in and from each other, about the shared caring, about the use of 'women's refuges' where a physical haven is given to women who are being battered, find themselves increasingly close to other women in a way that goes deeper than what their mothers and grandmothers allowed in their lives, at least after they were married. This may be because we are more outspoken and agonise more about the different roles that we play. It may also be the influence upon us of the whole psychotherapeutic movement, with its emphasis on not suppressing emotions, on pouring out feelings, a tendency women have always had, but now feel is respectable.

This is a great benefit that the women's movement has brought about. For women are undoubtedly enriched by this sense of the support of other women, and they have tended to understand the value of the reduction of isolation, the sharing of experiences, even when nothing else in the women's movement has begun to touch them. An excellent example is the growth of voluntary organisations, such as NEWPIN, a befriending organisation working primarily in south-east London, which has as its *raison d'être* the ending of the isolation of women, often women with small children, living in tower blocks. The remarkable thing about NEWPIN and others like it is that they genuinely operate as self-help groups, with professional, paid organisers maybe, but with the befrienders having originally been the befriended, and with the chain working on and on, bringing friendship and support and succour to countless women in an area. They have changed the social patterns not only of women isolated at home but also of men, if they have menfolk, going out and coming back home expectant, ready for food and sex and entertainment, to less isolated women, who now go out themselves and who function better in their accommodation and with their children and often with their menfolk too.

A large part of the thinking behind this is the fruit of the women's movement, with its late '70s and early '80s stress on consciousness-raising for feminism of the middle classes, on the whole, but its extension into extolling the virtues of female friends, female supporters and networking in all sectors of society. And although the networking and support works effectively and enrichingly for middle-class women, it probably makes even more difference in deprived areas and amongst economically deprived women. Although on the whole the women's movement has done very little seriously to tackle the problems of the very poorest women in our society and their children, this facet of setting up groups of women to support and help other women is probably the single most valuable contribution to the lives of those least able to campaign for themselves.

But female friends can bring their problems too, as Fay Weldon illustrated most entertainingly, and horribly vividly, in her novel of that title. There was affection and love and fun and dependence in *Female Friends*, but there was also fear and jealousy and sexual hostility. Women have always been friends with each other, historically, but in the first part of this century particularly, really intimate matters, such as sex and love and ambitions and disappointments, were not thought of as the matter for discussion with one's female friends, but only, if at all, with one's husband.

That is one view that many women in their seventies and eighties express, and it is largely a middle-class view of the world. Working-class women of the same vintage seem often to have thought and talked differently, spending perhaps more time in intimate talk and less in bridge-playing than their middle-class contemporaries, and they talked more about sex, personal matters, and to some extent contraception, than the others. That is well recorded in Angela Holdsworth's *Out of the Dolls' House*, with its magnificent cameo portraits of older women talking of their lives before the Second World War: 'Daisy Noakes' husband-to-be George "never had any thoughts of us sleeping together or getting together before we married. Never entered his mind. He never took very many advances to me at all." Margaret Wheeler tells the awful story of a friend she found in tears one day: "She'd had to ask her husband for sixpence for a packet of sanitary towels and she said she felt very humiliated and he'd ticked her off before because she'd spent all her twenty-five bob. . . ."'

Less intimate details are revealed in Janet Ford and Ruth Sinclair's *Sixty Years On*, a series of interviews with older women, talking about their experiences, and their conversations, throughout their lives, as they reflect on old age. Here is one woman, Maggie, on the subject of a husband she cannot stand:

> You know, I did realise my situation years ago, but you see, if I'd have left him, what was the chance of getting a roof over my head, no income and disabled? And there didn't seem anything I could do in between staying as I was and the very drastic action of going. That's why we've never had a row – we haven't, but that's because I've always let him have his way. I've been too easy, but because I've had no chance of being otherwise. . . .

Or Miss Stewart on the subject of missed opportunities, as she warns the young girls up the road not to abandon their education in order to get married with no skills: 'I don't think a girl can have too much education, any more than a boy. Mind you, I think girls should go in more for the sciences and that than they do. I think it's a good thing because that's the thing of the future for both boys and girls,' having previously said about not being a teacher: 'Well, I've been very upset about it in after years, but at the time it didn't bother me because we'd just had a piano and I was the one picked to take lessons for it. That's what my parents said to the school, even though the teacher said I could still have taken that on with my school work. . . .'

These were women confiding to later interviewers some of what they had confided to friends, perhaps, many years earlier. But from the late 1960s on, as the women's movement's philosophy of encouraging women to confide in each other began to take hold, women of every class and background began to talk. They talked to each other. Some of them also became professional talkers and listeners, and the growth of the 'counselling' movement, as it grew out of psychotherapy, may be tied in to the mushrooming of women confiding in each other. There was positive pleasure to be found in spending an evening with a group of women friends, and even a sense of joy when husbands were away, or busy, and the wives could go out with their women friends, or have a group of women friends to supper. It was no longer making the best of a bad job, having no man to go out with. Fay Weldon puts it very succinctly, quoted by Angela Neustatter in her *Hyenas in Petticoats*: 'For so long there was the sense of failure if you were in a room with a group of women; if Saturday night was spent with a girlfriend. Now the status of one's women friends is so much greater. It is true of me and I know it to be of others. We are nourished by our women friends.'

We are nourished by them and we learn from them. In the dedication to her volume of autobiography, *Before I Go*, Mary Stott, great feminist and editor of the *Guardian* women's page for thirteen years, lists the names of scores of women she had talked to and thought about and with and consulted and written to and read. Gradually more and more women see the work they produce, though essentially theirs, as the product of an interrelationship with other women, and the stuff of conversation, rather than necessarily the food of personal, isolated thought. There is less sitting in an attic, producing the great work, about many books written by women. In their novels, they use the stuff of their everyday lives, hence the growth, and success of, the domestic novel between the wars; and in their non-fiction, they do their research in books, but often find that it is their interaction with other women that makes the ideas stick and their words live. Four of the women I talked to, of whom three had been writing books on what the women's movement had done for them, made that point in very similar ways, because ideas flourish as a result of the conversations we have all been having with our women friends and acquaintances.

This is a direct result of the women's movement, though it predates the modern women's movement, as the phenomenon of the domestic novels makes clear. But the modern women's movement has encouraged it, and women now talk about important things, rather than about minutiae, and they are braver in revealing their inner feelings, and expressing their doubts, than they used to be.

Women whose marriages have broken down or who have been widowed or seriously ill, all add to that point. It is their women friends who have been important, and if they had neglected them – and many of them, particularly the older ones, still caught up in trying to live their husbands' lives to the full, had become distant from them – they regretted it, but found other women generous, willing to become close quite quickly, willing to support and to be warm and caring.

Time and again they have argued that women have been more generous in their relationships than men, and those with good, close relationships with husbands have nevertheless argued that their menfolk simply do not understand quite a lot of what they are saying, particularly about ambitions unfulfilled and expectations never realised. It has been women friends to whom they have been able to talk about those secret fears and doubts, and it has also been women friends who have carried them through the guilt and the grief of bereavement or divorce, and the pain of separation, as well as always being willing to talk about the affairs of the heart, lovers and men friends and women friends, even at a stage in life when such issues are supposed to be no more.

One woman apologised for describing some of the conversations and confessions she had with her women friends as being the stuff of a teenage affair, and into that statement there exploded a realisation on both of our parts that that is how affairs of the heart in older women are viewed – not sensible, not practical, not middle-aged; above all self-indulgent at a time of life when self-indulgence for women should be a thing of the past.

The same would not be felt of men. Men are constantly caricatured as little boys. Women, in talking about them, tend not to describe them as 'boys' except when they are going out with 'the boys', but they indulge them, along the lines of 'He does love his Porsche/bicycle/pint/pretty secretary. . . .' It is not a matter for criticism, any more than on the whole, except for a minority of vocal feminists, the soft porn magazines on sale at the average newsagent are thought to be other than an indulgence for men. The talk is of 'letting him have his little treat', where women of the same age are not expected to have their little treats (though it is hard to see what the equivalent might be) or to be indulged, or indulge themselves, in that way.

Unless, of course, they are the women who continue to play the little girl, who have learned nothing from the critique of male–female relationships that the women's movement has made. These are the women, however well educated, who play the part of the indulged, spoiled mistress even when they have become the wife, who fulfil all those expectations of 'an intelligent woman knows when to keep quiet and pretend that she cannot think', who wear pretty clothes and are beautifully made up, and flutter their eyelashes and twitter, so that their men can protect them and feel like great wild animals, fighting off attackers and nursing their nest at home.

That is still a relatively common phenomenon, but it is diminishing, partly because women are out in the workplace for economic reasons, partly because women have changed as a result of education and as a result of the women's movement, and many no longer have any desire to play that kind of role, a factor which clearly makes the critics of the women's movement wild with rage.

Isabella Mackey and others of the Moral Rearmament school of thought, a growing force in modern Europe and particularly, with the rise of fundamentalism in religion, in the United States, would argue that 'feminism is responsible for the rising divorce rate, abortion, child-molesting and also rape.'[1] She argued that 'somebody has to talk and somebody has to listen. Someone has to decide and someone has to give way. Men can't lose face – they find it difficult to admit mistakes even to themselves. If only women, and men too, would accept these different and complementary sex roles, male/female relations would be full of romance, chivalry, harmony and love.' The little girl would sit at home and listen to his every word and say: 'Yes, dear, no dear, three bags full, dear,' and all would be well.

That view has had precious little support. Much more damaging, although still very minor, has been the phenomenon of the PFW, the Post Feminist Woman, invented by the *Mail on Sunday* and criticised by Brenda Polan in *Cosmopolitan* in 1988: 'Post Feminist Woman clinches the deal and cooks *cordon bleu*. She flies first class and builds her own bookshelves. She pays the restaurant bill with her gold Amex card and she knits up Kaffe Fassett sweaters for her lover. She is hell in the office and heaven in bed. She doesn't exist.'

The main thrust of this is the idea that women do not need the women's movement at all – they can do it all on their own, and with the help of their lovers, and that somehow the support and help given to other women by women is a dangerous phenomenon that ought to be stopped.

For networking for women – operating an old girls' network as men do for each other, meeting for interest and advancement – is growing. It is an important phenomenon in the City, in the media, in medicine, in religion, in the law and in academe. By no means all women in any of these professional areas take part, but a significant number do, so that the Women in Media group, the Medical Women's Federation, the Financial Exchange and City Women's Network are all groups which give women strength from each other, which enable them to feel that there is a shared experience, and which allows them to put other women forward for jobs and positions. The immediate cry from men, including the most liberated and egalitarian, is that this is 'positive discrimination', or even unfair pandering to preferences, or prejudice. Yet men asked to put names forward for jobs and positions on public bodies do not usually cite an equal number of men and women, nor do they instantly think that it is important to have women on the boards of public companies, or on every government body, or in every high-flying position. Men have consistently put each other forward for jobs 'for the boys', and the resentment caused by a few women following that pattern and arguing for 'jobs for the girls' is quite out of proportion to the effect such a campaign can have.

Indeed, as one of the proponents of jobs for the girls, I am appalled at the numbers of times, when being introduced on some radio or television show, I am quoted as saying in my entry in *Who's Who* that one of my interests is 'setting up the old girls' network'. It is as if that is laughable, unserious, and yet there are few interests I have which I take more seriously, because I believe (as a result, no doubt, of the thinking of the women's movement, added on to my natural inclination to value women friends), that women have to support women to reach the top in a man's world. Until men willingly and freely move over and make space for equal numbers of women, campaigning, of the most polite and careful and civilised kind, to get women into top jobs or even more senior jobs and positions is a vital component of the continuing force of the women's movement, and something, some part, of what relationships between women, friendships and support systems are about.

There have been many earlier proponents of this thinking. Classic amongst them is Mary Stott, a doughty campaigner whose views about the women's movement are well recorded in her autobiography and in the pages of the *Guardian*. Then there is Barbara Hosking, vice-chair of the National Council for Voluntary Organisations and a great television senior manager, quiet in the way she works, but who has consistently put forward and encouraged other women, who knows that it is possible to get women into top positions by careful working and gentle persuasion, and who also knows that there are many men who share her concerns about women not being given sufficiently senior positions, and whom she asks to help. So does Katharine Whitehorn, *Observer* columnist, and so does Heather Brigstocke, ex-High Mistress of St Paul's School for Girls and now a peeress and director of Times Newspapers, and Mary Baker, director of Thames Television, and so on and so on. There is a significant group of older, more senior women, who have been doing it for years and whose networking has allowed younger women in. They in their turn have to do the same, to encourage younger women to come forward, to help them and to get them to do the same in due course, using their own ambition to help others reach the top.

It is vital that that task is carried out by women who believe that men can be, and often are, sympathetic to the cause of women's promotion. The classical radical feminist view, which is also a key factor in the exaltation of female friendship, is that men are the enemy and therefore all men are enemies. Those women think that the attempt to get on in a man's world is doomed to failure, that it is somehow selling out even to try, and that those women who try and persuade men to move up and make room are deluding themselves – and living a comfortable life in the process – because there simply is not a cat's chance in hell that men will be prepared to allow women any space at all, and that they would rather see women back in the home 'where they belong'.

This is one of the radical feminist views that is still, though less frequently, expressed amongst groups of women friends, and it is here, where women's friendships have become strong and supportive, that some of the keenest argument takes place. Many women reject the anti-men stand totally, but those women who have divorced and lived alone successfully for some years, whose experiences of marriage were particularly unhappy and debilitating, share something of the revolutionary approach. Though they laugh at what men put them through, or at what one particular man put them through, they tend now to believe in assertiveness training for women, in putting women first and in denying those men who have a different approach to women's issues any genuine belief in feminist at all.

Over the last ten years, this has caused immense problems amongst groups of women friends and colleagues. In the early days of the women's movement, it was possible, indeed essential, to argue that there must never be any criticism of what one group of women did by any other group of women. 'Sisterhood is powerful.' But it was only thought to be powerful if there were no rows.

This led to absurd situations, particularly as in the earlier, radical days there were arguments about all sorts of things, like whether there should be a new name for 'manholes', such as 'personholes', and whether people whose surnames ended in '-man' should change them, for common usage purposes, to '-person'. We knew the Whitepersons and the Persons (hitherto the Manns) and the Snowpeople, all of which seems absurd now, but was a very powerful facet of thinking in the '70s and one was not allowed to criticise it. In women's groups, one had to be very careful about what one said, or other women would say: 'But you don't really consider yourself a feminist, do you. . . ?' There was dogma and creed, rather as in religious faith or on the revolutionary or doctrinaire side of a political party. And relationships between women suffered when they did disagree, quite legitimately, because the fact of being able to disagree over a particular subject was seen as evidence of not being quite up to the mark, not somehow a 'true' feminist.

In 1977, it crystallised with Sheila Jeffreys speaking at the national conference of the Women's Liberation Movement against the liberal takeover of the movement itself. She argued that men were always the enemy, that they asserted their power over women by sex and violence and brute power. She called for 'a feminist revolution, not small tinkerings with the system, not small changes in sex roles, not just trying to make men clean the toilet, but actually really changing the system, pulling the plug out from male power over women.'[2]

Many women, seeing and hearing such talk, felt disturbed and frightened. This was not what they had had in mind at all. But most of that has now disappeared, partly because the revolutionary days of much of the feminist fervour are over, not because it failed, but because revolutionary fervour is hard to maintain twenty-five years on. But there is still a tendency to be very critical of, and very rude about, women who come forward with a wholly different view, or who change their minds. There has, for instance, been enormous criticism of Betty Friedan, for which I am partly to blame myself, for her views in her book *The Second Stage*, in which she advocated ending the war of the sexes, and instead striving together to build a better, safer world. She felt that the feminist mystique had replaced the feminine mystique, and she saw women damaged by everything they were trying to do. In many ways she was right, though she undervalued the extent to which economic oppression of women, and lack of national policy consideration on childcare, still affected women quite dreadfully, and she failed to realise that there are strong policy implications for women in the whole area of providing care for children, the sick, the handicapped and the elderly. Yet her message was to think again, to move on, and the criticism she received was vitriolic, unpleasant and unworthy, almost as if the principle of free speech did not apply where women's issues were concerned.

That same critical tone has continued to be used, levelled at those who have left their careers at forty-something and gone into the home to run it and to look after aged parents. Some women see this as a cop-out, others see it as a threat. The good opinion of other women has become an enormously important factor in many women's lives, often privately mattering to them a great deal more than men's opinion, unless that man is their husband or lover, brother or father. That is because of the high status women have put upon their friendships with other women, and the degree to which personal trust amongst women has grown over the last twenty years. It has been an almost unalloyed pleasure, this discovery of the value of women's friendships, and the way those friendships have withstood living in different countries, living different lives, being subject to varying political and social patterns of thought. But there is a downside to it, which has yet to be dealt with. The first problem is this immense criticism and the vitriol flung at anyone who oversteps the party line, even though the party line is ill-defined and there is huge variation in opinion about all sorts of things. The second is neglecting friendships with men, so that heterosexual women, all too often, have their sexual relationships with men, but their friendships with women, and do not seek support and succour and love – without sex – from men.

It is only in the last thirty years that it has been possible for women in the UK, with its tradition of single-sex education or segregation of the sexes even in mixed classes, to have friendships with men without sexual relationships developing, and the extent to which one can argue that there is never a sexual frisson there at all is likely to be fairly limited. Yet one thing the sexual revolution of the '60s did achieve, along with quite a lot of damage, was the ability to be open about sexual matters, and the chance, towards the end of the '60s and the beginning of the '70s, to make close friendships with people of the opposite sex whom one might have liked, at some stage, to have a sexual relationship with, which for one reason or another was impossible or inappropriate.

For many women, those friendships really started at university, or in early working days. Girls still at school now seem to report the same phenomenon, however, where groups of girls and boys go around together and there is no overt sexual relationship other than between those where the deal has already been done, and they are faithful to one another.

Those friendships of university days, and beyond, those relationships with male colleagues when there were few female colleagues about, are difficult to cherish, particularly when the drive of the women's movement has been to exalt friendship with women at the expense of friendship with men. Yet we do not live in a wholly female environment, nor, with the exception of the lesbian separatists, would most of us want to. To deny ourselves friendships with men because we have achieved real friendships with women seems somehow to dehumanise the men, seeing them, as the radicals did, and some still do, always as the enemy. Yet there is enormous pleasure to be had from friendships with men. There is an element of flirtation, often, and there is a teasing that one rarely has with women, but there is also the sense, all too rare for men in friendships with other men, of the establishing of intimacy, of the sort that women have learned to establish with one another, and which they so enjoy.

The women's movement, in its prejudice against friendships with men for women, has made an unholy alliance with religious fundamentalists who believe that there is something immodest in close relationships between people of the opposite sex unless they are married to one another, and who on the whole tend not to regard women as equals with men. After all the effort to get religious thinkers, in some schools of thought at least, to regard women as equals, after all the efforts of the women's movement to campaign for the equality of women, how crazy it is for women to argue that friendships with men are demeaning, or fundamentally a sell-out, because one cannot trust men, but only women. And how sad for men if they are not to be allowed to have friendships with women who will regard them as equals but no more, who will not require sexual activity, virility and proving of potency, but who will provide that delicious intimacy, that trust, that ability to talk about the things most personal to oneself, about hopes and fears and doubts, they get so little in any of their other relationships.

When we consider Betty Friedan's second stage and its relevance to the '90s, is the second stage not going to lie in making these close relationships with men? How else will they be able to tell us how they feel about women, as well as about themselves, honestly, without the mocking and spurning that has taken place in the public arena? And how else can we provide for them a sense of what women are about, and afraid of, and want, in a shared journey towards human development, and an end to the battle of the sexes, in a certainty that equality is right and obvious, and in a shared attempt to achieve it?

Endpiece

THIS IS WITHOUT doubt a very personal picture. The book came about as the result of conversations with women friends and men friends. It was born of the conviction that radical feminism, with its insistence either that men are violent and cruel and that they desire dominance above all things or that men are essentially the same as women, is wrong. It arose out of observing the real issues that confront us all, changing family patterns, divorce, unprotected children, the handicapped, the elderly, and believing that women and men have to think about these issues jointly. And my view was sharpened by the certainty that there is a peculiarly British cruelty to children, arising out of a sense that children are a personal, family matter and not the future of the society. Within the equation as well was the sense that there are still huge injustices in the political, economic and employment fields, but that the way to deal with them is to argue politely, to take cases to court, to campaign and persuade, and to believe that fair-minded men will ultimately agree with us.

These caring and family matters are the women's issues of the '90s. They are different from the issues that gripped the attention of women in the '60s and '70s. They are less radically based. They combine the interests of the individual with the context in which she is set – her family, friends, colleagues, employment. But if women's organisations do not pick them up and run with them, if political parties across the spectrum do not see the rightness in the sorts of proposals put forward by the Equal Opportunities Commission for childcare provision, or do not recognise the extraordinary inequalities in public life so brilliantly pointed out by the Hansard Society, or the government does not implement the community care proposals straight away, if more is not done to ensure proper counselling and conciliation in divorce cases, if children are not to be helped to see their absent fathers, and if women are not to be supported in taking on the plethora of roles society now demands of them, then we will see women yet again confined to the home, overloaded with caring, unappreciated, simply expected to function. And they will all too frequently collapse with depression and exhaustion. And that will be in no-one's interests, within society as a whole.

Yet the radical feminists have failed to see this as the key issue in women's lives, because they have largely ignored those family and social responsibilities most women gladly take on. Most of us, whether male or female, heterosexual or homosexual, black or white, Muslim, Jewish or Christian, do not want to see ourselves apart from our families, totally atomised, individualistic. For most of us, relationships, across age barriers, gender boundaries and with members of our family and friends, are in the end what makes life worthwhile. And that means being prepared to do some of the caring, some of the cherishing. But not all. It is the sharing of caring, the responsibility of the state versus the individual family, the woman rather than the man, the parents for the children and the children for the parents, that needs examining, and it is that sharing that it so difficult to achieve.

A new agenda for women includes achieving self-fulfilment without sacrificing others in the family and circle of friends. It includes ensuring that there is state support and state provision of care, for children, the old, the sick and the frail. It includes persuading men that they too want to share the caring, and encouraging them to show the gentler sides of their natures. It includes drawing up a new social contract that leads to optimum fulfilment and least exhaustion for everyone. It means men being more generous to women, moving up and making a bit of space. And it means women being less angry, but more persuasive, in encouraging them to do so. But in the end the essential requirement lies in realising the complementariness of the sexes, that there are differences, and it is those differences, those different approaches, that often make life worth living, providing one sex does not dominate the other all the time.

References

(Publication details not given here can be found in the Bibliography which starts on page 209.)

Chapter 1
1. Mary Wollstonecraft: *A Vindication of the Rights of Women* (1792)

Chapter 2
1. Family Policy Studies Centre: *Lone Parent Families* (March 1991)

Chapter 3
1. In *Some Day My Prince Won't Come: More Stories for Young Feminists*, ed. Rosemary Stones (Piccadilly Press, London 1988)
2. Published in *The Madwoman's Underclothes*
3. *The Body and Society — Men, Women and Sexual Renunciation in Early Christianity*

Chapter 4
1. See Feldman: *Birth Control in Jewish Law*
2. In *A History of Women's Bodies*
3. Quoted by Shirley Green in *The Curious History of Contraception* (Ebury Press, London 1971)
4. Mary Midgley and Judith Hughes: *Women's Choices: Philosophical Problems Facing Feminism*
5. Midgley and Hughes: *op. cit.*
6. 12 March 1972, quoted in *The Madwoman's Underclothes*
7. Germaine Greer: *Sex and Destiny*
8. Malcolm Potts in Malcolm Potts and Peter Selman: *Society and Fertility* (London 1979), quoted by Germaine Greer in *Sex and Destiny*
9. Greer: *Sex and Destiny*
10. Greer: *op. cit.*
11. In *Reproductive Technologies: Gender, Motherhood and Medicine*, ed. Michelle Stanworth
12. Michelle Stanworth: *The Deconstruction of Motherhood* in *Reproductive Technologies*, quoting *Newsweek*, 11 August 1986
13. *op. cit.*

Chapter 5
1. Shorter: *op. cit.*
2. National Childbirth Trust: *Pregnancy and Parenthood*
3. Sheila Kitzinger: preface to *The Experience of Childbirth*
4. Published by the Lisa Sainsbury Foundation, 1987
5. Shorter: *op. cit.*
6. *op. cit.*
7. Shorter: *op. cit.*
8. Quoted in Shorter: *op. cit.*
9. Jane Donegan: *Women and Men Midwives: Medicine, Morality and Misogyny in Early America* (Greenwood, Westport 1978)
10. Ann Oakley: *The Captured Womb*
11. Social Services Committee: *Perinatal and Neonatal Mortality* (Second Report 1979–80, HMSO London)
12. Ann Oakley: *From Walking Wombs to Test-Tube Babies* in *Reproductive Technologies: Gender, Motherhood and Medicine*, ed. Michelle Stanworth, quoting Alice Stewart on the cancer link (1956) and Carmichael and Berry on the survey of a group of British hospitals in the 1970s where one in three used foetal X-rays
13. *British Journal of Anaesthetics*, 17, 1053 (1975)
14. Polly Toynbee in the *Guardian* Monday Women, 20 May 1985
15. Jerome to Eustochium, quoted by Karen Armstrong in *The Gospel According to Woman*

Chapter 6
1. Gena Corea, quoting Jonathan Kandell in the *New York Times*, 17 March 1974.
2. Germaine Greer: *Sex and Destiny*
3. Warnock Report cmnd 9314 (HMSO, London 1986)
4. Quoted by Gena Corea: *op. cit.*
5. Quoted by Corea: *op. cit.*

Chapter 7
1. In Erich Neumann: *The Great Mother*
2. Quoted by Ann Shearer in *Woman: Her Changing Image*
3. Coote and Campbell: *op. cit.*
4. Shearer: *op. cit.*
5. Nicholas Davidson: *The Failure of Feminism*
6. Quoted in the *Independent*, 3 June 1991
7. Shearer: *op. cit.*

Chapter 8
1. Sir Patrick Forrest: *Breast Cancer: The Decision to Screen* (Nuffield Provincial Hospitals Trust, 1990)
2. In *Whose Body Is It? The Troubling Issue of Informed Consent*
3. *British Medical Journal*, 297, 1988, 533–9

Chapter 10
1. Stuart Smith: *Separate Tables? An Investigation into Single Sex Setting in Mathematics* (HMSO, London 1986)
2. 2 February 1991 in an article by Charles Bremner
3. Silvia Rodgers: *Women's Space in a Men's House*
4. Silvia Rodgers in the *Guardian*, 10 October 1979

Chapter 11
1. The *Sunday Times*, 22 December 1985, in an interview with John Mortimer
2. Eurostat figures, 1986

Chapter 12
1. General Household Survey (HMSO, London 1986)
2. R.M. Moroney: *The Family and the State* (Longman, Harlow 1976)
3. EOC: *Caring for the Elderly and Handicapped: Community Care Policies and Women's Lives* (1982)
4. General Household Survey (OPCS 1985, HMSO, London 1988)

Chapter 13
1. London *Evening Standard*, 8 May 1991
2. EOC: *Women and Men in Britain 1990* (HMSO, London)

Chapter 14
1. Quoted in *Cosmopolitan*, February 1988
2. Angela Holdsworth: *Out of the Dolls' House*

Bibliography

Alderson, Priscilla: *Choosing for Children – Parents' Consent to Surgery* (OUP, Oxford 1990)

Armstrong, Karen: *The Gospel According to Woman* (Elm Tree Books, London 1986)

Atkinson, Holly: *Women and Fatigue* (Macmillan, London 1985)

Ball, Jean: *Reactions to Motherhood* (CUP, Cambridge 1987)

Barr, Pat: *The Memsahibs – the Women of Victorian India* (Allied Publishers, Calcutta 1976)

Beauman, Nicola: *A Very Great Profession – the Women's Novel 1914–39* (Virago, London 1983)

Beech, Beverley Lawrence: *Who's Having Your Baby?* (Camden Press, London 1987)

Bennett, Gillian: *Traditions of Belief – Women, Folklore and the Supernatural Today* (Penguin, London 1987)

Bennion, Francis: *The Sex Code: Morals for Moderns* (Weidenfeld and Nicolson, London 1991)

Blixen, Karen: *On Modern Marriage* (Fourth Estate, London 1987)

Boswell, John: *The Kindness of Strangers* (Penguin, London 1991)

Brown, Peter: *The Body and Society – Men, Women and Sexual Renunciation in Early Christianity* (Faber, London 1989)

Brownmiller, Susan: *Men, Women and Rape* (Penguin, London 1976)

Bryan, Beverley, Dadzie, Stella, and Scafe, Suzanne: *The Heart of the Race – Black Women's Lives in Britain* (Virago, London 1985)

Campbell, Beatrix: *The Iron Ladies – Why Do Women Vote Tory?* (Virago, London 1987)

Carter, April: *The Politics of Women's Rights* (Longman, London 1988)

Clewlow, Carol: *A Woman's Guide to Adultery* (Penguin, London 1989)

Cline, Sally and Spender, Dale: *Reflecting Men at Twice their Natural Size – Why Women Work at Making Men Feel Good* (Fontana, London 1987)

Cockerill, Janet: *Second Chance – the residential working women's college and its contribution to the development of women's adult education* (Emberbook, Surbiton n.d.)

Commission of the European Communities: *Lone Parents in the European Community, Final Report, 1989* (Family Policy Studies Centre, London)

Conran, Shirley: *Superwoman* (Sidgwick and Jackson, London 1975)

Coote, Anna and Gill, Tess: *Women's Rights – a Practical Guide* (Penguin, London 1981)

Coote, Anna and Campbell, Beatrix: *Sweet Freedom* (Blackwell, Oxford 1987)

Corea, Gena: *The Mother Machine* (The Women's Press, London 1988)

Davenport-Hines, Richard: *Sex, Death and Punishment – Attitudes to Sex and Sexuality in Britain since the Renaissance* (Collins, London 1990)

Davidson, Nicholas: *The Failure of Feminism* (Prometheus Books, Buffalo, NY 1988)

Delafield, E.M.: *Diary of a Provincial Lady* (Virago, London 1984)

Dworkin, Andrea: *Right-Wing Women* (The Women's Press, London 1983)

Ehrenreich, Barbara and English, Deirdre: *Complaints and Disorders: The Sexual Politics of Sickness* (Writers and Readers Publishing Co-operative, London 1976)

Eichenbaum, Luise and Orbach, Susie: *Understanding Women* (Penguin, London 1985)

Equal Opportunities Commission: *Annual Reports 1983–90* (HMSO, London)

Equal Opportunities Commission: *Women and Men in Britain – a research profile 1985–9* (HMSO, London)

Faulder, Carolyn: *Whose Body Is It? The Troubling Issue of Informed Consent* (Virago, London 1985)

Feldman, David M.: *Birth Control in Jewish Law* (New York University Press, New York and London, 1968)

Ford, Janet and Sinclair, Ruth: *Sixty Years On* (The Women's Press, London 1987)

Forrest, Patrick: *Breast Cancer: the Decision to Screen* (Nuffield Provincial Hospitals Trust, 1990)

Forster, Margaret: *Significant Sisters* (Penguin, London 1986)

Fraser, Antonia: *The Weaker Vessel – Woman's Lot in Seventeenth Century England* (Methuen, London 1985)

Friedan, Betty: *The Second Stage* (Michael Joseph, London 1982)

Furlong, Monica: *Thérèse of Lisieux* (Virago, London 1987)

Gilbert, Harriett and Roche, Christine; *A Women's History of Sex* (Pandora, London 1987)

Glover, Jonathan: *Causing Death and Saving Lives* (Penguin, London 1977)

Greer, Germaine: *The Female Eunuch* (Paladin, London 1971)

Greer, Germaine: *The Madwoman's Underclothes: Essays and Occasional Writings 1968–1985* (Picador, London 1986)

Greer, Germaine: *Sex and Destiny – the Politics of Human Fertility* (Picador, London 1985)

Grove, Valerie: *The Compleat Woman – Marriage, Motherhood, Career – can she have it all?* (Chatto and Windus, London 1987)

Haddock, Lynda and Chappell, Adrian: *Staying On; Girls' Views about School, Family, Friends and Future* (GLC, London n.d.)

Henriques, Nikki: *Inspirational Women* (Grapevine, London 1988)

Henwood, Melanie: *Community Care and Elderly People* (Family Policy Studies Centre, London 1990)

Hewlett, Sylvia Ann: *A Lesser Life – the Myth of Women's Liberation* (Michael Joseph, London 1987)

Holdsworth, Angela: *Out of the Dolls' House: The Story of Women in the Twentieth Century* (BBC, London 1988)

Horney, Karen: *Feminine Psychology* (Norton, New York 1973)

Jolly, Hugh: *Book of Child Care* (Unwin Hyman, London 1985)

Kelleher, Anne: *Sex Within Reason* (Jonathan Cape, London 1987)

Kenny, Mary: *Abortion – the Whole Story* (Quartet, London 1986)

Kitzinger, Sheila: *The Experience of Breastfeeding* (Penguin, London 1987)

Kitzinger, Sheila: *The Experience of Childbirth* (Penguin, London 1985)

Kitzinger, Sheila: *Giving Birth – How It Really Feels* (Gollancz, London 1987)

Kitzinger, Sheila: *Woman's Experience of Sex* (Penguin, London 1985)

Lawson, Annette: *Adultery* (Blackwell, Oxford 1988)

Lerner, Alan Jay: *My Fair Lady* vocal score (Chappell and Co, London n.d.)

Lerner, Gerda: *The Creation of Patriarchy* (OUP, Oxford 1986)

Levine, June: *Sisters* (Ward River Press, Dublin 1982)

Liddington, Jill and Norris, Jill: *One Arm Tied Behind Us – The Rise of the Women's Suffrage Movement* (Virago, London 1978)

Meehan, Elizabeth M.: *Women's Rights at Work* (Macmillan, London 1985)

Menafee, Samuel Pyeatt: *Wives for Sale* (Blackwell, Oxford 1981)

Midgley, Mary and Hughes, Judith: *Women's Choices – Philosophical Problems Facing Feminism* (Weidenfeld and Nicolson, London 1983)

Miles, Rosalind: *The Rites of Man – Love, Sex and Death in the Making of the Male* (Grafton, London 1991)

Miles, Rosalind: *The Woman's History of the World* (Michael Joseph, London 1988)

Mill, John Stuart: *The Subjection of Women* and Mill, Harriet Taylor: *Enfranchisement of Women* (Virago, London 1983)

Miller, Alice: *For Your Own Good – the Roots of Violence in Child-rearing* (Virago, London 1983)

Millett, Kate: *Sexual Politics* (Rupert Hart-Davis, London 1972)

Mills, Jane: *Womanwords* (Longman, London 1989)

Mitchell, Juliet: *Woman's Estate* (Penguin, London 1971)

Moir, Anne and Jessel, David: *Brainsex – the Real Difference between Men and Women* (Michael Joseph, London 1989)

Morgan, Robin: *Sisterhood is Powerful – an Anthology of Writings from the Women's Liberation Movement* (Vintage Books, New York 1970)

Mullan, Bob: *Are Mothers Really Necessary?* (TVS Boxtree, London 1987)

National Childbirth Trust: *Pregnancy and Parenthood* (Oxford 1985)

Neumann, Erich: *The Great Mother* (Routledge and Kegan Paul, London 1963)

Neustatter, Angela: *Hyenas in Petticoats* (Harrap, London 1989)

Novarra, Virginia: *Women's Work, Men's Work – the Ambivalence of Equality* (Marion Boyars, London 1980)

Oakley, Ann: *The Captured Womb* (Blackwell, Oxford 1984)

Oakley, Ann: *Housewife* (Penguin, London 1976)

Perutz, Kathrin: *Beyond the Looking Glass* (Penguin, London 1972)

Petchesky, Rosalind Pollack: *Abortion and Woman's Choice* (Verso, London 1985)

Pitkeathley, Jill: *It's my Duty, isn't it?* (Souvenir Press, London 1989)

Pizan, Christine de: *The Book of the City of Ladies* (Picador, London 1983)

Richards, Janet Radcliffe: *the Sceptical Feminist* (Pelican, London 1982)

Rodgers, Silvia: 'Women's Space in a Men's House: The British House of Commons' in: *Women and Space*, ed. S. Arden, Oxford University Women's Studies Committee (Croom Helm, 1981)

Savage, Wendy: *A Savage Enquiry* (Virago, London 1986)

Seager, Joni and Olson, Anne: *Atlas – Women in the World* (Touchstone, New York 1986)

Segal, Lynne: *Is the Future Female? Troubled Thoughts on Contemporary Feminism* (Virago, London 1987)

Seltman, Charles: *Women in Antiquiry* (Pan, London 1956)

Shapiro, Rose: *Contraception – a Practical and Political Guide* (Virago, London 1987)

Shearer, Ann: *Woman: Her Changing Image* (Thorsons, Wellingborough 1987)

Shorter, Edward: *The History of Women's Bodies* (Penguin, London 1984)

Showalter, Elaine: *The Female Malady – Women, Madness and the English Culture 1830–1980* (Virago, London 1987)

Shuttle, Penelope and Redgrove, Peter: *The Wise Wound – Menstruation and Everywoman* (Paladin, London 1986)

Smith, Joan: *Misogynies* (Faber, London 1989)

Solomon, Juliet: *Holding the Reins – Parents, Children and Nannies in their Search for Domestic Salvation* (Fontana, London 1987)

Spender, Dale: *There's Always Been a Women's Movement this Century* (Pandora, London 1983)

Spender, Dale: *Time and Tide Wait for No Man* (Pandora, London 1984)

Stanworth, Michelle, ed.: *Reproductive Technologies – Gender, Motherhood and Medicine* (Polity, Cambridge, 1987)

Storkey, Elaine: *What's Right with Feminism* (SPCK, London 1985)

Stott, Mary: *Before I Go* (Virago, London 1986)

Vallance, Elizabeth: *Women in the House* (Athlone, London 1979)

Wandor, Michelene: *Wanted* (Playbooks, London 1988)

Warner, Marina: *Alone of All Her Sex – the Myth and Cult of the Virgin Mary* (Quartet, London 1978)

Warner, Marina: *Monuments and Maidens – the Allegory of the Female Form* (Picador, London 1985)

Warnock, Mary: *A Question of Life* (Blackwell, Oxford 1985)

Weldon, Fay: *Female Friends* (Pan, London 1975)

Wolf, Naomi: *The Beauty Myth* (Chatto and Windus, London 1990)

Index